THE NEW NOVEL
IN AMERICA

The Kafkan Mode in
Contemporary Fiction

THE NEW NOVEL
IN AMERICA

The Kafkan Mode in
Contemporary Fiction

By HELEN WEINBERG

CORNELL UNIVERSITY PRESS

ITHACA AND LONDON

First published 1970
Second printing 1970

Selections from *The Adventures of Augie March* by Saul Bellow, copyright 1949, 1951, 1952, 1953, by Saul Bellow, are reprinted by permission of The Viking Press, Inc., A. M. Heath and Co., Ltd., and Weidenfeld and Nicolson, Ltd.

International Standard Book Number 0-8014-0537-8
Library of Congress Catalog Card Number 70-87011

PRINTED IN THE UNITED STATES OF AMERICA
BY VALLEY OFFSET, INC.

*For my mother
and father*

"At a street corner Karl saw a placard with the following announcement: The Oklahoma Theater will engage members for its company today at Clayton race-course from six o'clock in the morning until midnight. The great Theater of Oklahoma calls you! Today only and never again! If you miss your chance now you miss it for ever! If you think of your future you are one of us! Everyone is welcome! If you want to be an artist, join our company! Our Theater can find employment for everyone, a place for everyone!"

—From Kafka's *Amerika*

CONTENTS

PREFACE

Alfred Kazin writes of Saul Bellow's "signature": he re-
marks particularly in Bellow's work a "somber, often desperate *individual* world, a world deeply and engravedly personal, aggrieved, heavy [contrasted] with an elegant wit, a
consciously unavailing, rueful curiosity that may be useless
in overcoming so much pressure, but which is sanctioned by
some larger spiritual world, outside the narrow circle of the
hero's own desperate existence. To this [spiritual world] he
seeks access." [1]

In the following pages I examine the novels of Bellow and
other Americans whose writing in the 1950's and early 1960's
represented a reaction against New Critical aestheticism and
the self-protectively thin academic novel to which that
aestheticism had brought the novel form. Individual desperation and the quest for access to some larger spiritual world,
which, coupled in a single narrative, were to become Bellow's
signature, were not exclusively Bellow's. Reaction against the
novel that had turned away from life toward aestheticism
brought with it the rebirth of the novel that turned toward
life. In this renaissance of human concern, various novelists
found their story in the self and its isolated, and therefore
private and personal, search for meaningful human value;
these novelists implicitly acknowledge that value resides in or
in relation to an undefined, often undefinable, spiritual re-
gion, not in or in relation to society.

In the movement against aestheticism in the novel, the modernist understanding of the universe as meaningless, which had brought the novel toward a little death, a dying into aesthetic concerns, had itself to be included in the novel that would now attempt valid, not merely sentimental, affirmations of human projects. I have used Franz Kafka's novels as an index to the ways that the modernist sensibility may yet write for the sake of life, not the sake of art, without self-deception or sentimentality: Kafka was the spiritual pioneer of the territory explored by the novelists of the fifties and sixties (Bellow, Mailer, Salinger, Malamud, Roth, Gold, Styron, Cassill), the territory of the quest for meaning, of the quest for access to the spiritual world, and of the human assault on the divine. It is on this Kafkan kind of novel that I have concentrated in order to make suggestions significant to our understanding of the "life," not the "death," of the modern novel.

The purpose of this study is to define and to distinguish between two types of contemporary novels, the absurdist and the activist, by reference to the novels of Franz Kafka, and to examine in detail the latter type with specific attention to the activist hero whose fictive process informs the activist novel.

The activist hero is defined in this study as the *spiritual* activist exemplified by K. of Kafka's *The Castle*. K. becomes the prototypal figure for this hero and is discussed in relation to the heroes of some recent American novelists—especially Saul Bellow, Norman Mailer, Bernard Malamud, Philip Roth, and Herbert Gold. I also examine certain variations of this mode of hero as presented in the work of J. D. Salinger, Walker Percy, James Baldwin, Ralph Ellison, William Styron, and R. V. Cassill.

In the first chapter I discuss the innocent victim-hero and the guilty victim-hero as they appear in Kafka's *Amerika* and *The Trial,* respectively. From this discussion of these two victim heroes I generalize about the nature of the absurdist novel as a type which has at its center the victim of worldly circumstances. The victim, whether innocent (guileless and unaware of the worldly circumstances which ensnare him) or guilty (cognizant of and in complicity with worldly ways), is caught in the absurd situation of trying to deal simply (if he is innocent) or rationally (if he is guilty) with a variety of worldly circumstances which pretend to represent objective truths but are in fact totally divorced from objective truth (if there is any) or from an ultimate ideality (if there is one). The world view of the absurdist novel sees the complete disjunction between the social-political systems of men in the world and a system of higher being: the focus of this novel's world view is on this disjunction. To live acquiescent to the terms of this world is to be passive; to allow the nonbeing of worldly routines and reasons to encroach upon the life of the self and its possibilities for true being is to become a victim.

The hero of the activist novel is in opposition to the pattern of the victim. He chooses, subjectively and irrationally, his self, his own being; he proposes the possibilities of his own being against the nonbeing of worldly schemes. He constructs an image of a transcendent self; he becomes a particular in absolute relation to an Absolute. Although the spiritual activist initiates his subjective quest for a transcendent self as an irrational choice, he is purposeful, willful, and conscious in pursuit of his goal. An anguished hopefulness, springing from this deliberate and conscious avoidance of nonbeing and despair, permeates *The Castle* and the recent American novels that share its vision. In the second chapter I discuss in detail K. of *The Castle,* in order to define the prototype of the spiritual activist.

The third chapter is an interlude: before I continue the examination of hero types, I compare Kafka's use of the novel as a form of metaphysical inquiry to Saul Bellow's use of the novel, hoping to clarify Kafka's relation to recent American novelists. I single out Saul Bellow because he seems most clearly concerned with Kafkan questions and

with the novel as a process of investigation and because he
may be considered the father of a school of writing in current American fiction.

In the fourth chapter I explicate the novels of Bellow in
order to substantiate my theories; in the fifth chapter I look
closely at some novels and other works of Norman Mailer,
with the same intention. The sixth chapter is an examination of J. D. Salinger's saintly heroes which resemble and
deviate from the spiritual activist prototype in significant
ways. The seventh, and concluding, chapter is a survey of the
heroes of other American writers: Malamud, Roth, and
Gold, who are in Bellow's (Kafkan) school, and Baldwin, Ellison, Styron, and Cassill, whose novels contain heroes in a
spiritual activist mode but heroes unlike the Kafkan in special ways which I categorize.

When I wrote this last chapter I attempted to separate
what seemed to me to be novels in the spiritual activist mode
and Kafkan from other novels that seemed to be in the same
mode but not Kafkan; I found that the existential expression
of the lives of the heroes of all these novels did reflect certain
broad characteristics of the Jewish (Kafkan), or the Christian, or the American Negro temperament. Although the
spiritual activist novel is an existential novel (the narrative
of a man's life as the process of becoming), it is nevertheless
inevitable that a remnant sense of the religious, or social,
"condition" of the writer should be expressively revealed in
the ways of seeing and moving described—religious formalities and rituals, customs and neighborhoods, distinct identity patterns of behavior, all these may have disappeared
from the lives of these writers, but a way of looking shaped
by an abiding, deep ethnicity remains. Clearly, I am not
talking about Jewish novels such as Chaim Potok's *The Chosen,* Christian novels such as J. F. Powers' *Morte D'Urban,* or
Negro novels such as Richard Wright's *Native Son;* these
novels take as their primary substance the answers to the
questions: What is it to be a Jew now? Or, a Christian now?

Or, an American Negro now? The spiritual activist novel asks more transcendent questions: What is it to be a man? What is it to be a particular in relation to an Absolute?—and really does not answer them but puts the questions vigorously rather than presents a picture with which to conjure answers.

Christian friends who have read this chapter have been dismayed by my assumptions about Christianity; they consider my assumptions to be dictated by what is really Roman Catholicism and not broadly Christian. It is true that to a degree I do assume the remnant motifs in Christianity to have grown out of Pauline concepts such as the Fall as the beginning of Original Sin; but these concepts, when put against Jewish concepts, do seem to be universal in Christianity and not exclusive to the Roman Catholic Church. To put it most simply, one need only look at the basic difference between the Hebrew "messiah" and the Christian "christos" to know that the salvation, the redemption, and the grace of which Christians speak depend on a concept of a soul locked in a condition of sin from which it must be loosed and is loosed by a savior-like figure, a Christ. Jews expect a messiah, but he is not clearly defined; he will be defined only when he *is*. The Jewish messiah's task is somewhat defined, but even this is a minimal and open definition. When the messiah comes he will unite the people of Israel in their own land, and he will bring peace to the nations of the world. About the salvation of the soul, there is nothing; and the reason there is nothing is that the Hebraic interpretation of the Fall was varied and did not settle on the idea of Original Sin, although speculations that the sin of Eve and the Fall may have introduced the universality of sin, and death, in the world do occur.[2] However, there is no established theological opinion on such subjects in Judaism; even on the laws of the Torah there is endless Talmudic comment. There is a continuing dialogue between the Law and the interpretations of the Law; the Law is not dogmatically fixed; it lives and changes. The vitality of dynamic law is at the heart of Jewish matters. There can be no generic sin because there is always room for comment.

On the other hand, some Jewish friends who have read my last chapter are dismayed that I rely so heavily on Martin Buber as a Jewish existential theologian: these friends feel that Buber was a Christianizer, a Jew who liberalized and softened too much the moral precepts of Jewish law and who interpreted the Eastern European Hasidic movement too much in accordance with his knowledge of Christian mysticisms. However, Buber had an obvious and popular appeal for many American Jews, and Christians, especially in the fifties; and Leslie Fiedler could even write in the early sixties:

Certainly, we live at a moment when, everywhere in the realm of prose, Jewish writers have discovered their Jewishness to be an eminently marketable commodity, their much vaunted alienation to be their passport into the heart of Gentile American culture. It is, indeed, their quite justified claim to have been *first* to occupy the Lost Desert at the center of the Great American Oasis (toward which everyone now races, Coca-Cola in one hand, Martin Buber in the other).[3]

Of course, Leslie Fiedler will write anything any time as long as it's witty, but he is also often right. In the case of Buber, he is, I think, right. And, given Buber's popularity and consequent influence, I find irrelevant to my particular concerns whether or not he is a Christianizer. My intention is to bring out the subliminal Jewish and Christian patterns which remain to shape the consciousness, choices, and styles of existential, fluid characters in the contemporary American novel. I have said that I thought the subliminal remnant in the recent Christian novelists to be from Pauline Christianity (for a larger discussion of this, see Chapter 7); and when I speak of the subliminal patterns *left over* from the Hebraic law, sense of life, and interpretation of the world, I am really thinking about the residual Jewishness in the non-orthodox, non-religious remnant of Diaspora Jews, such as Kafka, Bellow, Mailer.

Let me make a double confession. To my Christian friends: yes, I think Christianity is essentially Pauline. To my Jewish friends: yes, I think life in the (European and American) Diaspora has made assimilated (Christianized?) Jews of Buber, and Kafka, and Bellow, and Mailer. And, it is only a fine, very thin line of distinction apparent in certain metaphysically expressive novels that reveals the staying power of primary life-interpretations. These interest me.

Delmore Schwartz called Isaac Rosenfeld "the Jewish Franz Kafka," [4] a telling *mot* from my point of view: Isaac Rosenfeld is *too* Jewish in some ways to be included in this discussion. His one novel, *Passage from Home,* while not like Potok's novel of specifically Jewish subject matter, is a *Bildungsroman* about a specifically Jewish youth. It is a novel of psychological realism more than one of primarily metaphysical, or spiritual, concerns. Rosenfeld's shorter fiction does, incidentally, recall an aspect of Kafka's writings—the dark, surreal quality of the parables, paradoxes, and short tales— which is more commonly thought of as Kafkan, or Kafkaesque, than the Kafkan mode of the novel which I consider in my text. The dark and surreal are also apparent, though less distinct, in the novels *Amerika* and *The Trial,* and I deal with them, and with what they represent thematically, calling these novels absurdist, in my first chapter. That line of Kafka's American heirs which comes down through Rosenfeld—the Jewish Franz Kafka—rather than down through Bellow are somewhat neglected in my book, however.

One other prefatory observation might be made concerning some novels that are not discussed in this book though they are by writers discussed here. I am thinking especially of Norman Mailer's *Why Are We in Viet Nam?* and *The Armies of the Night;* of Bernard Malamud's *The Fixer;* of Herbert Gold's *Fathers;* of William Styron's *The Confessions of Nat Turner;* of Philip Roth's *When She Was Good* and of his *Portnoy's Complaint.* These later novels represent yet another turning—a shift away from the personal spiritual activist hero who essentially shuns social-political values for the sake of his own life, or of his self. In these later novels one is often given a picture of that hero, but he is transformed from a seeker after self in a larger spiritual world to a self that confronts a whole complex of social and political structures and conventions.

From Kafka one could not have predicted this turning in the later novels of these American writers: the enlarging of the personal quest to permit the past (history, tradition, inherited ethnic custom) and society to function once again, at least as a variable in the personal life. No longer does the personal-metaphysical continuum dominate those new novels that are for the sake of life. Made bold by *The Adventures of Augie March* and *Henderson,* with their pastless activist heroes looking always forward, Bellow is able to look fully at a person whose past and the past of his own Jewish people in a community are relevant to him as an individual, at a Herzog. Mailer, after *An American Dream,* has been capable of *Why Are We in Viet Nam?,* which, for all its campy, potboiler effects and its ambiguities, is a magnification and glorification of primitive human energy as it continues to exist, remains alive, in spite of but nevertheless *inside* of a modern technological society. And Mailer's latest novel, *The Armies of the Night,* is a successful attempt to make a novelistic history of the confrontation of society by a spiritual activist hero, a willful self, a gigantic ego—in brief, Mailer himself, but Mailer transformed into the imaginative and imagined hero of the novel-as-history. Malamud's *The Fixer* is a historical novel of sorts, and its hero, Yakov Bok, though he shares some of the characteristics of such a lone spiritual adventurer as S. Levin in *A New Life,* comes to the conclusion that "the purpose of freedom is to create it for others" and that "there is no such thing as an unpolitical man."

Herbert Gold in *Fathers* and Philip Roth in *Portnoy's Complaint* investigate particular personal histories as they took shape in and out of Jewish communities in Cleveland

and Newark, New Jersey, and, simultaneously, in the world, while William Styron explores the spiritual and political activism of a Negro slave of the American past in *The Confessions of Nat Turner*.

If the rebirth of the novel as an instrument for exploration and discovery in the realm of human concern was achieved by the spiritual activist novels of the fifties and early sixties described in detail in this book, the most apparent recent consequence of that achievement has taken the novel into a renewed and ever extended inquiry into man's relation with his history, his society, his politics.

If at first it seemed necessary after the hell of Europe, the Holocaust and the concentration camps—it is no accident that the modernist imagination is most pronounced in Jewish writers—to start bare and to focus purely on individual man's isolated position and to look at that place where modern man's consciousness overlapped with the absence of given meaning in all communities and in the universe, it now seems possible to talk once again about a social environment and to take a stand in it and on it, whether the stand be an affirmation or an attack.

The process through which the novel went in the fifties and early sixties was a purifying one; and as a result there has been strained out of the picture of the personal encounter with the social and political worlds, presented in the most recent novels of, for example, Bellow, Mailer, and Malamud, any adherence to a defined political-social system, to simplistic formulas, to utopian solutions, or to easy ideas of political or communal salvations. If each of the novelists discussed in this book now seems in his later work more political or more aware of the public lives of men, he is yet a radical spirit, an anarchist, and his novel is still open-ended, inconclusive, urgent, somewhat desperate, but not entirely without some hope for the lives of men.

H. W.

Cleveland, Ohio
March 1969

ACKNOWLEDGMENTS

It would be immensely difficult for me to acknowledge properly or to express the gratitude I feel for all the useful conversations with generous friends and teachers that have gone into the making of this book.

My thoughts about Kafka's novels were first discussed with Albert S. Cook, whose advice was very valuable at the beginning of the undertaking. Joseph Friend, who saw the manuscript through its first draft with patience and kindness, has my gratitude; Peter Salm and Lyon Richardson made very useful suggestions.

Finally, the book would not exist at all in its present form without the readings, comments, and concern of David L. Stevenson. To him, Cynthia Ozick, and my husband, Kenneth, are addressed my most special thanks: they know how they helped.

THE NEW NOVEL
IN AMERICA

*The Kafkan Mode in
Contemporary Fiction*

1

Amerika and *The Trial:*
Preliminary Studies
in Innocence and Guilt

If Franz Kafka was the most private of modern writers, driven by some deeply personal impulse to polish his language and his stories so that they might dazzle with truth, he has also become the twentieth-century writer whose impact on modern literary consciousness is most vividly felt. More than Proust, Joyce, or Mann, he appears to anticipate in his work a postreligious spiritual awareness that is ever more present in literature as the century ages. His influence, if it may be called that, is indirect and not of the manner proposed by historians of national literary periods. As a regionalist of the spirit, Kafka evades categorizing in any of the textbook ways. He had a primary, pure, and intuitive—some say neurotic—grasp of those themes that belong to all of us in the modern world, and by articulating them he has also in a way given them to us. It is, therefore, appropriate to analyze his most extended and complex works—his novels—in connection with those of recent American novelists to see in what ways they are his inheritors.

Kafka wrote three novels, all unfinished at his death, although their effect is of the wholeness of a special vision; all were unpublished during Kafka's lifetime, and his final instruction to Max Brod was that the manuscripts of the novels be burned.[1] "The Stoker," the first chapter of *The Man*

Who Disappeared, the original title of the novel we know today as *Amerika,*[2] was the only significant part of Kafka's novelistic work to appear in print during his lifetime. *Amerika* was begun in the autumn of 1912, when Kafka was twenty-nine years old. ("The Judgment" and "The Metamorphosis," two stories concerned with the father-figure, were written about the same time as "The Stoker.") *The Trial* was begun in 1914 and *The Castle* [3] in 1921, a year after the writing of "In the Penal Colony" (1920). The simplest distinction between the early and the later work is in the views they take of authority, of the father-figure: in the early stories and *The Trial,* authority is clearly and unambivalently oppressive; in the later work—even in "In the Penal Colony"—the hero cannot, or will not, define authority even as oppressive. The Kafkan hero, always uncertain, extends his uncertainty in the later work to the source of uncertainty, the primary authority in the world. This leaves him a razor's edge of hope.

This change may be attributable to the influence of Søren Kierkegaard, whom Kafka had started to read in 1913 and whose biographical speculations he found relevant to his own life problems. That he continued to read Kierkegaard is attested to by several entries in his diaries, the last being a note that he had been ill, in bed, reading *Either/Or,* in December, 1923, a year and a half before his death on June 3, 1924.[4] Kierkegaard's writings have a cumulative effect on Kafka's work. Philip Rahv suggests that the increased metaphysical speculation in *The Trial*—the movement away from a literal dealing with the father and the family, even through the metaphors of metamorphoses—was in some degree due to the first reading of Kierkegaard in 1913.[5] By 1921, when Kafka wrote *The Castle,* Kierkegaard's thought had taken an important place in the shaping of Kafka's own vision, as I will attempt to show in detail in the following chapter which deals at length with *The Castle.* What began as a "biographical," or psychological, affinity for Kierkegaard's writing [6] became an interest that, at least partially, led the way to Kafka's use of his personal dilemma in an expanded metaphysical vision of the total human dilemma.

Although "The Stoker" was written in 1912 and published in 1913, the rest of *Amerika* was still a "projected novel" in 1917.[7] Kafka, however, had been working on the novel, on and off, and concurrently on *The Trial*, in the intervening years. "The Stoker," in itself, may be considered a transitional piece: it stands between the abbreviated, concretized vision of the short-story writer, the fabulist, and the projecting, more ambitious vision of the novelist. The story of the stoker is a completed tale of the ambiguity of innocence and guilt. A sea voyage, which carries Karl Rossmann, the innocent hero, from an old, wicked Europe and its seductions to the New World with its miracle of salvation and its Uncle Jacob, marks a rebirth for Karl, from his old, soiled European innocence to a new, American innocence. His innocence, tainted in Europe by the family maid's seduction of him, has prompted his parents to send him to America; the parents have in effect disowned him for what they see as his guilt, and he is an orphan. During the ocean voyage the time of his stay with the stoker in the hold of the ship is a dark womblike time before his emergence on the shore of America. With the stoker, Karl has confronted the injustice of the world which would call the stoker guilty; he has confronted the guile and guilt of Schubal, the stoker's enemy; he has witnessed the "human tribunal" of justice in the captain's cabin: a trial serious to him, a joke to many of the others on board ship. The human tribunal is interrupted by Karl's American uncle, Jacob, who has been informed of Karl's arrival by a letter from the motherly servant-seductress, who is now pregnant. Uncle Jacob has come; an instrument of miraculous intervention, he saves Karl. The trial of the stoker, who has come to seem a father to Karl, and of Schubal, the schemer, is "provisionally postponed" by this interruption; it is clear, however, that the confrontation of the stoker and Schubal, their mutual accusations and declarations of innocence, will continue after Karl leaves the ship with his Uncle Jacob to enter the New World. Karl, the perpetual innocent to whom things happen, who makes nothing happen himself, who is not even responsible for his own sexual acts, is saved by his Uncle Jacob from this scene of accusation and guilt; and when the scene disappears, so does its significance: "It was now as if there were really no stoker at all." [8] Yet another father for the boy has presented himself: Uncle Jacob, about whom Karl wonders "whether this man would ever be able to take the stoker's place." [9] The story ends, and the novel begins.

Essentially pastless and fatherless as Karl is, his experience of the claims of innocence and guilt in this first chapter opens the investigations of not one novel but the two novels that precede *The Castle: Amerika* and *The Trial*. Karl escapes the human and divine mechanisms of the law as Joseph K. does not; Karl is saved and resumes his innocent wandering. In *The Trial*, begun in 1914, the paradigm for the investigation of guilt, the trial in "The Stoker," is deepened and expanded. In 1915, while working on both novels at once, Kafka said of his two heroes in *Amerika* and *The Trial*: "Rossmann and K., the innocent and the guilty, both executed without distinction in the end, the guilty one with a gentler hand, more pushed aside than struck down." [10] This, of course, is not the way these (unfinished) novels actually conclude, for Joseph K. is struck down, not pushed aside, and Karl Rossmann finds himself in the Nature Theater of Oklahoma, not struck down. But their basic helplessness, their essential victimization at the hands of the world, whether they are innocent or guilty, is what Kafka asserts in this concept of what the conclusions must be for Joseph K. and Karl. Only Kafka's manic dream of salvation (Chapter 7 of *Amerika* ends with Karl falling asleep, still in the prison of Delamarche's and Brunelda's schemes, and Chapter 8 records the dreamlike fantasy of the Nature Theater of Oklahoma) keeps Karl from his inevitable end as an innocent victim. Both Karl and Joseph K. are victims, Karl of the worldly schemes of others, such as the maid, Uncle Jacob, Robinson, Delamarche, and Brunelda; while Joseph K. is victimized by his own worldly schemes, his sacrificing of himself to the rationalistic, dry-souled routines of the bank and to its petty contests for meaningless power. Their stories, however, are very different from one another; one is the story of innocence, the other, of guilt.

In his innocence, his marginality, his insubstantiality of character, his random, free-floating adventures unguided by any principle or purpose, neither wishing nor needing to prove himself innocent, Karl becomes the hero of a rambling, picaresque story. His world is shifting, ever changing and chaotic, but open. Though victimized by the worldly people he meets, there is always the hope, the dream, of identity and freedom in the Nature Theater of Oklahoma. The recurring "rebirths" implicit throughout the novel—leaving Europe; being rescued from the ship by Uncle Jacob; finding the Nature Theater—symbolize this ephemeral, ever present hope before the fully developed denouement of the Nature Theater chapter itself. Kafka's foreboding gloomy awareness that even the sweet fool, the vulnerable boy, must be struck down was offset by his instinctive awareness of possibility in a new land like America. Max Brod says, "Kafka knew quite well, and discussed the fact, that this novel was more optimistic and 'lighter' in mood than any of his other writings." [11] There is a crucial contradiction between what Kafka has told us of his pessimism—his plan that Karl be struck down—and what Brod has told us of his optimism. The novel is ambivalent: both pessimism and optimism are present in it. Kafka does not sacrifice what he knows of life and of the world to what he hopes for from a new world; however, he does let a surrealistically transcribed suggestion of possibility reside in his narrative to explode at the end in a (dreamed) one-day fulfillment. "Today only and never again! If you miss your chance now you miss it forever!" [12] This reversal of the planned consummation of the innocent victim's wandering, the inevitable striking down, is a miracle of earthly salvation, and it repeats the scheme presented in the first chapter when Uncle Jacob suddenly arrives at the scene of the stoker's trial on the ship.

Amerika has its own completeness in spite of its rambling episodic form; and it has its own complexity of intertwined, contradictory themes in spite of its seeming simplicity. This strangely unified picaresque novel was inspired, Kafka tells us, by *David Copperfield*. In comparing his own novel to that of Dickens, Kafka reveals how his novel works toward a totality of meaning:

"The Stoker" is sheer imitation of Dickens, the projected novel even more so. The story of the trunk, the boy who delights and charms everyone, the menial labor, his sweetheart in the country house, the dirty houses, *et al.,* but above all the method. It was my intention, as I now see, to write a Dickens novel, but enhanced by the sharper lights I should have taken from the times and the duller ones I should have got from myself. Dickens' opulence and great, careless prodigality, but in consequence passages of awful insipidity in which he wearily works over effects he has already achieved. Gives one a barbaric impression because the whole does not make sense, a barbarism that I, it is true, thanks to my weakness and wiser for my epigonism, have been able to avoid. There is a heartlessness behind his sentimentally overflowing style. These rude characterizations which are artificially stamped on everyone without which Dickens would not be able to get on with his story even for a moment.[13]

Kafka's whole does make sense because it evolves without overelaboration of plot and avoids arbitrary insistence on a narrow interpretation of any character. If Karl is duped by many grotesquely "evil" characters, it is not so much that they are stereotypes of wickedness, but that he is innocent and therefore has no schemes of his own with which to encounter, and counter, theirs.

Karl is more used than misused or abused: when no longer of use, he is free to go his own way. There is as little true malice as there is true goodness in the worldly schemers, even in the robbers, he encounters. Although Karl may appear again and again to have been betrayed, those who use him usually intend to help him in some way, according to their own lights. The Nature Theater of Oklahoma is the revelation of what Karl has avoided throughout his wandering—a personal way. A way must be chosen if he is not to be the victim of the purposes of others. Karl, who has not been able to imagine his own way, finds an attractively transcendent one offered at last in the theater of angels and trumpeteers, an expansive community in which there is a place and a part for everyone, everyone who wishes to be an artist, the epitome of role and nonrole at once. "If you think of your future you are one of us! Everyone is welcome! If you want to be an artist, join our company!" [14] It is, however, only a theater, a world of illusion and fantasy, after all: it claims to be the Nature Theater of Oklahoma, but it is hiring its artists at the Clayton race course in upper New York state. Nevertheless, it offers the vision of a way in an ideal community that is better than the schemes of the worldly community with which Karl has been presented. An interesting question arises when, confronted by this promise of a part in a theater that seems to recreate the Garden of Eden, Karl hesitates and gives the name of "Negro" rather than his own. It is not surprising that he does not give his real name, since he is being hired as an actor and since he is also skeptical, after his many earlier experiences, of the generous promises made by the theater. Why the name of "Negro," however, which he says is his nickname? Perhaps he is not as skeptical of the theater as one might assume from the evidence of a false name. Perhaps he is throwing off the past entirely, assuming a new identity for the new community and choosing his future in

a new, world. With his sixth sense of prophecy, Kafka seems
to have realized that the Negro, enslaved and exploited,
would become ultimately the fullest embodiment of a new,
hopefully free, characteristically non-European man in America.

  The Trial is another story, the story of guilt and of Europe. Its guilty victim-hero, Joseph K., reflects the other side
of "The Stoker" coin. In Europe, and even on the European
ship halfway between Europe and America, all men are am-
biguously guilty: they share in a generalized system of petty
connivance that the Americans Robinson and Delamarche,
real thieves though they are, can never quite share in, simply
because they live in a different world. But The Trial is not
only about the burden of guilt the long history of Europe
puts on a man; and it is not merely the story of the absurdly
inept and unjust workings of the Austrian bureaucracy, as it
is sometimes supposed to be. It is partially these stories, but
at the center of the narrative is Joseph K., not only the victim of an inexplicable system but also the inherently guilty
man. His guilt may simply be his literary characteristic, a described attribute, as Karl's innocence seems to be his literary
characteristic in Kafka's study of innocence.[15] Guilt is more
complex than innocence, however; guilt implies complicity.
Things do not happen to the guilty man; he has made, and
does make, things happen. He has chosen the wrong way, in
Joseph K.'s case the routinized, legalistic, respectable, commonplace life of the bank clerk. Since this is his way, after he
is accused he pursues a verdict of "not guilty" by following
the very procedures that have estranged him from the source,
wonder, and divine law of life. His progress is increasingly
involved, therefore, in legalistic, mystifying, labyrinthine
procedures, none of which can possibly absolve him of guilt,
all of which, in fact, serve to intensify his guilt. Joseph K. is
as foolish and simplistic as Karl, but he is guilty and Karl is
innocent. Joseph K. is the foolish one slaughtered in the end;
he is not pushed aside finally. Only a miracle could save him,

and miracles are unavailable in the Old World of Modern Europe. (For Kafka, as we have seen in *Amerika,* they are never really available even in the New World, except in dream or fantasy.) Though it forms a counterpart to the investigation of innocence, the investigation of guilt in *The Trial* is a much less literary work and a much more deeply felt spiritual research for Kafka than *Amerika.*

Joseph K. is perhaps no more guilty of routinizing his life, thus losing himself, than his fellow workers at the bank; yet he is, seemingly arbitrarily, and certainly suddenly, accused one morning. (His arrest on the morning of his thirtieth birthday is a kind of sudden and arbitrary salvation, of the sort Karl experiences, in reverse.) What establishes his guilt is his acknowledgment of the accusation and his willingness to engage in legalistic procedures in pursuit of a favorable judgment. His acknowledgment grows out of his fear of any authoritative voice; his pursuit of a favorable judgment is motivated by the desire to save appearances. He is entirely mystified when the priest in the cathedral, in the crucial episode toward the end of the novel, tells him the parable of the Law, which shows that the final truth of the Law is its mystery.[16] He does not see mystery as truth; he can only be mystifed by such ultimate, nonrational truths. He is a reasonable man, condemned to die in an absurd world.[17] Only the acceptance of mystery, the pursuit of the dangerous unknown, the giving up of one's past and its procedures, the giving up of the world and the world's meretricious embodiments of the mystery of the Law are the heroic attributes of a struggle that may not lead to salvation but saves one from meaningless annihilation at the hands of impersonal executioners.

Of Kafka's three novels, *The Trial* is the most self-contained, complete, and conclusive, the most fable-like, the most similar to such short tales as "The Metamorphosis" and "In the Penal Colony." The passively guilty victim-hero, trapped in an absurd situation and unable to extricate himself by rational means (*his* only means), also would seem to be the prototype for the hero of many self-enclosed stories in recent American fiction. Acceptance of reason as the governing force in the world is at the base of the guilty victim's situation in such novels. Joseph K. sees the gap between the real and the ideal manifestations of the Law as part of an order which may be understood in a systematic way, and thus he tries only to get things right in reasonable, worldly terms, approaching the highest court through the gestures of a worldling: fawning, flattery, bribes, seduction. His case, therefore, is hopeless, and he enacts the prototypical absurd drama of our times. All his feverish activity is a kind of inactivity in the eyes of an ultimate, remote, probably indifferent, mysterious judge. When the hero refuses finally—on no better grounds than the subjective truth of his own will toward being—to accept passively the terms of the world, and when, in spite of the empirical evidence of the apparently real world, he chooses to will himself to go through the open door, to seek his private, mysterious truth, *then* the novel changes not only in theme but in structure. From Joseph K. to K., from *The Trial* to *The Castle*.

The activist hero, epitomized by K. in *The Castle*, wills a private truth and consequently cannot be encompassed any longer by the traditional form of the novel with an older social, moral, or religious system at the heart of its vision.

The Trial and *The Castle*, both pivotal modernist novels, thus adumbrate two distinct forms that have taken shape in the recent American novel: the absurdist and the activist. At the core of the absurdist novel is a vision of the absurd disjunction in the world, the disjunction between the probable and the wonderful, a disjunction seen through the eyes of a "probable" man, creating a situation that we may, with Albert Cook, call comic, in the broadest, or highest, sense of comedy.[18] The comic vision of absurdity in the modern novel may or may not be manifested by a stylized, absurd surface. Some absurdist novels are more realistic than stylized:

The Trial, Camus' *The Stranger,*[19] Sartre's *Nausea,*[20] Bellow's *The Victim* [21] (and, to a lesser extent because of the hero's intense self-awareness preserved by the journal form, *Dangling Man* [22]), Friedman's *Stern,*[23] Malamud's *The Assistant,*[24] Mailer's *Barbary Shore,*[25] and Salinger's *The Catcher in the Rye* [26] (in which the hero actively engages in the pursuit of a private truth but is at the same time the victim of the absurdity promulgated by the "sensible" world of adults).

These novels are informed by a vision of absurdity and have at their center a passive, rationalistic, or hopelessly ineffectual victim-hero, dominated by his situation rather than creating or acting to change it. They have a more or less realistic surface, with somewhat surrealistic elements. Realism of detail, rather, underscores the madness of the world, its grotesque comedy.

This is true even of *The Trial.* *The Trial,* however, is as much a forerunner of the absurdist novel with a stylized absurd surface as it is a forerunner of the aforementioned absurdist novel with a realistic surface. The absurd surface exaggerates. Through exaggeration and repetitions; grotesqueries; unique, exotic, bizarre, or strange symbols (the whippers in *The Trial,* for example, or the mechanical executioners), the absurdity found in life is transcribed through surreal descriptions. Special surrealistic situations, too, are created to embody the inexplicable; and somewhat common situations, such as those of war, are exaggerated and distorted to produce a heightened effect of the sort experienced in dreams. Representative of the absurdist novels using surreal means to present the victim-hero's situation are Pynchon's *V,*[27] Hawkes's *The Cannibal* [28] and *Second Skin* [29] (indeed, all Hawkes's work may be included in this category), John Barth's *The End of the Road* [30] (and, to some extent, *The Sot-Weed Factor* [31] and *Giles Goat-Boy,*[32] although these seem *tours de force* more indebted to eighteenth-century satire and other ancient and modern literary conventions than to their admittedly dark modernist view of man's absurd position in

an incalculable world), and Joseph Heller's *Catch-22*, which
has an activist victim-hero similar to Holden Caulfield.[33]
    These are, of course, not all-inclusive categories, nor can
any categorizing help us to apprehend truly the unique qualities of the individual novels named. The only reason that I
have attempted to define some novels of recent American fiction as absurdist is to make a distinction between the absurdist novel and the activist novel. The activist novel, the definition of which is my larger purpose in this book, is postab-
surd and starts with a disavowal of the absurdist world and
its destructive terms. Whether the absurd terms of a rationalistic and materialistic world still govern that world or not is
not at issue in the activist novel. The activist hero, fully as
alienated as any innocent or guilty victim-hero, chooses to sustain his alienation in order to assert his own subjective truth
and to seek for himself a wonderful, improbable, transcendent self, an authentic identity he has created for himself, a
self that refuses to participate in the schemes of a madden-
ingly reasonable world's failures and successes. He turns inward in an attempt to turn fully outward, in an attempt to
put his own particular truth against the banalities of world-
lings and the nihilism of a world of undiscoverable or "lost"
values. Whether he truly achieves the ideal being of his personally defined transcendent self (he does not) is not at issue
here either. What is relevant is his choice, his goal, his actions,
his exploration of possibles beyond the givens and beyond
the probable, and his putting himself, a particular, beyond
the confines of the absurdist realities.[34]
    K., in *The Castle,* is a germinal presentation of this activist
hero. He is neither an innocent nor a guilty victim: he is
counterposed to the innocent Karl and the guilty Joseph K.
His triumph is not assured, but there is a little triumph in
his initial choice to seek directly a wonderful goal, to make a
wholehearted assault on the castle. In my next chapter, K.
will be discussed as the activist hero, and the form his novel
takes to accommodate his peculiar spiritual adventure in a

secular world will be considered. Albert Camus has suggested that *The Trial* describes the modern disease and *The Castle* prescribes a treatment for that disease.[35] While Kafka never seems prescriptive, *The Castle* nevertheless does turn from the labyrinthine ways of an imprisoned self to the labyrinthine ways of a free one, and in so doing proposes a hero who has become—especially in American novels of the fifties and sixties—a viable alternative to the victim-hero of modernist fiction.

How directly Kafka's work has influenced American novelists since World War II is difficult to say. Kafka's work was first translated into English and published in America in the thirties and forties; it was not until the forties that it captured the attention of the avant garde in this country, primarily through publication of the stories and of evaluative comments on the work in *Partisan Review*. During the forties, Bellow, Mailer, Malamud, and Salinger were writing their first stories and novels. Bellow's *Dangling Man* was first published, in a shorter form than that of the finished novel, as "Notes of a Dangling Man" in *Partisan Review* in 1943.[36] But more significant than any external evidence of Kafka's direct influence is the impress of the Kafkan hero on the minds of American writers who, from the internal evidence of their work, demonstrate that they share his sensibility. These American writers have inevitably transformed the Kafkan vision by using it in a way that coincides with American consciousness and with their own native perceptions.

2
The Kafkan Hero K. of *The Castle*: Prototype for a Modern Spiritual Activist Hero

The Kafkan hero K. of *The Castle* has by his struggle for a definition of the self changed the shape and ground of many of the serious novels of the recent decades of the twentieth century. With the breakdown of traditional systems of philosophy, religion, and ethics, the values of the individual man have been cut loose from universally accepted systems of thought which he might use as his own frame of reference for his intercourse with God and with other men. As once the microcosm was held to mirror the macrocosm, now the macrocosm mirrors the microcosm: man makes his own world in which he functions. Moreover, he makes it as he moves; he creates it in action. His main quality, in existential terms, is the kinetic one of "becomingness," his struggle is toward "beingness." When the existent man going toward being, and shaping the world in his terms, is a fictive hero, he gives his container, the world of his novel, a new literary shape that departs from older literary forms as much as he departs from older hero forms.

To be sure, this hero is not wholly new. He is related to an older hero of romance, and his quest is basically the older one: the quest for an absolute sense of significant meaning in life, the search for some ultimate answer that man is more than physical being and is in some way divine or somehow partakes of the divine. But this new quest is a question; it is open-ended. Furthermore, it must be undertaken without the traditional markers of the way—or with the traditional markers there but pointing, absurdly, in wrong or ambivalent directions. The modern knight finds the true way as he goes, by the markers of his immediate experience; or he may not find the true way. It is the purpose of this study to examine this new hero, his way, his actions, his goals, and his world—fictive and, by implication, real.

The Castle's K. is an existential hero; his acts lack conclusive meaning, for they are acts in process. The single act's "meaning can only be given by more process, which in turn lacks meaning to be given by more process." [1] By examining Kafka's hero, in his intensive process of self-definition, I intend that analogies with him will show the peculiar characteristics of some of the later heroes of Malamud, Salinger, Bellow, and other recent American novelists in their special insistence on openly confronting the basic moral and spiritual problems of modern existence and their peculiar blend of European pessimism and American optimism.

The heroes of Kafka's novels, *Amerika, The Trial,* and *The Castle,* are characterized by their solitariness, which, even when they are in social contexts, is intensified by their inwardness, their immediate "feel" of self, and their involvement with their personal struggle toward some goal of their own. But it is K. in *The Castle* who escapes the confines of an absurdist world, most clearly strikes out on his own, and has a subjective but definite image of his goal before him. In *The Castle,* K.'s goal, the castle itself, undergoes change and definition through K.'s experience; however, as a fundamental goal, it is consistent from the beginning of the book. He knows what he wants. In another sense, his ultimate goal is self-definition; the movement is toward a point of rest in which the self may be finally complete and may sit quietly and alone, letting the world "offer itself to [him] to be unmasked; it [the world] can't do otherwise; in raptures it will writhe before [him]." [2]

In this Kafkan hero is found not a "unitary character with his unitary personality," as Saul Bellow calls the traditional fictional hero, but "an oddly dispersed, ragged, mingled, broken amorphous creature whose outlines are everywhere . . . and who is impossible to circumscribe in any scheme of time. A cubistic, Bergsonian, uncertain, eternal mortal someone. . . ." [3] He is a protean hero who, in his openness, opposes, is over-against, the traditionally designed or the more recent mass-produced image of civilized man. The modern novelist intends that a fresh truth will issue forth out of the adventures of an open hero who defies the formulas and types to be found in and out of fiction. It becomes the novelist's paradoxical task, with this sort of hero, to structure the chaos of human experience, while still preserving the chaotic feel of that experience. The experience of the open hero in his indeterminate struggle toward completion takes place in a world that he defines in terms contingent upon the nature of his forays into it. In this novelistic situation the form of each particular novel changes with the hero: the traditional structure of the novel does not allow room for the unique, asocial movements and choices of a protean hero or for the metaphysical ideas his singularities initiate.

Along with the play of opposing ideas resulting from the presentation of a process of multiple choices and the inconclusiveness inherent in a story of existential becomingness (two of the marked characteristics of the form of *The Castle*), there is in the style of the activist novel an insistent and deliberate attempt to destroy aesthetic distance. In *Fear and Trembling*, Kierkegaard emphasizes that a story is one thing at a distance and another at close, or intimately involved, range. In telling the story of Abraham, Kierkegaard tries to make the reader realize Abraham fully as an existent man, with the possible choices of all men, in order that the reader may ultimately perceive and understand Abraham's final choice of faith. Perhaps the reader cannot understand fully, as Kierkegaard says he himself cannot: instead he knows a blinding truth and has a sense of absolute value in a particular situation. At a distance we all know it as story; as Kierkegaard says, "it was only a trial" in the simple story. But, "Who gave strength to Abraham's arm? Who held his right hand up so that it did not fall limp at his side? He who gazes at this becomes blind.—And yet rare enough perhaps is the man who becomes paralyzed and blind, still more rare one who worthily recounts what happened. We all know it—it was only a trial." [4]

Kafka in his storytelling attempts to escape aesthetic distance, to engage the reader passionately with the hero and in the hero's quest. After *The Castle* is finished, one cannot say "it was only a trial." (Bellow, Mailer, Malamud and, to some extent, Salinger are capable of risking, and in their later works do risk, formal considerations in order to reach out and pull the reader in. In their faithfulness to the existential demands of their hero, these writers, as well as Kafka in his activist novel, *The Castle*, renounce a sense of aesthetic distance in order to give us a closer view of existential reality.)

The Kafkan hero of *The Castle*, K., is a Kierkegaardian hero, a hero over-against universals who, in his immediacy, defies easy categories. He is a very particular consciousness, but without static characteristics; we know him only by his choices and his actions. He is a particular process of continuity that defines the Kafkan view of the human condition, so that through his particularity K. comes to have symbolic meaning. We cannot label and set aside this hero as representing simply this or that—a formula; even Max Brod comments on the impossibility of assigning allegorical terms to Kafka's work,[5] although at times this is precisely what Brod does. The most we may do with the Kafkan hero is describe his choices and actions and the significant areas in which these choices and actions occur.

In *The Castle,* the areas of action are the moral and spiritual; K.'s significant choices in these areas are all for the spiritual: they represent K.'s absolute relation to the Absolute through K.'s particularity.[6] The Absolute, which is symbolically presented in the castle, is K.'s goal. His choices are toward this goal, often at the expense of the moral, always at the expense of the Kierkegaardian ethical. The interpretation of being for K., then, is in spiritual terms: he will be defined, rather than be inside a process of definition, when he knows himself to belong absolutely and irrevocably to the castle; when he is what he now merely says he has been called to be: the castle's Land-Surveyor. He seeks a spiritual relationship with the castle; in his relationships with other individuals, those relationships in which moral action or ethical behavior is involved, he insists on the primacy of his pursuit of acceptance from the castle. With his affairs in the village, those community affairs through which the Kierkegaardian ethical is expressed, he is almost totally unconcerned. Only insofar as they are connected with the castle do the villagers interest K.

K. comes to the village on his way to the castle, having chosen to come and having given up his past. Karl, who has not chosen to come to America but has been flung into his strange situation, keeps his past in memories of Germany and in a photograph of his mother and father, which, however, is soon lost. Joseph K., a hero halfway between Karl and K., is accused, but in his recognition of his trial he accepts the new strange situation through which he must encounter reality in his life. In Joseph K.'s new situation his past functions as the time of irrevocable guilt. In the fact that K. is pastless, and by his own choice, lies the distinction between him and the earlier heroes: in K.'s fundamental crucial choice to sacrifice his past and to be pure becomingness or being-toward-the-future, in answer to what he has interpreted as a summons from the castle (but which appears later to have been perhaps an enticement of an "evil day"[7]), he is exercising that first kind of free will which Kafka says, in an aphorism, a man potentially has:

A man has free will, and this of three kinds: first of all, he was free when he wanted this life; now, of course, he cannot go back on it, for his is no longer the person who wanted it then, except perhaps in so far as he carries out what he then wanted, in that he lives.

K. has sacrificed his past in his choice to live, to move toward the castle. His present life is the consequence of that choice. The aphorism continues:

Secondly, he is free in that he can choose the pace and the road of this life.

Thirdly, he is free in that, as the person who will sometime exist again, he has the will to make himself go through life under every condition and in this way come to himself, and this, what is more, on a road that, though it is a matter of choice, is still so very labyrinthine that there is no smallest area of this life that it leaves untouched.[8]

K. is free in the second and third way as well. He alone chooses his pace and road, and he makes himself experience fully all that lies on his labyrinthine way, in the act of defining his being so that he may finally *be*—that is, "the person who will sometime exist again." He accepts no simple truths such as the villagers, and especially the landlady of the Bridge Inn, might give him from their lore of legend or from their general experience; he insists on testing all things by his own experience.

By his freedom of choice, K. put his solitary self outside of what Kierkegaard calls the ethical circumference of universally understood and accepted duty in the community when he sacrificed his ordinary past in order to struggle toward the castle. In his continued struggle in the village, K. constantly refuses ethical guidance, preferring his own experience of reality. This is justified, primarily, by his insistence that he has an absolute relationship to the castle, which summoned him to be its Land-Surveyor. Thus, he is akin to Kierkegaard's Knight of Faith, best represented in Kierkegaard's work through the figure of Abraham in *Fear and Trembling*. K. is *not* a hero who may be identified by the universally understood terms of the serious hero of tragic vision, although he may appear to be similar. Kierkegaard says of Abraham: "Abraham's whole action stands in no relation to the universal, [it] is a purely private undertaking. Therefore, whereas the tragic hero is great by reason of his moral virtue, Abraham is great by reason of a purely personal virtue." [9] It is not through moral action, with other persons as central, or through a universally acknowledged moral concept, but through his personal action in respect to the castle that we must see K. To have put himself thus above the ethical and moral may be a sinful evasion of objective reality in K.; however, he seeks the subjective truth of his own reality; he seeks himself in his personal reality, which is spiritual.

The subjective, or relativistic, nature of K.'s quest puts the whole quest in doubt. K. is never certain from the outside that he has been summoned. He recognizes that he may have been "enticed" to put himself above universal, moral concepts of duty. The possibility of temptation is expounded by Kierkegaard: "If Abraham would express himself in terms of the universal, he must say that his situation is a temptation (*Anfechtung*), for he has no higher expression for that universal which stands above the universal which he transgresses." [10] In the mayor's bedroom, K. acknowledges to the mayor, an interpreter of the ethical, that he may in fact have been enticed to leave his home and make this " 'long, difficult journey' " toward the castle. The mayor assures K. that it is the " 'very uncertainty about [his] summons' " that guarantees him the " 'most courteous treatment' " in the village.[11]

The contingent nature of the summons as an immediately felt, subjective response of the particular man is recognized by Kierkegaard as dangerous; he says, "Though Abraham arouses my admiration, he at the same time appalls me," and adds: "He who denies himself and sacrifices himself for duty gives up the finite in order to grasp the infinite, and that man is secure enough. [Abraham] gives up the universal in order to grasp something still higher which is not universal—what is he doing?" [12] K. has put himself in jeopardy, outside and above the life of the ethical, with nothing but a subjective belief in the validity of his summons to the castle. The landlady defines his situation from her community viewpoint: " 'You are not from the Castle, you are not from the village, you aren't anything. Or rather, unfortunately, you are something, a stranger, a man who isn't wanted and is in everybody's way, a man who's always causing trouble, a man who takes up the maids' room, a man whose intentions are obscure. . . .' " [13] K. is thoroughly alienated and alone because of his goal; only he truly believes that he has a right to pursue this goal of belonging and being. (There is irony in the fact that his alienation stems from his goal of belonging; however, true being is the larger goal—belonging, incidental.)

He recognizes, however, that his uncertainty in the eyes of the community and its law gives him the freedom to believe in the validity of his struggle toward the castle. He has made his choice and intends to continue his private pursuit of the castle and its recognition of himself. When the landlady, in a friendlier moment, suggests that he submit to an official routine for gaining an interview with Klamm, a high official of the castle, K. chooses his own way:

"My decision is made, and I would try to carry it out even if an unfavorable answer were to come. And seeing that this is my fixed intention, I can't very well ask for an interview beforehand. A thing that would remain a daring attempt, but still an attempt in good faith so long as I didn't ask for an interview, would turn into an open transgression of the law after receiving an unfavorable answer. That frankly would be far worse." [14]

K., then, does not wish the certainty of the ethical or universal code, since that might put him into a condition of sin and into a state of despair without the belief in the validity of his quest. Also, he must remain a particular in absolute relation to the Absolute, without codified sanctions, or he will lose his inward sense of self. This hopelessness in himself would be worse than uncertainty and suffering, which leave him at least free to strive, and worse than "ignorance," which makes him at least daring. Significantly, K. flings open a door as he ends his first interview with the landlady and answers:

"Of course I'm ignorant, that's an unshakeable truth and a sad truth for me, but it gives me all the advantage of ignorance, which is greater daring, and so I'm prepared to put up with my ignorance, evil consequences and all, for some time to come, so long as my strength holds out. . . . an ignorant man thinks everything possible." [15]

Uncertainty gives K. freedom; ignorance gives him daring. As long as he is strong, strong in his resolve, he can continue to try; this is all he asks: the freedom to try, to control his own destiny to this extent. And his uncertainty is the foundation of his hopeful activity.

Indeed, in an aphorism, Kafka says, "The fact that there is nothing but a spiritual world deprives us of hope and gives us certainty." [16] K.'s uncertainty is not only the basis for his hope in the routine world but also in the spiritual world: "The fact that there is nothing but a spiritual world" is the premise on which K. acts; however, it is the personal and subjective, not the factual, reality of this premise that is vital for K. Paradoxically, if this "fact" were no longer a relational one but became an objective one, then K.'s activity and his personal awareness of himself in it might lead him to despair. Certainty would deprive K. of hope. The text of *The Castle* supports this interpretation of K.'s preference for his dual consciousness and his uncertain and subjective relationship with the castle when, on K.'s first day in the village, he hears a bell from the castle ringing merrily "as if to give him a parting sign till their next encounter." But "its tone was menacing, too, as if it threatened him with the fulfillment of his vague desire." [17]

K. does not want absolute certainty from outside, then; he wants his own subjective resolve in relation to the Absolute. He is responsible for himself, even when there are "evil consequences." Furthermore, K.'s insistence on the solitary nature of his way comes when he links his ignorance with his daring and suggests that " 'these [evil] consequences really affect nobody but myself, and that's why I simply can't understand your pleading. I'm certain you would always look after Frieda, and if I were to vanish from Frieda's ken you couldn't regard that as anything but good luck. So what are you afraid of?' " [18] This action is entirely spiritual. K. rejects the ethical behavior of universally accepted procedures at the same time that he rejects the moral choice of responsibility for Frieda, who loves him and whom he supposedly loves. In the world of the Kafkan hero there is little room for an expanded description of the intimate relation of two individuals; least of all is there room in the world of the activist Kafkan hero as he seeks the realization of his being in an absolute relation to the Absolute, alone.

Interludes with Frieda do describe particularized tenderness or passion; they do add concrete detail to our knowledge of what happens between persons; however, what happens between persons is momentary and secondary to the meaningful, purposeful design of the hero. When, in Chapter 13, Frieda accuses K. of "profiteering by possessing" [19] her, and he answers with a compelling description of their love, even then his answer, in its simplicity, reveals his first awareness of his own goal, as well as his willingness to include Frieda if she can come along naturally, unconsciously, easily on the way. K. says:

"But if it wasn't as bad as all that, if it wasn't a sly beast of prey that seized you that night, but you came to meet me, just as I went to meet you, and we found each other without a thought for ourselves, then, Frieda, tell me, how would things look? If that was really so, in acting for myself I was acting for you too, there is no distinction here, and only an enemy can draw it." [20]

But Frieda cannot always be the unconscious other half of his wholeness. Frieda is suspicious of his "hidden intention," which at times seems to her full of guile, in spite of K.'s actual astonishing openness.[21] She is ambivalent: she feels owned, used, hurt, while at the same time she recognizes his goal and knows she does not help but hinders him. He, on the other hand, feels a responsibility for her, which he does not fully really affectively assume. He is anxious, rather than really responsible, about food, shelter, and his janitorial duties, but anxious about these things only in relation to Frieda. It is the petty annoyances of life, the routines, that become connected with Frieda. He does not mind those, in fact, for he has not come to this place to lead "an honored and comfortable life." [22] (Respectability is the precise opposite of his goal.) However, the petty annoyances are endured only for Frieda, and he abandons them, and Frieda, when he gives himself up to "new hopes" that he feels he must follow with *all* his strength.[23] The relationship with Frieda underscores more severely the necessity for the hero to undertake his task alone, to make himself by himself, to keep his strength for his commitment to his absolute goal. Without that, he is a nothingness rather than an incompleteness. The theme of love as a predominant theme disappears in the fiction of Kafka. Preoccupied with metaphysical goals, the Kafkan hero is only momentarily seduced by earthly love, by the others.

About K., Kafka says:

K. fought for something vitally near to him, for himself, and moreover, at least at the very beginning, on his own initiative, for he was the attacker; and besides he fought not only for himself, but clearly for other powers as well, which he did not know, but in which, without infringing the regulations of the authorities, he was permitted to believe.[24]

Here is the Kierkegaardian Knight of Faith, alone and without sanction; but K. is "permitted to believe." The more his freely chosen, pure drive toward an absolute relation to the Absolute becomes mixed with ethical or moral motivations and sanctions, the more blurred becomes his vision of the castle, the less clearly seen his goal. Any freedom in the village, given by the authorities, paradoxically limits his freedom in the struggle toward his ultimate goal: the villagers tolerate him and give him light duties; thus, they "pampered and enervated him, ruled out all possibility of conflict, and transposed him to an unofficial, totally unrecognized, troubled, and alien existence." [25] Although at the very first K. thinks that his struggle toward the castle is best served by work in the community, his nature and the nature of his quest is repeatedly affirmed as nonethical, alien to the village and its life; the villagers view him as a stranger in the unique role he claims, and he feels that their easy acceptance of him as a mere individual hinders him in the crucial conflict by which alone he may attain his goal. The villagers must accept him as the Land-Surveyor appointed by the castle or reject him completely, in order that he may do battle with them, or with the codes they represent, and thus prove and keep his faith. Thus, when the villagers do not alienate him, he must alienate himself and choose always the alternative that maintains his pure relation to the castle. Consequently, he repeatedly chooses against the others and for himself, so that his progress in *The Castle* is toward total alienation, toward the man who has lost the whole world and yet not lost his self, toward a pure freedom in which there is "no room for any will, free or unfree" (the end of aphorism 89).

K. seems to have reached this pure freedom, momentarily, at the end of Chapter 8 in *The Castle,* when, after drinking Klamm's brandy, he finds himself alone in the courtyard of the inn where Klamm stays, and it seems to him as if at last those people had broken off all relations with him, and as if now in reality he were freer than he had ever been, and at liberty to wait here in this place, usually forbidden to him, as long as he desired, and had won a freedom such as hardly anybody else had ever succeeded in winning, and as if nobody could dare to touch him or drive him away, or even speak to him; but —this conviction was at least equally strong—as if at the same time there was nothing more senseless, nothing more hopeless, than this freedom, this waiting, this inviolability.[26]

As K.'s habitual shedding of the past, his choosing not to accumulate goods, and choosing not to make social and ethical commitments become more apparent, more intensively willed choices rather than seemingly accidental happenings, K. becomes more obviously a bare potentiality, the essential state of his inviolable freedom. Intuitively this is recognized by the boy who, when he grows up, wants to be like K. Hans is attracted by K.'s

absurdly distant future and the glorious developments that were to lead up to it. . . . that was why he was willing to accept K. even in his present state. The peculiar childish-grown-up acuteness of this wish consisted in the fact that Hans looked on K. as on a younger brother whose future would reach farther than his own, the future of a very little boy.[27]

This naked free self, which is as a "very little boy" in its inviolable freedom, has also an innocent yearning for the mere animal presence of other people. At the beginning of Chapter 9, after the vision of isolated freedom at the end of Chapter 8, K. feels a need to be once more in touch with the human; he wants "to see human faces." [28] He does not really wish to experience the others, but only to know that they are there so that he may not realize his actual alienation so acutely as he has done in the desolate courtyard of the inn. This is an impulse toward animal warmth. It is this impulse toward "company," as well as his tracking down of all clues that may lead to nearness to the castle, that takes him finally to Barnabas' house, to the alienated family of the village, where he hears Amalia's story. Amalia, though ostracized and despised by the villagers, mainly because she refuses to pretend that nothing has happened when something has happened, is, ironically, truly in the spirit of the village as it represents the Kierkegaardian ethical, since she sees the summons from a castle official which she has received as a temptation. Indeed, Olga, Amalia's sister, characterizes the castle official Sortini's summoning of Amalia as a satanic "abuse of power." She says: " 'The very thing that failed this one time because it came naked and undisguised and found an effective opponent in Amalia might very well succeed completely on a thousand other occasions in circumstances just a little less favorable, and might defy detection even by its victim.' " [29]

Amalia's plight leads to the consideration of the castle and its representatives: Whether the castle is divine or diabolical is, as Paul Goodman suggests, irrelevant; in either case, it is to be regarded only as K.'s goal.[30] The relevancy here is that Kafka makes the castle not only mysterious but also ambiguous. It is near and far, remotely indifferent and vitally concerned with the village affairs and the villagers, divine and diabolical—all these things at once. Kafka insists on the nonallegorical, undefinable nature of his hero's goal. All that is given is the castle as the Absolute, beyond and above the villagers and K., physically and spiritually.

This insistence on the paradoxical nature of this Absolute keeps Kafka's tale open to the play of opposites. He is existentially faithful to all that he knows of man's situation. When the Kierkegaardian idea of the particular in absolute relation to the Absolute—a teleological idea that, with the Absolute-as-divine, answers the question of what man is if he loses the world and yet keeps his self—is tested in the context of *The Castle*, it is no longer merely an abstract idea; it becomes a concretely realized view of life itself, a view related and opposed to other views of life. That there is no single, certain way of the self; that the self in its striving must embrace uncertainty and paradox, and strive toward the Absolute in spite of the fact that God may indeed be dead; that it is in the striving that the self exists and not in the end, not in the realized goal; that man is a becomingness and not a beingness and that in this fact lie his hopefulness and his freedom—all these inconclusive suppositions issue forth from the Kierkegaardian conclusions when they are tried in Kafka's existential context. Because Kafka is capable of allowing his Absolute to be paradoxically divine and diabolical, near and distant at once, as artist he achieves a detachment, an aesthetic structuring, which his and the reader's immediate involvement with K. might belie. *The Castle* has an open-ended hero in process—an immediately felt presence, in the Kierkegaardian sense—who is, nevertheless, enclosed by the ultimate irony that his spiritual goal, very real to him, is eternally unknowable and paradoxical in the world's terms. But it is outside and above K.'s struggle that the reader comprehends the final irony of this total view.

Finally, the very openness of the protean hero pushes against the conventional novel form and insists upon the play of opposites and the nonallegorizing fidelity to experience that exposes the paradox in every situation. K.'s striving, his successes and failures, his various confrontations of villagers and castle officials produce the cumulative, particularized awareness of the castle itself in its representation of the spiritual paradox. This attribute in the reader's understanding of the castle derives from K.'s outwardly uncertain, subjective, relational experience, in spite of the fact that his experience also ultimately reflects that one thing about the castle which is sure: that it is Absolute. Although the tale of K.'s adventure is inconclusive in terms of the hero's decisive victory or failure, the coexistence of opposites is so vitally maintained that the work has a tension that gives it an organic wholeness and clear aesthetic structure even though the tale is not shaped by any traditional concept of novel form.

3
Kafka and Bellow: Comparisons and Further Definitions

One of three fragments printed at the end of the definitive edition of *The Castle* starts: "Yesterday K. told us of the experience that he had had with Bürgel." [1] An unidentified storyteller is introduced as the narrator in this fragment, and it is probable that Kafka intended to make another separate tale of it. As it stands, it comments on and elucidates the whole narrative venture that Kafka undertook when he started to write *The Castle*. The fragment ends:

And now I am going to tell you the story as well as I can word for word, and as much in detail as K. told it to me yesterday with all the signs of mortal despair. I hope he has meanwhile been consoled by a new summons. But the story itself is really too funny; just listen: What is actually so funny about it is, of course, his own painstakingly detailed account, and a good deal of that will get lost in my retelling it. If I could really bring it out, it would give you a full-length picture of K. himself, though of Bürgel hardly a trace. If I could bring it out—that is the precondition. For otherwise the story may equally well turn out to be very boring, it contains that element too. But let us risk it. [2]

The nature of the Bürgel story, which is *not* told by the unidentified speaker in this fragment, is to be comic, and its comedy lies in the very fact that K. tells it so "painstakingly," as if his life depended on it. And K.'s life does depend on it, on the Bürgel story and on the whole story given in *The Castle*, for *The Castle* is a life history with a special emphasis: the quest for the self, the true self that "belongs," which is in a state of grace, or simply of rest, serenity, and completion, if we do not wish to use the specifically religious term *grace*.[3] The life depends on the telling of the life story because, though the goal is the transcendent one of a fulfilled self (which K. considers his true destiny or fate and to which he has given subjectively, and perhaps arbitrarily without any external confirmation, the name of Land-Surveyor), the only events of this life history are, paradoxically, nontranscendent ones, the facts of his struggle in the village. Each fact, furthermore, is without meaning except as a part of the process of becoming, a process dictated by the transcendent idea of being, which remains unattained and, by implication, unattainable. The process itself would be nothing if K. did not preserve painstakingly all the details of his life story as the above quotation indicates he does. In the whole of *The Castle* it is Kafka who preserves the details of K.'s struggle and makes the seriocomic story of the attempt to wrest a transcendent fate from a naturalistic world—a comic story, indeed, a spiritual tale which can only take place in a natural world. The importance of the story as story is apparent: a story is all it is. Not a mimetic representation of external reality, not an allegory, but the record of a subjective spiritual truth, realized in daily process in the secular world. If it is not recorded, made story, put into words that preserve the process, it does not exist at all anywhere in the world. The factual process might exist in some real life, but meaninglessly, for the secular process must be seen in the light of the transcendent goal or it has no meaning. Hence, the fictive life story is the only way that this particular process can exist and make a claim of immediacy, if not of objective truth, on the world.

Furthermore, the validity of the existence of subjective truth through the word stands for life and against death, as

Augie March declares when he speaks of the record he has made of his life story:

I have written out these memoirs of mine since, as a traveling man, traveling by myself, I have lots of time on my hands. For a couple of months last year I had to be in Rome. . . . Therefore I got into the habit of going every afternoon to the Cafe Valadier in the Borghese Gardens on top of the Pincio, with the whole cumulus Rome underneath, where I sat at a table and declared that I was an American, Chicago born, and all these other events and notions. Said not in order to be so highly significant but probably because human beings have the power to say and ought to employ it at the proper time. When finally you're done speaking you're dumb forever after, and when you're through stirring you go still, but this is no reason to decline to speak and stir or to be what you are.[4]

That death, the common doom, comes to each individual, to each self, and eventually blots out the distinctions between person and person is not a reason to choose death-in-life, to decline to say what *you* are, to move as *you* are, or to be what *you* are. The subjective truth of each individual is created out of the process of his life, and this process is only made manifest through the verbalized story that includes both the process and the vision of a transcendent self.

Like *The Castle*, *The Adventures of Augie March* is the life history of a particular self. But *The Castle* is not a story of secular adventures but rather the depiction of an inner life through its manifestations in movements, gestures, choices, and acts in the world; *The Adventures of Augie March* is in this same pattern, as a close look at the novel itself will show, though on the surface *The Adventures of Augie March* may be easily summarized as a "picaresque tale of a Jewish Huck Finn who bounces about the U.S. and Mexico sampling and quickly tiring of all manner of jobs, creeds and persons." [5]

Such a summary, though glib, includes the germ of much of the more serious critical comment that has been written on *The Adventures of Augie March*. Augie is Jewish, although nothing is made of his Jewishness; it is simply a personal fact. He is like Huck Finn in his peculiar brand of American innocence, which is in Augie, however, an innocence held obstinately, intentionally, and in spite of his recognition of the foolishness of such innocence in the modern, urban world—his is a *conscious* innocence. And the tale is picaresque in its detailing of adventure in a chaotic world. It is also, as Bellow has said of it, " 'all rhetoric.' " [6] It is, however, essentially in the Kafkan pattern of the manifestation of inner life through surface action; and the picaresque quality and the rhetoric are there to lessen the risk of being boring.

The unidentified speaker of Kafka's fragment says: "If I could bring it out—that is the precondition. For otherwise the story may equally well turn out to to be very boring, it contains that element too. But let us risk it." While Bellow risks it,[7] he knows that if the inner life of Augie March or any man is to become existent, it must be brought out, it must make its imprint on the world as story. Bellow has said, speaking against the excessive intellectuality of the *nouveau roman* in France, "A literature which is exclusively about itself? And boring, to boot? Intolerable!" [8] Neither did Kafka wish to write boring literature, since he recognized that to be boring was to defeat the purpose of storytelling; nor did Kafka write literature about literature, literature about culture, literature about history, literature about theology.[9]

Hardly ever have there been more intensely personal novels than Bellow's and Kafka's. Paul Goodman says of *The Castle* that it is concerned with character, not theology, and that it is *not* "imitating some absurdity at the heart of life" but is rather an effort to come to terms with "his [Kafka's] own lamentable character which he knows to be lamentable." [10] Kafka's writing may, then, be seen as an accident of personality, not as a self-conscious literary or artistic event. The novels are personally compelled and are personal histories—storytelling with a personal purpose. However, Kafka's work is always transvalued from neurotic self-awareness to meaningful fictive forms, as Philip Rahv makes clear when he says:

That Kafka was among the most neurotic of literary artists goes without saying. It accounts, mainly, for the felt menace of his fantastic symbolism and for his drastic departure from the well-defined norms of the literary imagination. For all its obviousness, however, the fact of Kafka's neuroticism presents a danger, if not a vulgar temptation, to the unliterary mind, which tends to confuse a fact so patent with critical judgment and appraisal. No greater error is possible in our approach to literary art. To avoid that common error it is above all necessary to perceive that Kafka is something more than a neurotic artist; he is also an artist of neurosis, that is to say, he succeeds in objectifying through imaginative means the states of mind typical of neurosis and hence in incorporating his private world into the public world we all live in. Once that is accomplished, the creative writer has performed the essential operation which is the secret of his triumph as an artist, if not as a man; he has exorcised his demon, freed himself of his personal burden, converting us into his accomplices. And we, as good readers, as willing accomplices, have no real reason to complain. Neurosis may be the occasion, but literature is the consequence. Moreover the creative writer is the last person we may look to if our concern is with drawing a line between the normal and the abnormal. For whatever the practicing psychologist may make of that crude though useful distinction, the artist cannot attend to it without inhibiting his sense of life in its full concreteness and complexity.[11]

Kafka is a personal and private writer "in the metaphysical mode, whose concern is with the ultimate structure of human existence."[12] So private a writer was he that he asked his friend Max Brod to burn the manuscripts of his novels at his death. But he converted his private, personal, metaphysical speculation into literature so that his heroes become, for all of us, seekers after the answers to the universal questions: What is man? What is real in the world?

Bellow's fiction seems less neurotic in initial impulse and, because of this, more optimistic about the nature of man. His seeming optimism also springs from his American spirit. Bellow chooses to write not from the Kafkan "inner need for it" [13] but because of a moral obligation on the part of a writer to investigate the same questions: What is man? What is real in the world? Bellow does say that he writes because he "must," [14] but in the same essay, he says that he writes for someone and that he writes not only because of his personal need to write: he writes a book to manifest love, to affirm human existence. He says:

> The objective conditions necessary for its [the novelistic imagination's] existence are supposedly gone. I've never heard it stated in the same circles that money is obsolete or that social advancement and distinction are obsolete. Apparently these things are hardier and don't require the same agreement as to the nature of the Universe.
>
> Well, such an issue can never be settled in debate. Neither the denials of academic people nor the affirmations of writers can make much difference. "To believe in the existence of a human being as such is love," says Simone Weil. This is what makes the difference. It is possible—all too possible—to say when we have read one more modern novel: "So what? What do I care? You yourself, the writer, didn't really care." It is all too often like that. But this caring or believing or love alone matters. All the rest, obsolescence, historical views, manners, agreed views of the Universe, is simply nonsense and trash. If we don't care, don't immediately care, then perish books both old and new, and novelists, and governments, too. If we do care, if we believe in the existence of others, then what we write is necessary.[15]

Bellow's personal impulse to write, whether out of a need to come to terms with "his own lamentable character" [16] or not, has been converted through conscious moral justification into an almost religious impulse of caring, loving, believing in the existence of others, in the affirmation of the existence of all men. A similar justification of the writer's activity is made in "The Writer as Moralist." [17] Walt Whitman, Bellow says, charged writers with the highest of moral duties. "The priest departs, the divine literatus arrives," he wrote in a prophetic spirit. This particular brand of Romanticism held the poet (the writer) to be the new spiritual leader and teacher of a community freed from slavery and superstition. Very often, and this was certainly true in Whitman's case, the poet offered himself as a model. In effect he said: If you want to know what an American of this democracy might be like—here I am. What I assume you shall assume and whoever touches me touches a man.[18]

In this same essay, Bellow expands what seems to be an essentially Whitmanesque position into a modern position of his own, which excludes theories of art-for-art's-sake, art-for-ideas'-sake, and art-for-didacticism's-sake, when he describes the moral nature of the activity of writing thus:

Either we want life to continue or we do not. If we don't want it to continue, why write books? The wish for death is powerful and silent. . . . But if we answer yes, we do want it to continue, we are liable to be asked how. In what form shall life be justified? That is the essence of the moral question. We call a writer moral to the degree that his imagination indicates to us how we may answer naturally, without strained arguments, with a spontaneous, mysterious proof that has no need to argue with despair.[19]

Whether the impulse to write is neurotic or otherwise contrived in order to come to terms with one's own character in the world or whether the justification is purely personal, based on the urgent need of the writer to write or on an enlarged moral and religious view of the writer's activity as meaningful, the point to make about Kafka and Bellow, and other writers of the activist modern novel, seems to be that they write novels not for the sake of art or for the sake of ideologies. Bellow categorizes Flaubert and Joyce as the novelists in recent literary history who explicitly rejected moral purpose —or life purposes—in favor of an art-novel that would evoke a pure, static, "aesthetic" response in the reader. Although he says this may be the satisfactory end of a poem,[20] Bellow contends "the novel meets life at a commoner level where confusion is inordinate." He says, "The art-for-art's sake novelist believed in pure form, classical order. Order of this sort is seldom available, and in chaotic conditions such beliefs must inevitably lead to disappointments." [21] He himself believes that the novelist moves toward order out of chaos in his work,[22] but Bellow does not think possible in the modern novel the complete artistic unity and harmony that results in aesthetic stasis.

An alternative to the art-for-art's-sake novel is the novel of ideas, which Bellow also discredits:

> What we sense in modern literature continually is not the absence of a desire to be moral, but rather a pointless, overwhelming, vague, objectless moral fervor. . . . In this sphere we see a multitude of moral purposes in wild disorder. For as long as novelists deal with ideas of good and evil, justice and injustice, social despair and hope, metaphysical pessimism and ideology, they are no better off than others who are involved cognitively with these dilemmas. . . . It is then scarcely possible for [their] art to avoid the fate of [their] ideas. They triumph together or fall together. Novelists as different as Camus, Thomas Mann, and Arthur Koestler are alike in this respect. Their art is as strong as their intellectual position—or as weak.[23]

What he specifically discredits here is the adoption by the novelist of a particular ideology or external structure of ideas about the world, even such an open philosophical system as Sartre's existentialism or Camus' idea of the absurd. Any ideological construct that pre-exists the novelistic task is a given; and it is the nature of Bellow's work to shun all givens, to explore, without the confines of a system, the texture of life and the nature of existence in order to discover, inside the novel's material, the possible, available, parallel forms in which life itself may continue. Exploration of the varietal forms of self becomes Bellow's pervading theme, as well as his method; his vision affirms the possibility of new forms for human life in the modern world, the possibility of vital human existence. Because of this theme and vision, he calls himself as writer a "teacher," but he emphasizes that he does not wish to be didactic: he will not offer moral constructs or lessons as patterns to be learned. The writing is explorative, not didactic; its moral fervor is in its storytelling energy, not in its position-taking. Moral "commitment in a novel may be measured by its power to absorb us; by the energy it contains. A book which is lacking in power cannot be moral. Dullness is worse than obscenity. A dull book is wicked." [24]

In his definition of his activity as a writer, Bellow starts with the assumption that old forms for fiction, as old value systems for life, are lost; he refuses, however, to assume, with "metaphysical pessimists," that therefore everything—God, man as an individual self, meaning, value—is dead. He sees that other writers are convinced, in the ideological terms of our time,[25] "that the jig of the Self is up." But he himself is "not convinced that there is less 'selfhood' in the modern world." He says:

We have so completely debunked the old idea of the Self that we can hardly continue in the same way. Perhaps some power within us will tell us what we are, now that old misconceptions have been laid low. Undeniably the human being is not what he was commonly thought a century ago. The question nevertheless remains. He is something. What is he? [26]

The question remains, and it is this question, as well as the manifold corollary questions, that engross Bellow—the question and the mystery:

. . . this question, it seems to me, modern writers have answered poorly. They have told us, indignantly or nihilistically or comically, how great our error is, but for the rest they have offered us thin fare. The fact is that modern writers sin when they suppose that they *know*, as they conceive that physics knows or that history knows. The subject of the novelist is not knowable in any such way. The mystery increases, it does not grow less as types of literature wear out. It is, however, Symbolism or Realism or Sensibility wearing out, and not the mystery of mankind.[27]

The emphasis on questions and mystery pervades all of Bellow's definitions of the novelistic venture. The openness of that venture, excluding past answers to the problem of form and tone (Symbolism, Realism, Sensibility) and excluding past answers and some new ideological answers to the problem of man's nature, suggests that the novel is a way of investigation, an open field of exploration and possible discovery (or discovery of possibles). The novel becomes a form of inquiry.

Kafka, whose personality was more reserved and self-enclosed than Bellow's, did not write the sort of public statements justifying his private commitment to literature that Bellow has written. Both commitments are private, however. The above quotations from Bellow's public statements about writing underline the privacy of his commitment and the nature of his "teaching" as the giving of personal truth only, after the manner of Whitman's "Touch me and you touch a man." Kafka thought of his writing as a prayer and his commitment to literature as a personal salvation.[28] What he did not do was understand himself as a "teacher" in Bellow's Whitmanesque way. However, in writing he gave to the world his personal truth, as he discovered it through writing. In reading Kafka's novels one has the immediate sense of touching a man. (My comments here refer to *Amerika, The Trial,* and *The Castle,* not to the more enclosed short stories such as "In the Penal Colony" and "Metamorphosis," nor to the short "lyrical dialectics"—Paul Goodman's term in *Kafka's Prayer*—such as "The Investigations of a Dog" or "The Burrow." Although all these, too, give the sense of Kafka's personality, they are not as urgent and immediate. They more clearly reflect the externalized *conclusions* to which Kafka came, rather than the struggle toward or against those conclusions. The struggle itself, in all its urgency, is embodied in the longer work of the novels.) But Kafka wrote not to "teach" but to "breathe" [29] and to exist. "Everything that is not literature bores me and I hate it, for it disturbs me or de-

lays me." [30] Both Kafka's and Bellow's commitments to literature are for the sake of life, one's own and all life, not for
the sake of art or ideology.

The personal is transformed in the novel from the initial
impulse to make art for life's sake into a form of art and a
kind of metaphysical truth. In Kafka's and Bellow's novels
one perceives the metaphysical presence in the work, finally,
as a skeletal structure of strong significance, in spite of the
original intensely personal impulse with which the writing was
undertaken and in spite of the intention to write in order to
come to terms with oneself or to teach by presenting forms
for man's existence. The bare metaphysicality of the action is
apparent also in spite of the realistic, densely secular scenes
which make up the setting. What is arrived at through the
actions of the hero of the novel are suppositions, but the importance of these suppositions, or questioned and uncertain
formulations, consists in their metaphysicality. And to this assertion I add that those suppositions are about the spiritual
nature of man without being about God. It is not the ontology of God but the ontology of man, specifically in an agnos-
tic, open, questioning state, that is here presented.

It may be necessary to say more about what I mean by
metaphysical and by *spiritual* as well as to show the way the
personal in Kafka and Bellow inevitably becomes metaphysical and spiritual.

Kafka's dictum that writing is a prayer and Bellow's statement that he wishes to investigate the mysterious "something" that is selfhood are both earnest starting points par-
taking of the spiritual. Both depend on a kind of faith in the
viability of personal truth as it may be realized in literature.
This is something more, as I've already said, than a commitment to literature or art: it is metaphysical and spiritual.[31]
However, these two terms are not synonymous and must be
distinguished.

Metaphysics is that part of philosophy which includes ontology (the study of the nature of being) and cosmology (the

study of essential causes and processes). In the widest sense the word *metaphysics* suggests any abstract philosophical truth, and in the narrowest sense the word refers only to ontology. Kafka and Bellow are not metaphysical in their reasoning: they do not reason in abstruse, abstract, or ideological systems, but the truths they seek and find are metaphysical, even though they are not enclosed in a system. Bellow would repudiate any systematized findings, even the modern ones of existentialism; and it is the modern existentialist metaphysics, of Sartre and other atheistic existentialist thinkers, that he repudiates in his chastisement (noted above) of position-taking based on ideological opinion in the novel. "To look for elaborate commitments [inside the novel] is therefore vain. Commitments are far more rudimentary than any 'position' or intellectual attitude might imply." [32] A similar repudiation of the use in the novel of external metaphysical systems arrived at intellectually and philosophically—separately from the act of writing the novel—is apparent in this dictum: "For as long as novelists deal with ideas of good and evil, justice and injustice, social despair and hope, metaphysical pessimism and ideology, they are no better off than others who are involved cognitively with these dilemmas." [33] In spite of this repudiation of a preconceived metaphysics, Bellow, in all his novels, fundamentally asks the ontological questions: What is man? How does he exist? Bellow's novel is a special form of inquiry, comes to no systematic conclusions, and is a metaphysical process in fictive terms; it is not a metaphysical construct, conclusion, system, or statement, nor does it exemplify any system elaborated outside of and prior to the novel's internal process.

Literary metaphysicality emerges through the hero's actions in relation to his environment, but these actions must be in the form of questions; the vision must be embodied in speculations. The result is an overwhelming sense of inconclusiveness, which suggests that the answers exist in the repetition of the primary questions, that man's quest for fulfillment is constant and unfulfilled. Here the spiritual impinges on the metaphysical, for spiritual striving is implicit in the affirmation of constant quest: the activist heroes of *The Castle* and of Bellow's *The Adventures of Augie March* and *Henderson the Rain King*,[34] for example, will not take an eternal "no" for an answer. They will not accept the dry, atheistic, empirical answers of modern times, nor will they accept, without testing, a simple affirmation of historical religion's tenets. They wish to realize what is possible in their own lives, and what is possible as the "more" beyond their secular environments.

In a discussion of Kafka, Eliseo Vivas says of Joseph K. and K., two characters whom he assumes to be essentially the same character (an assumption I do not share): "He [Kafka] grasped clearly the meaning of certain phenomena as constitutive of normal human development in its break from what Kierkegaard called the 'aesthetic' stage, But he was not able to concede what is demanded in order to reach the 'ethico-religious' stage."[35]

I agree with Vivas' description of the Kafkan hero as it pertains to Joseph K. in *The Trial;* however, the distinct difference between Joseph K. and K. in *The Castle* is that K. makes a leap of faith and puts himself, as a particular, in an absolute relation with the Absolute. Leaving the aesthetic stage of natural, rational, empirical, merely secular understanding behind, he enters the ethico-religious stage, believing in his summons from the castle, even though he knows it may have been a temptation. The ethical seems to be represented by the village, where K. is constantly forced to inspect and reject aesthetic and secular demands and to choose, constantly, himself in his relation to the castle, the transcendent or spiritual element, the Absolute. But the village itself is at a remove from the simple aesthetic sphere, sitting as it does close to the castle; it is the place between the aesthetic and the religious: it is the ethical. While in the village, however, K. does not participate in its activities: he is always alien, always the stranger. His quest is spiritual and will not be satisfied by aesthetic sureties, which still lurk in the village, half hidden, or with the ethical sureties of the villagers. (See my Chapter 2.)

To discuss *The Castle* in terms of Kierkegaard's philosophy would appear to assign it an external metaphysics; clearly, however, no matter how much affinity one might show between the Kierkegaardian hero and Kafka's K., the latter is never to be understood as purely Kierkegaardian. He is not, as hero, an allegorical projection of Kierkegaard's Knight of Faith. He partakes of and impinges on the Kierkegaardian idea and through his actions changes our understanding of that idea and of the Knight of Faith, for through his actions he shows us how it *is* to be such a one on such a quest, not how it should be. How it is can emerge only through the story. As Vivas himself points out, Brod, in his *Biography*, cites Kafka as having said, "Our art consists of being dazzled by truth." [36] Life may not be captured whole, but some dazzling truth about it may reside in the telling of it. If Kafka's view of life was informed by Kierkegaardian philosophy, it is nevertheless a vision of life, not a philosophical view of it, that he attempted to record.

The hero on a continuing quest—the spiritual-activist hero always in process—is one aspect of literary metaphysicality. Another aspect is the presentation of the environment in which or against which the hero acts. In the world of Kafka and Bellow, the secular world has two characteristics, one dependent upon the other: it is always changing, and it is in flux because it is always relative to the hero's perception of it. It is part of a subjective, not an objective, or objectified, reality: it is made up of human facts and is not an ideological or scientific representation.

In *Nausea*, Sartre's journal-novel, on the other hand, Sartre's view of the universe is an ideological construct imposed upon the text of the novel. Bellow's journal-novel, *Dangling Man*, deals with the environment not as part of an ideology outside the consciousness of the hero, Joseph, but as a fact of his consciousness. Joseph, regarding a dark Chicago scene, says:

The sun had been covered up; snow was beginning to fall. It was sprinkled over the black pores of the gravel and was lying in thin slips on the slanting roofs. I could see a long way from this third-floor height. Not far off there were chimneys, their smoke a lighter gray than the gray of the sky; and, straight before me, ranges of poor dwellings, warehouses, billboards, culverts. . . . These I surveyed, pressing my forehead on the glass. It was my painful obligation to look and to submit to myself the invariable question Where was there a particle of what, elsewhere, or in the past, had spoken in man's favor? There could be no doubt that these billboards, streets, tracks, houses, ugly and blind, were related to interior life. And yet, I told myself, there had to be a doubt. There were human lives organized around these ways and houses, and that they, the houses, say, were the analogue, that what men created they also were, through some transcendent means, I could not bring myself to concede. There must be a difference between things and persons. . . . Otherwise the people who lived here were actually a reflection of the things they lived among. I had always striven to avoid blaming them. Was that not in effect behind my daily reading of the paper? In their businesses and politics, their taverns, movies, assaults, divorces, murders, I tried continually to find clear signs of their common humanity.[37]

This long passage is worth quoting here since it shows the way Bellow deals, in *Dangling Man* and in *Herzog*,[38] an epistolary novel similar to the journal-novel in several respects, with the environment through the consciousness of the hero: the hero speculates about it, more philosophically than not, because it is a part of his life. It is interesting to note that the city environment on which Joseph speculates above is man-made, not separate from man. Yet man, in his "common humanity," is, *must* be, Joseph thinks, more than the city environment, with all its man-made ugliness. In thus doubting that man is to be equated with the thing he makes (the city, the society, the man-made environment), Joseph rejects an easy pessimism. However, he is not a simple, easygoing optimist; he is filled with doubts and questions. He reads the newspapers avidly in search for possible clues to man's human identity. He wants to know what is the common humanity at the base of the city's generalized activity. Joseph's speculation about the environment is metaphysical; but the metaphysical element is inextricably attached to a subjective, human consciousness.

In a review of *Herzog,* the novel by Bellow most like *Dangling Man,* Tony Tanner also suggests the way in which the city environment becomes more than a naturalistic Dreiseresque presence in *Herzog.* He points out that the significant action in the whole novel takes place in Herzog's head and adds that

People and incidents teem through his memory, precipitating great bouts of agitated soul-searching and pounding speculation. More than that, his mind heaves under the pressure and weight of the modern city and the innumerable problems of the modern age. Ultimately he finds himself struggling with the deepest questions and mysteries of human existence. He constantly returns to that central problem in Bellow's work—what is it to be truly human? [39]

Since the city environment of *Herzog* is more than objective physicality (as in Dreiser) and less than objectified ideology (as in Sartre), it has not its own nature with which man must come to separate terms outside of his immediate experience. The city environment is always subordinate— though often an accent—to the subjective questions and to the quest of the hero in *Herzog.*

The Victim and "Seize the Day," [40] two other novels by Bellow with urban settings, have the same interaction between hero and environment that *Dangling Man* and *Herzog* have, although *The Victim* and "Seize the Day" are more dramatic than speculative. However, in *Augie March* and *Henderson,* where the environment is more than the city and its vistas, environment does play a metaphysically symbolic role which goes beyond the speculations of the hero. But in these novels, too, environment is symbolic and suggestive, not an absolute part of an external ideology. It is still only important in what it symbolizes in relation to the struggle of the hero. *The Castle* environment of snow, which is a larger background to the hero's struggle than are the village scenes, where K. comes into contact with man-made things, is similar to the larger backgrounds of *Augie March* and *Henderson*. These larger environmental backgrounds, which are more than the city or the village, are where ideas about nature are symbolically transcribed. In such treatment of environment lies a metaphysical awareness of the universe similar to that in Sartre's *Nausea*, but there are two differences between the environment of *Nausea* and that of such books as *The Castle* and *Augie March*. Sartre, in *Nausea*, makes no distinction between the man-made and natural environments: city and nature become one, a single centralized sordidness representing the arbitrary, alien, hostile universe in which men must live. As I have suggested above, this lumping together is not found in Kafka's or Bellow's work. The second inherently different emphasis in *Nausea* grows from the first. Though an existentialist, disavowing systems, Sartre is first a philosopher and then a storyteller; consequently he is willing to generalize his view of environment as he does in *Nausea* without making the artful distinctions of the storyteller who is concerned that the truth dazzle, not convince.

A closer view of the way in which nature, that part of man's environment which is not man-made, not the city or the village, functions symbolically in *The Castle* and in the activist novels of Bellow—*Augie March* and *Henderson*—must be taken to show how these three novels differ from Sartre's. I wish to look at the similarities between the larger environments of snow in *The Castle* and of "a darkness" in *Augie March*. It would be simplest to call the snow and the darkness symbolic and omit specific metaphysical significances. Snow is more organically symbolic than the *gemütlich* but ambiguous detail of village inns and kitchens in *The Castle*, and the generalized darkness is more symbolic than the particularized city streets and stores in *Augie March*. But it is precisely the coexistence of all-enveloping snow with *gemütlich* kitchens or the coexistence of darkness with city streets and stores that gives the environment of these novels their special kind of metaphysical significance. Kafka's snow and Bellow's darkness make the village and the city seem un- alterable facts—perhaps eternal facts—in the whole scene; but the symbolic emphasis on the snow and the darkness in- sists that the total environment is *not* a part of a system of ideas as, for example, the bleak streets of *Nausea* are a part of the Sartrean existentialist idea. In *Nausea* the streets are an ideological representation of the separate world of objects which man must hopelessly confront.

The snow and darkness are unsystematized and *twofold* in their symbolic suggestions: they are there to suggest the ex- ternal background for the human endeavor, and they are there to be transcended. Though external and generalized backgrounds, they throw the emphasis back on the heroes' subjective and isolated consciousness. K. and Augie recognize the snow and darkness, and in their recognitions lie their knowledge of themselves and their world. They realize the snow and darkness through their consciousness, not through their actions. They recognize the natural environment as dif- ferent from the human, man-made fact, which is to be chal- lenged. Consciousness of the natural environment as larger- than-city fact and consciousness of it as unalterable fact lead to action not in response to it but in response to the purposes of the transcendent self, self that is more than any environ- ment, not self that is conditioned by it, trapped by it, or forced to act "constructively" through interacting with it. Since these heroes are not victims, not men "fallen in the [man-made] world of appearances," [41] but are rather heroes in the pursuit of a transcendent selfhood, their lives are given to the search for their own reality which defies the appearances given by the cities of the world. Their acknowledgment of the nonhuman reality outside of themselves and others only sharpens the affirmation of the self and maintains the *felt* metaphysicality of the work.

The snow in *The Castle* is an ever present, unchanging, season-defying, boundary-hiding presence of silence, colorlessness, and coldness.[42] Snow is the background against which K. strives for himself. It is the symbolic presentation of the nothingness against which the tiny figure of the Kafkan hero must assert himself. As a natural phenomenon, snow suggests the neutrality of nature in respect to man's quest. Nature's immutability and silence are perhaps extensions of the castle's immutability and semisilence, a silence broken by noises and messages which are meaningless to K.; their meaning is more related to the timelessness and limitlessness of the snow than to the time and place of the village, whose specificity captures K. since it is within and through the village that he must operate.

Two attributes of the snow that seem of particular importance are its denial of seasonal, rhythmic changes in nature and its boundary-hiding, limitless expanse. These two attributes make contributions to the text in separate ways, although they are both held within a single, unified symbol. First, the absence of seasonal, rhythmic changes in nature, which the constantly present snow portends, suggests the impossibility of rebirth as a recurrent part of nature's cycle. Yet K.'s struggle is for a kind of rebirth: he has left his past and come to the village, his present, in order to redeem his future by making direct contact with the castle. He has announced that he is reborn as ideality, that is, as the Land-Surveyor for the castle, an especially appointed servant of that high place. But the title of Land-Surveyor, it becomes apparent in the story, is not his to claim blithely. He must struggle for it, struggle to be reborn. This struggle progresses against the background of a rebirth-denying nature.

It is ironic that in the text of that struggle there should be the suggestion, contained in four lyric interludes,[43] that the way to the castle, to the desired connection that would validate the quest, is not through consciousness such as K.'s but through unconsciousness, semiconsciousness, or a relaxing into the natural process. The struggle-to-become is graced by these four stops, pauses that manifest the loss of self-consciousness or purposefulness and show a kind of sleepiness or relaxation into the natural self as the way to true being. However, given the snow as the prevalent symbol of a re-birth-denying, deathly silent nature, the loss of purposefulness in the lyric passages becomes not a promise of the viability of the natural process available to all men if they will only give in to it, but rather a temptation away from the true path of the conscious, purposeful, ever watchful hero, who must await the main chance and seize what he wishes from an, at best, neutral universe—a hero whose life is defined by the process of becoming without which he is not pure being but ceases to be, even as a process, and is dead.

The other attribute of the symbolic snow—its boundary-hiding, limitless expanse—also makes a metaphysical contribution to the total text. As with the rebirth-denial attribute, the contribution is again in the form of an ironic contradiction. The place to which K. has come to be a Land-Surveyor is boundary-less. His definition of his own identity of being is thus subverted immediately by the natural condition of the environment. But, as in the case of the rebirth-denial attribute, so it is in the case of the boundary-less, limitless expanse of the snow: K. is not interested in the objective or phenomenological evidence which may be provided by nature; he is concerned only with his subjective perception of a truth toward which he supposes he moves, although he may in fact be only in a static relation to that truth. In the process which is K.'s character, subjectivity in the apprehension of his own truth is more important than regard for the phenomenological facts. What appears at first to be an ironic contradiction in the total text evolves as an underscoring of K.'s purposeful subjectivity, his main characteristic. What would K. be if he attempted to take clear, rational, logical notice of what would seem to be factual evidence? Nothing. He would be cancelled out by the evidence that there was no need for a Land-Surveyor.

In much the same way as snow in *The Castle* functions as an open metaphysical symbol, evading the exigencies of allegory, so darkness functions in *Augie March*. Bellow, like Kafka, converts through his symbolism the ironic confusion between the real and the apparent into an affirmation of the way it is for a particular man. The darkness of nature underlying the appearances of the city, which is established in *Augie March* as an adjunct of the city crowd, is an outer reality Augie perceives but finally refuses to be determined by when he asserts himself as one in search of a "fate good enough," as one who refuses to lead a "disappointed life."

A closer examination of the darkness symbolism in *Augie March* suggests a distinction between the use of snow in *The Castle* and the use of darkness in *Augie March*. In *The Castle*, the snow is a material part of the natural environment, objectively seen from an omniscient point of view, while in *Augie March*, which is written from the first-person point of view, the darkness which is finally symbolic of the external world of nature is also Augie's way of describing the deterministic and materialistic stuff of the world. An example of Augie's description of the darkness occurs in this passage:

However, as I felt on entering Erie, Pennsylvania, there is a darkness. It is for everyone. You don't, as perhaps some imagine, try it, one foot into it like a barbershop "September Morn." Nor are lowered into it with visitor's curiosity, as the old Eastern monarch was let down into the weeds inside a glass ball to observe the fishes. Nor are lifted straight after an unlucky tumble, like a Napoleon from the mud of the Arcole where he had been standing up to his thoughtful nose while the Hungarian bullets broke the clay off the bank. Only some Greeks and admirers of theirs, in their liquid noon, where the friendship of beauty to human things was perfect, thought they were clearly divided from this darkness. And these Greeks too were in it. But still they are the admiration of the rest of the mud-sprung, famine-knifed, street-pounding, war-rattled, difficult, painstaking, kicked in the belly, grief and cartilage mankind, the multitude, some under a coal-sucking Vesuvius of chaos smoke, some under a heaving Calcutta midnight, who very well know where they are.[44]

The darkness that is for everyone and is a constant presence becomes, through the imagistic transmutations of this passage, and others like it, connected with the city so that the natural material of the universe seems to come to fullest fruition in the modern, crowded, smoke-choked city, where it forces itself upon mass-man. But that it is a natural fact *first*—that it is prior to cities—is what Augie makes evident in the passage quoted above.[45]

The external realities of the snow and darkness which present denials of man's possibility are ignored for the sake of the personal quest. In both these novels, the objective or natural world becomes connected with the world of appearances—that is, with the world of the village or the city, the man-made world of things—but it does not become identical with it. In neither the natural nor the man-made world will K. or Augie fall. They refuse to fall in or be circumscribed by either world as the nonactivist heroes of Kafka's *The Trial* and Bellow's *The Victim,* for example, are finally circumscribed by both because of their reliance on the man-made world and on what they can empirically discover there. K. and Augie insist on their own subjective reality: they insist on themselves and announce their denial of that which denies their individuality or predetermines them in shapes and roles they have not personally chosen. Freedom of the self against the circumstantial necessities of all environments is what they enact. They cannot be cheated since they, alone, define their possibilities. If they do not reach their envisioned ideals of true being—for K., the transcendent role of Land-Surveyor to the castle; for Augie, the similarly transcendent role of creator and director of the perfect, pastoral foster home—these ideal visions, self-constructed, inform their quests and raise them to the level of undefeated men who persistently move toward a self-conceived ideality. They say no to nihilism in all its forms.

The darkness and the snow deny the possibility of eternal values or absolutes in nature which are *meaningful to man.* Joseph Wood Krutch has remarked the absence of nature in Kafka's work, although he does not speak of *The Castle*'s snow, and he comments that, without nature, man is lost.[46] Krutch, of course, means the glorious nature, or Nature, of America's nineteenth-century Transcendentalists through which man might join with the Oversoul and, perhaps, God. Kafka's work does not simply omit this but denies its possibility. Bellow, with *Augie March*'s darkened urban setting, which is not contradicted by the dryness of Mexican landscape or the vast meaningless expanse of the sea in the rowboat scene or the vistas of modern Europe after the war, similarly denies the possibility of divine intuitions in man's apprehension of nature.

This stance toward nature is maintained in all of Bellow's novels except the last, *Herzog,* in which God and nature do come together in Herzog's lyrical acceptance of the present as complete in itself—at least for the moment—at the end of the book. Lyrical, euphoric endings, which are inconclusive in terms of the whole work and represent only a pause in the struggle of the hero, a struggle which must be supposed to continue after the last page, are the pattern for Bellow's last three novels, *The Adventures of Augie March, Henderson the Rain King,* and *Herzog.*

The euphoric hopeful note at the end of *Augie March* is sounded, literally in song, in a frozen barren field of the French countryside across which Augie, with Jacqueline, a French maidservant, hikes toward a farmhouse after his car has stalled on the road. A dark, cold day and a bleak, frozen setting, it offers nothing of comfort to men on their way. To oppose the cold and bleakness, Jacqueline suggests singing, a French folk cure against freezing. A Mexican song leads to talk of dreams—Jacqueline's dream of Mexico and Augie's dream of not leading "a disappointed life." And with this notice of man's dream poised against the background of indifferent nature, Bellow proclaims, through Augie, his belief that men continue their quest for their own lives, in this optimistic passage:

I thought if I could beat the dark to Bruges, I'd see the green canals and ancient palaces. On a day like this I could use the comfort of it, when it was so raw. I was still chilled from the hike across the fields, but, thinking of Jacqueline and Mexico, I got to grinning again. That's the *animal ridens* in me, the laughing creature, forever rising up. What's so laughable, that a Jacqueline, for instance, as hard used as that by rough forces, will still refuse to lead a disappointed life? Or is the laugh at nature—including eternity—that it thinks it can win over us and the power of hope? [47]

It is interesting that in this scene at the end of *Augie March,* Bellow repeatedly uses the words *dark, white,* and *cold*—which sustain the image of a generalized and neutralized background against which Augie moves throughout the novel.

The use of nature, the African landscapes, in *Henderson the Rain King* is symbolically the same as in *Augie March,*[48] and the ending of *Henderson* is strikingly similar to the ending of *Augie March.* Henderson, returning from his African quest for an answer to the question of what his spirit really wants, finds his plane stopping to refuel at a Newfoundland airport. He wraps the Persian child, who has sat unknown and silent beside him on the trip, in a blanket and carries him outside for a breath of fresh air. Here the cold air is refreshing, unlike the cold at the end of *Augie March,* but the picture is still one of man's spirit set against a nature eternally gray, neutral, cold. With the child in his arms, Henderson runs around the plane, taking pleasure in his physical movement:

Laps and laps I galloped around the shining and riveted body of the plane, behind the fuel trucks. Dark faces were looking from within. The great, beautiful propellers were still, all four of them. I guess I felt it was my turn now to move, and so went running—leaping, leaping, pounding, and tingling over the pure white lining of the gray Arctic silence.[49]

This is a less verbally specified but more imagistically effective picture of man's energy posed against a neutral nature than the one at the end of *Augie March*.

Herzog, a personalist letter-novel that only sporadically resembles the two activist novels which precede it, does maintain the pattern of euphoric ending. However, *Herzog* concludes on a note of man's reconciliation with nature. The euphoria at the end of *Augie March* and *Henderson* is the euphoria of the undaunted self; the euphoria at the end of *Herzog* is the euphoria of the daunted self, resigned, submissive, reconciled to natural force in the universe; nature is now seen as a benevolent force.

At the end of *Herzog*, there is a shift to seeing nature not as coexistent with cities but as an entirely separate and different entity: nature is the antithesis of the man-made world of the cities, not the force underlying them. Nature is not, through its neutrality, a complement to man-made sordidness but is opposed to that sordidness. Suddenly, at the end of *Herzog*, nature emerges as a nineteenth-century Transcendentalist's Nature which man accepts as good.

The end of *Herzog* occurs in a pastoral summer setting: in the woods after having written his last letter—to God ("'How my mind has struggled to make coherent sense. I have not been too good at it. But have desired to do your unknowable will, taking it, and you, without symbols. Everything of intense significance. Especially if divested of me.'"[50])—Herzog picks flowers, feels at peace, needs no one and has no need to send messages, write letters. He is content in the serenity of the pastoral present, forgetting the past and making no urgent promises for the future. This is a new note in Bellow's work, and is characteristic of the difference between this last novel and the earlier ones.

That this latest of Bellow's novels should conclude with some sort of communion with God and some sort of rest in a benevolent nature is not surprising, since the quest of the activist hero for his self has, in *Augie March* and *Henderson,* a spiritual proportion. Augie and Henderson insist, as Herzog finally does not, that the spiritual must be found through human action if it is to be realized in the world. Like K. in *The Castle,* they strive toward the fulfillment of a transcendent goal: they cannot simply believe, accept, live a life of faith. They know their particularity and through it they wish to affirm their own connection with a transcendent principle, something which is more than man-made or natural materiality.

Finally then, these metaphysical life stories are stories of the spirit. The curious contradiction inherent in the *willing* of the spirit, which the spiritual activism of K. represents, pervades Western literature; but the painstaking examination of the process of willing the spirit as the center of a story is a modern tradition initiated by Kafka and continued by various American writers, among whom Bellow figures prominently. In the next chapter I will discuss, among other things, this phenomenon of spiritual will as it is presented through Augie March and Henderson. Meanwhile, I have tried in this chapter to provide a link between Kafka and Bellow, which may serve to justify the connections I will make between their texts, by comparing their initial impulses and motives for storytelling; their definitions of storytelling; their uses of a felt metaphysicality functioning as symbolic meaning; their avoidance of systematic ideology; and their strategies for telling the spiritual story in a modern manner.

4
The Heroes of
Saul Bellow's Novels

The Victim-Hero in Bellow's Early Novels

In *Dangling Man*, Saul Bellow works with the themes of Kafka's *Trial*: arrest, guilt, self-victimization, alienation, and the inability to use freedom positively and creatively when relieved of routine occupations. Joseph K. in *The Trial* is placed under a curious arrest which "frees" him from his routines at the bank; however, he uses his "free" time to investigate the reason for his arrest, his alleged guilt, and the way in which he may legally establish his innocence. He wastes himself and is constantly frustrated in his attempt to deal rationally with the system under which he lives, to establish, *within* it, his legal innocence. By staying inside the system, he compounds the guilt of his prior unarrested life: the guilt of the unimaginative timeserver who does not create new and positive forms for his life but lives only according to the roles society has assigned him. This guilt and his compounding of it lead to the death of the self, worked out in the middle of the novel as a process and at the end of the novel by the killing of Joseph K. at the hands of the servants of authority.

Joseph in *Dangling Man* is in a crucial situation similar to Joseph K.'s. When first encountered, he is starting a journal, the novelistic record of his situation. He, too, is under "arrest" and has been for seven months. After his draft call into

the United States Army, he has given up his routine obligations as a clerk at the travel agency; but his induction has
been delayed by a bureaucratic investigation of his Canadian
citizenship by Army authorities. His "normal" life brought
to a standstill, Joseph decides to use his free time to read, to
write essays on the Enlightenment, and to pursue rational, humanistic, intellectual concerns and thoughts which have always been his style. He finds he cannot continue in his old
terms without his old routines: without his daily life of
friends, jobs, community interests (he had been a Trotskyist),
the optimistic thoughts of those simpler, routinized times
have gone. He gives himself to inward speculation, attempts
to understand rationally the mistakes of the "old Joseph"
and to find alternatives for the "new Joseph," who seems
more alienated than free in spite of his release from former
obligations. Bellow's Joseph engages in two dialogues with
the Spirit of Alternatives, dialogues that explore the problem
of how to live. The first of these contains an important exchange between the new Joseph and *Tu As Raison Aussi,* as
the Spirit of Alternatives is called, probably a reference to
the old Joseph's humanistic interest in the French Enlightenment and its philosophers. This exchange centers on man's
historical need for an ideal construction by which to shape
his life and by which to live. Joseph says:

"Well, it's a lovely phrase. An ideal construction, an obsessive device. There have been innumerable varieties: for study, for wisdom, bravery, war, the benefits of cruelty, for art; the God-man of
the ancient cultures, the Humanistic full man, the courtly lover,
the Knight, the ecclesiastic, the despot, the ascetic, the million-
aire, the manager. I could name hundreds of these ideal constructions, each with its assertions and symbols, each finding—in conduct, in God, in Art, in money—its particular answer and each
proclaiming: 'This is the only way to meet chaos.' "

Tu As Raison Aussi asks:

   "Do you want one of those constructions, Joseph?"
   "Doesn't it seem we need them?"

"I don't know."

"Can't get along without them?"

"If you see it that way."

"Apparently we need to give ourselves some exclusive focus, passionate and engulfing."

"One might say that."

"But what of the gap between the ideal construction and the real world, the truth?" [1]

The implied conclusion of this dialogue is that the ideal construction, a structure *external* to the particular man—the social, political, or religious cause to which the particular man may attach himself deliberately in order to find a way to live (may it not be the Law in *The Trial?*)—is no more effective a way of life than the routinized role-playing way of the common man. The absurd contradiction between the ideal construction and the truths of the existential world is all too apparent to the modern man.

Joseph finds no answer for his question, How does man live as a free man in the modern world? He is progressively alienated from society as his "freedom" from work, old friends, and old political ideas continues; yet he does not find any self-fulfilling way to use his freedom. He is his own prisoner, and his rational attempts to solve the philosophical problems his situation imposes on him fail. Finally, sick of self and irritable with all others, from whom he has become increasingly cut-off by his profitless self-concern, he gives himself over to the authorities by enlisting in the Army and demanding to be taken immediately. He no longer waits but symbolically kills the self which has become a burden. The last words of Joseph's four-and-a-half-month journal, and the novel, are:

I am no longer to be held accountable for myself; I am grateful for that. I am in other hands, relieved of self-determination, freedom canceled.

Hurray for regular hours!

And for the supervision of the spirit!

Long live regimentation! [2]

The spirit has *not* triumphed, so it might as well be relinquished to the authorities ready to receive it, its killers, the forces of regimentation.

Bellow's *Dangling Man* has more verbal reasoning than Kafka's symbolic presentation of Joseph K.'s dilemma in *The Trial;* Bellow here, as elsewhere, makes statements directly *about* the dilemma. (In later, more activist novels, Bellow makes his hero more a symbol for the dilemma than he does here, but the tendency to give the hero conscious and completely verbalized concepts to accompany his acts is always present in Bellow's novels.) While Bellow's Joseph seems to be victimized by a narrow, rationalistic concept of self, he nevertheless has an awareness of what the true alternative may be to ideal constructions, on the one hand, and to mediocre norms and routine roles, on the other hand. His post-Kafkan recognition of the cure for his dilemma is couched in these words, which provide a clue to Bellow's later breakthrough, activist novels:

If I had *Tu As Raison Aussi* with me today, I could tell him that the highest "ideal construction" is the one that unlocks the imprisoning self.

We struggle perpetually to free ourselves. Or, to put it somewhat differently, while we seem so intently and even desperately holding on to ourselves, we would far rather give ourselves away. We do not know how. So, at times, we throw ourselves away. When what we really want is to stop living so exclusively and vainly for our own sake, impure and unknowing, turning inward and self-fastened.

The quest, I am beginning to think, whether it be for money, for notoriety, reputation, increase of pride, whether it leads us to thievery, slaughter, sacrifice, the quest is one and the same. All the striving is for one end. I do not entirely understand this impulse. But it seems to me that its final end is the desire for pure freedom. We are all drawn toward the same craters of the spirit —to know what we are and what we are for, to know our purpose, to seek grace.[3]

The essential ideal, then, says Bellow's protagonist, is not the personal passion linked to an external social or religious cause, but rather the personal passion, not entirely understood by the dangling hero, for pure freedom for the self so that the self may know its own unique identity and purpose; in this knowledge there may lie the birth of grace or rest from striving. Because this grace seems to him to be the final end of all quests, regardless of the worldly terms in which the quest is carried on—money, notoriety, thievery—it is common humanity's quest for pure freedom, for pure spirit, for transcendence over deterministic circumstance, which is seen at the bottom of all man's striving. Each man's attempt to find the free and ideal self is the acting out of all men's ideals; hence the quest is not to be realized through empirical, inward-turning, self-fastened self-knowledge but through the action of the individual man in the world as being-in-the-world, not being-in-the-midst-of-the-world.[4]

The old Joseph was a liberal humanist, a man optimistically devoted to causes that made promises of progress toward utopian communities by political and social means; the new Joseph is pessimistic about the natural goodness of democratized man on whom his old hopes rested. The old Joseph was guilty of living an unexamined life, simplistically relying on social and political means to effect progress for all men. The new Joseph, though he sees the fallacies of his old optimism, still relies primarily on reason to show him the way to authenticity. Through reason, however, he finds only his old guilt and creates new frustrations, irritabilities, and guilts for himself. The reasonable inward-turning man who examines his past and present experience empirically and tries, on empirical evidence, to clear and free himself, is doomed to ultimate failure. Only the disavowal of the past, a leap of faith, and the quest for the spiritual self, his and all men's, can purify and free. The new Joseph of *Dangling Man* sees this but does not do this. He fails, as Joseph K. does, to free himself, remains imprisoned inside himself, and finally gives himself to the authorities of social death. K. and Augie March make the leap that Joseph K. and Joseph are unable to make.

But *Dangling Man,* Bellow's first novel, is followed by one more novel with a victimized and self-victimizing hero before Augie March appears in the third novel to seek freedom and self. Asa Leventhal, the hero of the second novel, *The Victim,* is, like Joseph in *Dangling Man,* caught peremptorily and arbitrarily in an imprisoning situation that disrupts his routine life and forces him to re-examine his motives and goals. *The Victim* is a dramatic concretion of the situation as the journal form of *Dangling Man* is not; consequently, in Asa's plight there is a much closer resemblance to that of Joseph K. Unlike Joseph in *Dangling Man,* Asa is not able to *see* the leap to the quest for pure freedom even as a possibility beyond him. The self-awareness of Joseph, who knows his guilt of the past, his sins of the present, and the possibilities of other men's futures, is not found in the protagonist of *The Victim* or *The Trial.* Joseph's situation may be similar to Asa's and Joseph K.'s; however, the freedom to say all there is to say about that situation, made possible by the journal style of *Dangling Man,* is not accorded Asa or Joseph K., who remain tightly kept within the confines of their fables and their situations.[5]

Augie March breaks through these confines, and the most productive way to examine the activist hero in the recent American novel is to look closely at Augie March, who comes upon the American literary scene as the first explorer of a new way. There is a rightness about Augie's comparison of himself to Columbus in the book's final words:

Why, I am a sort of Columbus of those near-at-hand and believe you can come to them in this immediate *terra incognita* that spreads out in every gaze. I may well be a flop at this line of endeavor. Columbus too thought he was a flop, probably, when they sent him back in chains. Which didn't prove there was no America.[6]

There is in Augie's *seemingly* random, but actually willful, purposeful, and stubborn insistence on freedom to define his own goals, a sense of new and optimistic discovery of possibilities in the face of the unknown, the *terra incognita*. This hopeful spirit of *Augie March* differs very much from the European pessimism that pervades *The Castle* and casts the shadow of desperation over K.'s purposefulness. However, the ways of Augie and K. are the same, their goals are comparable, and their abilities only to achieve a state of becomingness, never the complete ideal beingness they visualize, are similar in spirit if not in tone.

That Kafka recognized America's expanded possibilities— those inherent possibilities of a new world that give to the fiction of Bellow, Mailer, Malamud, Roth, Gold, and other American activist novelists its optimistic tone—is clear in his picture of the Nature Theater of Oklahoma at the end of *Amerika,* when Karl Rossmann, the innocent victim-hero, finds or dreams a better, more abundant place with more ways of belonging to a utopian society, an ideal community in which the ideal being of each man is fulfilled.

Karl, whose innocence is like Augie's, and the end of whose novel shows us Kafka's awareness of the differences between the European experience and the American experience, is, nevertheless, in spite of his joyful moment at the end, a victim. Karl's innocent victimization seems best mirrored by yet another hero of Bellow's, Tommy Wilhelm in "Seize the Day," the novella that follows *Augie March* and precedes *Henderson*. Tommy Wilhelm is, like Joseph and Asa Leventhal, a victim-hero; however, Tommy is the innocent victim, more the marginal man, the free-floater, than the trapped man whose own rationalistic consciousness further engulfs him in spirit-restricting procedures.

Tommy is not a character caught in a crucial separate time in his existence when he is on trial and knows his freedom to be at stake. Tommy is in crisis, but his is an endgame crisis that comes after a sequence of unfortunate incidents in his always marginal life as a man who hopes to get into the movies, as a salesman, as a player of the stock market, as a divorced man, as a son whose father does not understand him. He is not the victim of the world's absurdity, not a man conscious of being arrested and forced to seek ways to clear himself. He is more the innocent at the mercy of his own inadequacies, his failings as a too human, too simple man—he is a slob or a *schlemiel,* and he suffers for it. At the end of the story he weeps at a stranger's funeral for his own spoiled life. His confrontation of death in the culminating funeral scene suggests that Tommy may do the only thing he can to leap out of his marginality—seize the day and live at the center of his life rather than living on its margins in the innumerable social roles at which he has failed.

Tommy is like Karl Rossmann in that a series of things simply happen to him because of his innocence; he cannot examine his guilty past for he truly has none. He is free, even though his freedom rests, ironically, in his being marginal and tentative, a failure. He has finally more in common with Augie March than with Joseph and Asa. If Augie had remained an innocent victim rather than a rebel for himself, he would have been, like Tommy, marginal and wandering, as indeed Augie seems to be on the simplest level. Augie has something of the innocent victim-hero, the *schlemiel,* about him. Tommy, although a victim-hero who may be viewed in the light of the two earliest novels, nevertheless occurs in a novella written after *Augie March* and can be regarded as being as much an extension of the new view that *Augie March* represents as another manifestation of the victim-hero. Tommy's suffering is the other side of the coin to Augie's pilgrimage. Both "Seize the Day" and *Augie March* pronounce the absolute need to discover the self, the former by showing the effects of not trying to discover the self and the latter by showing the quest for discovery. In a review of *Seize the Day,* Herbert Gold says of the title story "that it is one of the central stories of our day," and that the book represents "an extension of Bellow's view of contemporary life." [7] This extended view of the contemporary world shows a movement away from mysteriously guilty victims such as Joseph and Asa and toward the innocent victim Tommy Wilhelm as well as toward the innocent who refuses to be victimized, the good-natured rebel Augie.

The Emergence of the New Hero from the Victim-Hero

This new, hopeful emphasis that asserts the truths of the self seems partly to grow out of the philosophizing of the Jewish storyteller, philosopher, and authority on the mystical Hasidic movement, Martin Buber, whose book *I and Thou* and whose translations and interpretations of the Hasidic tales [8] have had a profound influence on many American writers. (Buber's similarities to Kierkegaard, who seems to have influenced Kafka's *The Castle,* are documented by Malcolm L. Diamond.[9]) Buber's mystical ideas include the doctrine that man's first responsibility is to realize the "I" so that the "I" may participate in a dialogic relationship with a "Thou," and finally with the "Eternal Thou," or God. The object of Buber's philosophy is the immediacy of dialogic communication with God; however, the process of becoming an "I" is paramount, since only from it the ability to say "Thou" to others and to God follows. The responsibility to be oneself is exemplified in one of the *Tales of the Hasidim* in which the zaddick, or rabbi, Zusya, who fears his own death, is asked by friends if he is afraid God will reprimand him for not having been Moses. Zusya's reply is that he fears God will reprimand him for not having been Zusya.[10] This parable, called "The Query of Queries," elaborates the philosophy of Buber and emphasizes not merely man's responsibility but also his fearful, even awesome, obligation to be himself, to be human and to achieve his unique human identity by refusing to give up his will before the arbitrary, impersonal, gigantic power of social and political forces, the worldly forces of party, corporation, state, and ersatz community.

The turning from the victim-hero toward the hero who wills himself comes in Kafka's work in the last novel, *The Castle,* and in Bellow's work in *Augie March,* a book that not only represents a turning for Bellow but is also considered by many to be a breakthrough in the development of the American novel.[11] Whether Kierkegaard in Kafka's case and Buber in Bellow's are directly influential is not a major concern here. However, that Kierkegaard and Buber were presences in the *Zeitgeister* inhabited by Kafka and Bellow as well as in the particular lives of Kafka and Bellow is significant information to the student of twentieth-century literature when he comes to a consideration of the new subjective hero who wills himself in order to confront the Absolute— that which is beyond all material schemes.

When the victim-hero rebels, when he does at last seize the day and assert himself as more than a person with a series of social roles or functions, Augie March appears. When Karl Rossmann, at the end of *Amerika,* gives his name as "Negro," he seems to say that he is independent of his old name and of his past and that he wills himself a free man who is yet to be fully freed in the new place of the promised future; so does Augie defy the past that would imprison him and put himself outside and beyond the imperatives of the social-political milieu into which he was born. He recognizes his own uniqueness. He is from the very beginning of his adventures more than an innocent victim such as Karl Rossmann or Tommy Wilhelm, who only disavow their passivity in the final scenes of the Nature Theater and the funeral parlor.

Augie March is above social, political, and communal roles because he has chosen to be, and therefore he is free of their impositions, the suffering they cause, the gifts they give, and the promises they make. Even at the conclusions of their novels, Karl and Tommy are still bound by communal considerations: the promise of the Nature Theater is, finally, not the promise of complete freedom but of complete belonging, a kind of grace, but not the same grace as that of the earned separate self. Tommy's recognition when he confronts death at the stranger's funeral is twofold: his personal need to seize the day, to live for himself, and his need to become one with other men, to recognize his sharing in a common humanity. Completely alone; bereft, not by death but by circumstance and emotion, of wife, father, and last advisor-friend Tamkin; stranger in a crowd, Tommy sobs in the funeral parlor:

> The flowers and lights fused ecstatically in Wilhelm's blind, wet eyes; the heavy sea-like music came up to his ears. It poured into him where he had hidden himself in the center of a crowd by the great and happy oblivion of tears. He heard it and sank deeper than sorrow, through torn sobs and cries toward the consummation of the heart's ultimate need.[12]

Tommy, alone in a crowd, mysteriously belongs to all humanity; only thus can he find "his heart's ultimate need." Here, as in *Amerika,* the mysterious gracelike belonging of the individual, not the freedom of the separate self, provides a solution to the innocent victim's plight.

K. and Augie more clearly demonstrate the two goals of the rebel hero: first, freedom to become oneself, and, second, the ideal being that each has envisioned. K. envisions the ideal being of Land-Surveyor to the castle, not jobholder in the village. K.'s rejection of the Mayor's proposal that he consider himself the village school's janitor makes this distinction clear. He will accept no village function; his ideal being can only be realized through belonging on a higher plane. For Augie, the ideal being which he envisions for himself is that of founder and director of a foster home for orphans. His idyllic description of the foster home manifests its dreamy ideality for him: "What I had in mind was this private green place like one of those Walden or Innisfree wattle jobs under the kind sun, surrounded by velvet woods and bright gardens and Elysian lawns sown with Lincoln Park grass seed." [13] With its pastoral mood and lyrical quality, this vision of the foster home which Augie, the orphan, wishes to found is a vision of the place to which his own true being mysteriously belongs.

The vision of ideal being as a state of completion and grace through belonging to some ideal place is found, then, in *The Castle* and *Augie March* as well as in *Amerika* (the Nature Theater) and "Seize the Day" (the funeral parlor as the symbolic "oceanic" place of the common heritage). However, in *The Castle* and *Augie March* the goal is more clearly coupled with the process through which it is sought: it is not a new or sudden given of which the hero, suddenly alone, free of his victimized past, becomes almost miraculously aware. K. and Augie do not suddenly achieve grace. Nothing is given or granted in the rebel hero's quest for the self. There are hints—I have elsewhere called them, using Paul Goodman's terminology, "lyric interludes"—that if the hero would relax in his quest, if he would sit still or lapse into a dreamy somnolent state, he might achieve, suddenly and automatically, what he strives for so unceasingly. (Cf. K.'s scene in Bürgel's bedroom and Augie's recognition, while resting on the sofa, that if one simply relaxed and allowed the "axial lines" of his existence to come together, harmony, love, justice, and all the goods of the spirit would be available at once, without striving.) But what this hero fears is that a relaxation from his willing of himself may make him a victim. He is faithful to his goal of ideal being, which has spiritual significance, but his faith is a strange one, for it is willed, and it is a faith that does not accept miracles.

Frederick Hoffman, whose perceptive book *The Mortal No* [14] contains an analysis of the way in which the concept of self in modern literature has taken over and included the spiritual considerations of religion, discusses the willing of belief. He says:

Quite aside from all speculations about creation, the questions are reduced to one: *does* eternity, or *can* it, reside in time? If it does, then movement through time *may* involve the experiencing of eternity, and the religious quality of experience *may* "save the self" from extinction. But even when one is willing to accept this possibility, the general tendency is to make the act of acceptance an act of *will* [italics mine], a "leap" from disbelief to belief.[15]

Continuing this discussion, Hoffman says that the general attitude in modern literature toward the self has "changed from regarding it as substance to analyzing it as process" and attributes this change as it is manifested in American culture first, and then in twentieth-century literature, to the psychology of William James. He says:

James is an interesting example of the Victorian scientist whose researches lead him away from convictions he prefers to hold and land him in an uncomfortable situation, from which he hopes to *will* his escape. In this respect volition becomes a surrogate agent of belief: the quality, power, and energy of the will, in its projections into possibility, become the means of identifying and measuring the self. More important for modern literature, however, is his having helped in shifting the perspective upon the self: from the self at center projecting outward [the substantial self], to the self as an inner center, as a focus of analysis [the self-in-process]. . . .[16]

Two points Hoffman makes which contribute to the discussion here are that will, or volition, is a surrogate agent of belief; and that there has been a shift from a concept of self as substantial to a concept of self as process.

In the novelistic presentation of the process of the activist hero, the freedom of the self and the envisioned goal of the willed ideal self coexist, and paradoxes consequently proliferate. Three paradoxes in the existential situation of this hero are: he is always in some symbolic way what he wishes to become; he becomes what he wills although he does not know he has; and his conceptualized ultimate goal, if realized in a literal way, is just that which would negate the freedom which is his way of becoming what he wishes to be, which in fact he *is* in his existential being at every moment.

The first paradoxical outgrowth, that this hero is always what he wishes to become, involves his wish to become himself projected in an ideal image. When K. answers a summons to be Land-Surveyor to the castle and gives up his past in his native village to come to the site of the castle, he has in effect made himself the Land-Surveyor. Who else is? The people of the village are right when they call K. the Land-Surveyor, even though they do not recognize his absolute claim to the official title. Augie March, an orphan, wishes to be the founder and director of a pastoral, idyllic, carefree, happy, irresponsible, bee-keeping foster home for the care and education of orphaned children. He wishes to be the father he never had, to be the father of himself: and insofar as he makes himself what he is, he is the father of himself. (Ironically, he is also, like his actual but never-present father, a traveling man.) The choice of the particular goal of ideal being is dictated by the free self's original uniqueness: the goal is only a symbolic projection of that original existential uniqueness. Existence is prior to essence or ideality.

That existence is prior to essence is also an underlying factor in the second paradoxical element. The self must somehow be what it envisions as its essence or ideality, before it can choose and project that goal; and now one sees that it also becomes more fully what it is in the process of becoming what it has envisioned. As K. and Augie move with ease or with difficulty through the situations that they find or create, they superficially appear to be moving away from their professed goals. In reality, however, they are moving toward them, for they are becoming more what they have claimed they will be. As his quest progresses, K. becomes more clearly the true Land-Surveyor, the man who surveys the land of the castle, not that of the village. He is the one who scrutinizes and measures the spiritual landscape with complete and con-

scientious exactitude. Both his initial choice and his subsequent actions pronounce him existential Land-Surveyor for
the castle though the title which would define the final essence of his being evades him. His life and his freedom to
pursue himself are his reward, *not* the miraculous granting
of grace that comes from outside the self. As Augie's quest
progresses, he becomes with every act more the father and the
teacher of himself, the orphan, till, at the end of the novel, he
is far from the realization of his conceptualized dream. In Europe with his wife Stella, a singularly transient and ephemeral creature and, appropriately, a film star, he has only himself, the self as discoverer of "those near-at-hand." He has become a lover of those transient ones found "in the immediate
terra incognita," found "near-at-hand" outside of social or
political contexts. He has become the idyllic foster parent,
existentially, though his foster home is not made of bricks
and boards but of himself. He becomes that which he has
willed himself to be, but he does not seem to know it.

The third paradox is that the realization of the ultimate
goal as conceptualized by the hero would be precisely what
would negate his freedom, which is necessary to his becoming
what he wishes to be. Realization of the goal would conclude
his quest; and he is nothing without that quest—a quest only
informed by the envisioned goal, a quest through which he
can become what he wishes to be existentially but not essentially. To achieve pure essence is to die.

K. and Augie possess the only being possible in their novelistic worlds: being manifested through the acts of the fluid,
constantly choosing, Heraclitean self which must willfully assert its own imperatives in order to maintain its unique humanity. The only way to justify the single self's existence is to
live, and the only way for man to come to spiritual affirmation is through that which it is his to explore and test,
human experience. So, at least, these two novels demonstrate.
Their heroes, K. and Augie, live in a state of self-awareness
and questing tension in order to live according to their own

lights. They are tempted by the natural ease of the simple, sleepy, relaxed unconscious, or semiconscious, life in which they might lose themselves. They might lose themselves in bliss, but the point is *not* to lose the self, not even in bliss. K. refuses to stay, relaxed and sleepy, in Bürgel's bedroom and gain automatic access to the castle. Augie recognizes the validity of the "axial lines" but does *not* sit still and let them pass through him. He is soon up and after his better fate.

These heroes are threatened not only by the givens of the natural life into which they will not relax, but also by the actual realization of the ideals they have proposed. If the ideals were realized rather than kept in an open process of becoming, these heroes would cease to be what they are, and what they are is men who make themselves through choice and movement, men who consciously will themselves not as political or social activists (the activism that Buber has called "the glorification of self-confident virtue" [17]) but as human activists with the hope of achieving the spirit.

Augie March: An Examination of His Activism

The rich and dense particularity of Augie and his quest cannot be entirely revealed by comparing him with K. as I have been doing so far in this chapter. Both Augie and K. are complex characters in their own ways, though both seem even more complex than they actually are to the villagers and to those Bellow has called the Machiavellians in *Augie March*. They are really very ingenuous men with simple purposes. However, both refuse to be defined in any of the usual terms; and so, though they are innocent (deliberately innocent) of malevolence, they seem, in the eyes of the world, either fools or evil schemers. They are, of course, neither. The varietal situations into which they enter or which they create make their single-purposed characters complicated. Augie, who calls himself a "varietal" man, is different from K.; as a post-Kafkan hero, he includes, comments on, and goes beyond this prototype.

Augie says, "a man's character is his fate," and he often says as well that he, Augie March, wants "a fate good enough." These statements form an at times harmonious, at times discordant, set. Augie's textual character, that character revealed through surface situation uninformed by the will and intent of the deeper character seen in the whole of the novel, appears foolish, uncorrected, blundering, provisional, unreliable. And the apparent foolishness of the textual character is Augie's character as it appears to those of his Chicago world, the Machiavellians.[18] Is this character his fate? Or is his fate a chosen one, a "fate good enough"? It is only as textual character on the surface of the novel and as his persona materializes in the world of the Machiavellians that Augie's foolishness is his character and, therefore, his fate. He achieves a "fate good enough" by saying "no" stubbornly to all the worldly schemes with which others would encompass, define, and thus limit him. His supposed foolishness is his defense against the world's schemes and is his protection for his "fate good enough."

Among the Machiavellians (Grandma Lausch, the Coblins, Einhorn, and so forth) of the Chicago slum in which he lives as a boy and young man, Augie, an orphan, first learns to say "no" to the customs, practices, and idols of the material world, though he is not so stupid that he does not recognize, especially in his association with Einhorn, its positive glories. Saying "no" becomes Augie's way of keeping himself free of binding social contracts while he seeks his true self. Living among Machiavellians who wish always to recruit him to their schemes and to bind him in business, political, sexual, or family deals, all usually as much to his worldly advantage as to theirs (the Renlings even wish to adopt him and make him their well-dressed son and heir), he has every opportunity as a young man to become adept in the ways he must use to strengthen his will against the temptations to lose himself in the easy roles of a seductively available and comfortable life. If he is to survive as a pilgrim of self, he cannot succumb to these temptations; being the rich, well-dressed, well-educated son of the Renlings would never be "a fate good enough."

Augie's orphaned condition is somewhat metaphorical. He thinks of himself as an orphan because he is alone and also because he is constantly meeting people who wish to adopt him, in one way or another. He is more a natural-born adoptee than he is an orphan since he does in fact have a mother, though she is mentally defective—sweet and silent with a kind of perpetual sadness. He and his two brothers are the bastard sons of a traveling man—merely by-blows, Augie says —and are born into an undefined situation. Of his resultant open, undefined condition, Augie makes an advantage. He accepts, indeed prefers, his heritage of illegitimacy and his nonrestrictive, nondefining family. Augie's two brothers in the same situation represent alternative fates. Augie's older brother Simon is an Horatio-Alger opportunist from the start; he readily cooperates in Machiavellian schemes. When he is a grown man he marries a shrewish, domineering woman for her money, which he uses to start a coal business of his own and make a financial success, a success as much dependent on his own ruthless, sometimes sadistic, shrewd business ability as on her money. At the end of the novel, it is clear that Simon has sold his self: he is a stone, his life a living death. The other, younger brother, Georgie, is the polar opposite of the worldly wise Simon; born an idiot, he fully realizes, without striving, the potential of his natural self. He is trained as a shoemaker in a home for the mentally deficient, and he is happy, at ease; he is almost enviable to Augie, who can never achieve the simplicity of the original natural self of the "axial lines" because he must always *strive* for his better fate.[19]

The dream of returning to "the axial lines of life," occurs

at the climactic moment of the novel, after the Mexican adventure with Thea and before his marriage to Stella. Since in this quiet moment between adventures, Augie feels he has discovered something essential and since this discovery would suggest an end to his quest for self, it is pertinent to look closely at the "axial line" passage:

"I have said 'no' like a stubborn fellow to all my persuaders, just on the obstinacy of my memory of these lines, never entirely clear. But lately I have felt these thrilling lines again. When striving stops, there they are as a gift. . . . Truth, love, peace, bounty, usefulness, harmony." [20]

The "fate good enough" for which he must strive by saying "no" to his persuaders is this natural self defined by the "axial lines of life." "A man's character is his fate" becomes, by this definition, "a man's life is his fate." The sense of completed being, which the revelation into the way of the "axial lines" gives, is the predominant motif here: within the completely natural, simple, unstriving self are wholeness, harmony, and the peaceful coexistence of truth and love. But this substantial self, similar to that of the early nineteenth-century Transcendentalist vision, is lost in the diffusion of the modern world—the modern self is a self of process and will. Though Augie may feel longing for his substantial self, an inevitable longing and almost a commonplace in the anguish of modern existence, he can only achieve completion through willing it, *not* by relaxing into it. Simple being is for idiots without acute perception, such as his brother Georgie (or the saintly fool, Gimpel, of Isaac Bashevis Singer's "Gimpel the Fool" [21]). Augie does, however, persistently and consciously maintain himself as the world's fool. He partakes of the fates of both his brothers: he is the middle child. Through a conscious process in the secular world (Simon), he wills himself completeness of being (Georgie), by proposing a transcendent goal (his self).

The vision of the "axial lines" is followed in the novel by

a significant passage that illustrates Augie's consciousness that he cannot simply rest and have these "axial lines" without a volitional effort; he is not an idiot, and he must make an image of ideal being in the world, even if the image is in the world's terms or in imitation of them. It is at this point that he imagines his personal scheme of the idyllic foster home:

"All I want is something of my own. . . . I'd never loan myself again to any other guy's scheme. . . . I aim to get myself a piece of property and settle down on it. . . . I'm not thinking about becoming a farmer . . . but what I'd like most is to get married and set up a kind of home and teach school." [22]

He also says:

"I'm looking for something lasting and durable and trying to get where those axial lines are. . . . This may not sound like such a great scheme to many people. But I know I can't have much of a chance to beat life at its greatest complications and *meshuggah* power, so I want to start in lower down, and simpler." [23]

In Augie's novelistic surroundings, the foster home is not visible, even indistinctly, as the castle is visible, and so he must, from his inward self, entirely define what he seeks by defining what he will be.

Before this verbal recognition of what he has been in some way doing, and now commits himself to do, Augie has evaded the schemes of Chicago Machiavellians only to fall, through love, into another's mad scheme: Thea's plan to go to Mexico with a trained eagle to hunt iguanas. That Augie is limited, trapped, and deprived of his freedom to choose for himself and to make himself by his love for Thea (and, later, by his love for and marriage to Stella) is a corollary theme in the novel. If the primary theme has to do with the nature of the free self in its becomingness the secondary theme has to do with love and its impediments to the self. Prior to love's first appearance in the novel, with Thea, Augie has tentatively allowed himself to fit for a moment into others' schemes, to play the game, to taste and test alternatives, but he has made only provisional commitments. (The complexity and variety of testing in the novel are extensive—romance, thievery, immigrant-running, union-organizing, reading, and poker-playing abound. The episodes involving these various, tentative adventures add greatly to the picaresque surface of the novel. They may be compared to K.'s provisional relationships with the villagers and to his adventures with them in the inn, on the road, and in houses—all worldly and social experience that he uses to find out what ways are available to another sort of experience, the castle experience, the spiritual experience.) Love, however, is a different matter and involves automatic commitment to another and that other's schemes. Especially for Augie love is involuntary; he does not have the opportunity to say "yes" or "no" when Thea recruits him, but falls immediately, dizzily in love. It is in love that one aspect of Augie's character shows itself most clearly: his *amor fati,* his "mysterious adoration of what occurs," his ready response to dreams of blessedness.[24] This makes for an undefined hopefulness, an optimistic quality in Augie's character, which permeates the book and almost conceals with cheerfulness the anguish in the pilgrimage of the self.

Love, more than any other human possibility, holds forth the promise of blessedness, to the dream of which Augie is so susceptible. This is not unlike K.'s hope that Frieda's relationship with Klamm will bless his own pursuit of self in relation to the castle. In neither novel is the love of women strictly for its own sake; however, it appears to be more so in *Augie March.* In Augie's tale, as in K.'s, love does not bring what it promises: it becomes a burden to which the lover must submit. Through his love for Thea, Augie goes to Mexico with her as an accomplice in her eagle-training, iguana-catching scheme; he becomes a mere acolyte, and by submitting to her scheme he is in danger of totally losing himself in farcical situations with the eagle, with the iguanas, and with the snakes which Thea keeps after her eagle scheme fails and no iguanas are captured. Thea finally saves Augie from herself by dismissing him, in a jealous rage, after he has done a favor for Stella, a chance acquaintance in the Mexican village, whom he will meet again later in his travels and marry. Although Thea never wished to marry Augie, her rejection of him, because of his presumed infidelity, is complete, and with the loss of love Augie is thrust into a dark time of self-analysis. He tries to understand his character in relation to love, which has disappointed him; he tries to correlate his lovingness and his freedom-willing self.

If the novel, which has a loose and inconclusive structure of sequential episodes in order to accommodate the process of becoming, can be said to have a traditional climax, Augie's dark time of self-analysis after his parting with Thea and his conclusion concerning the "axial lines" must be considered that climax, since here, in the crisis of identity, Augie understands himself in relation to freedom and love: his thoughts are the product of, as much as a reflection on, the opposition between these two goods that the self covets.

Augie speculates in an introspective monologue:

And was it true, as she said, that love would appear strange to me no matter what form it took, even if there were no eagles and snakes?

I thought about it and was astonished at how much truth there actually was in this. Why, it was so! And I had always believed that where love was concerned I was on my mother's side [that is, that of simplemindedness], against the Grandma Lausches, the Mrs. Renlings, and the Lucy Magnuses [the Machiavellians].

If I didn't have money or profession or duties, wasn't it so that I could be free, and a sincere follower of love?

Me, love's servant? I wasn't at all! And suddenly my heart felt ugly. I was sick of myself. I thought that my aim of being simple was just a fraud, that I wasn't a bit good-hearted or affectionate. . . .

Now I had started, and this terrible investigation had to go on. If this was how I was, it was certainly not how I appeared and must be my secret. So if I wanted to please, it was in order to mislead or show everyone. . . . And this must be because I had an idea everyone was my better, and had something I didn't have. But what did people seem to me anyhow, something fantastic? I didn't want to be what they made of me, but wanted to please them. Kindly explain. An independent fate, and love too—what confusion! [25]

This self-analytical passage speaks for itself; however, it has several curious aspects. Augie remembers that Thea has told him love would always appear "strange" to him: it does. As a pilgrim of the self he is never comfortable in love, though he is a naturally loving man as the rest of the passage attests. A naturally loving man, a man influenced by women who seems to have, as K. has, some trust in their peculiar powers, Augie says, "I tried not to reject the truth in what I was told, and I had a lot of regard for the power of women to know it." [26] He is nevertheless incapable of a complete and satisfactory relationship in love. Love is always for Augie domination by an external scheme, a hindrance to his unique ends: "An independent fate, and love too—what confusion!" Bellow keeps the conflict between these opposites, love and freedom, alive throughout the novel. Augie's nature is an excellent ground for that conflict.[27]

The contemplation of his way in love leads Augie to a more intense evaluation of his nature:

My real fault was that I couldn't stay with my purest feelings. This was what tore the greatest hole in me. . . . Everyone got bitterness in his chosen thing. It might be in the end that the chosen thing in itself is bitterness, because to arrive at the chosen thing needs courage, because it's intense, and intensity is what the feeble humanity of us can't take for long. . . .

As for me personally, not much better than some of the worst, my invention and special thing was simplicity. I wanted simplicity and denied complexity, and in this I was guileful and suppressed many patents in my secret heart, and was as devising as anybody else. . . .[28]

That he should want simplicity is an ironic element in Augie's situation. It is, however, relevant to the total paradox of
the seeker after self: the self can only be realized continually
in process, never grasped as concretized ideal being; character is fate, but character is in a state of flux. To continue to
pursue "the chosen thing" under these circumstances, a man
must be courageous and undaunted, must have an unremit-
ting faith in his quest. Augie says:

> Tell me, how many Jacobs are there who sleep on the stone
> and force it to be their pillow, or go to the mat with angels and
> wrestle the great fear to win a right to exist? These brave are so
> few that they are made the fathers of a whole people.
> While as for me, whoever would give me cover from this
> mighty free-running terror and wild cold of chaos I went to, and
> therefore to temporary embraces. It wasn't very courageous.[29]

After these reflections on his own nature, Augie concludes
that the only way to achieve true being is to get where the
"axial lines" of one's existence meet, through relaxation into
a natural condition; that is, to reach that place where all opposites are reconciled in the serenity of completion—or grace.
Augie's self-defined ideal is his personal description of a state
of grace: he concretizes this with his vision of the idyllic foster home. To the foster home Augie plans to bring an unknown wife, his mother, who is now blind and in a home for
the aged, and his brother Georgie, who is in a home for the
mentally   defective.   (Institutionalized   homes   afflict   the
Marches, which may be the reason that Augie structures an
idyllic and personal foster home as the concretization for the
simplicity of his ideal being, his own state of grace.) His in-
clusion of others in his own self's idealized goal is interesting;
it emphasizes his loving, warm nature which dreams of blessedness and of belonging to a true community, though a true
community of his own making. A meaningful comparison to
The Castle is possible: K.'s true community is that of the castle,
a community outside his own making (though it is somewhat

shaped and subtly transformed, in the world of the novel, by
K.'s subjective understanding and definition of it), through
which he wishes to affirm himself by certain belonging. Although K., like Augie, rushes to temporary embraces, seeks
the truth from women, is loved by women, and is finally
impeded in his personal quest by his close association (similar to marriage) with Frieda, there is no family to which he
looks backward or forward in his courageous and lonely
quest. K. *does* wrestle with angels; he does "wrestle the great
fear to win a right to exist." As novelistic hero he does this
metaphorically for all of us; however, Augie, as a personality
in his novel, specifies (self-deceivingly?) that when he does it
he does it not only for himself but also for others, his unknown wife, his mother, Georgie. "The one thing I could say
was that though I wanted this independent fate it wasn't
merely for my own sake I wanted it." [30]

After this important section of Augie's introspection, the
world intrudes: the Second World War begins, taking away
everyone's right to pursue an independent fate. Augie joins
the Merchant Marine in order to protect his fate, and he
raises the issue of war from the level of the merely political
to that of the spiritual when he says,

I went around and made a speech to my pals, much to the amaze-
ment of people, about the universal ant heap the enemy would
establish if they won, a fate nobody could escape then, mankind
under one star of government, a human desert rolling up to the
monster pyramids by power. A few centuries after, and on this
same earth's surface, under the same sun and moon, where there
once had been men like gods there would be nothing but this
bug-humanity that would make itself as weird as the threatening
universe outside and would imitate it by creating human mechanical regularity as invariable as physical laws. Obedience would be
God, and freedom the Devil.[31]

Unlike the insight of Joseph in *Dangling Man,* who joins the
Army to become regimented and lose the anguish of self-de-

termination, Augie's view is that he must fight the forces of "human mechanical regularity."

During his military experience Augie meets the Stella of his Mexican misadventure again, falls in love once more, and this time marries. The romance with Stella is a sequel to the romance with Thea—the second romance underlines the difficulties of the love relationship for the seeker of the self; the first romance has defined them—just as K.'s experience with Pepi is the sequel to the romance with Frieda.

Stella and Pepi are something of footnotes or auxiliary comments to the central concepts of romantic love embodied in the relations between Augie and Thea, K. and Frieda. Stella and Pepi are women *without* higher schemes of their own. They are seemingly more loving, simpler women than the first loves. Pepi, who has taken Frieda's place at the bar in the inn, has no designs on the castle or castle officials; she loves K. and decides that her love will be pure, independent of any desire for honorable positions in the world.[32] Stella tells Augie that he and she are alike in being *simply* warm and loving and that they are alike in being natural adoptees. She says, " 'One of the things I thought is that you and I are the kind of people other people are always trying to fit into their schemes.' " [33] But as it turns out, Stella does have an ambition, if not a higher scheme, which triumphs over everyday reality, and Augie in marrying her finds that in love what happens to one happens of necessity to both. Married to Stella, the warm and loving one, he loses his freedom as much as he lost it with Thea, although with Stella he has no confining, janitorial-like duties, routine or otherwise. No householding is necessary with Stella, whose career as a film star is a metaphor for her own illusive character. Accompanying Stella to Paris, where her film career has taken her, Augie travels around Europe, buying and selling the scrapped junk of the war as the representative for a New York lawyer, Mintouchian. The fragmentary, temporal, and alienated quality of his situation at the end of the novel prompts him to say, before the final euphoric pages of the coda, "I'm in the bondage of strangeness for a time still. It's only temporary." [34] Marriage to Stella has again stolen his freedom, not through the burdens of householding in the name of another's higher scheme but through his estrangement from his own announced goal.

K.'s Pepi also declares that she is like the man she desires: " 'We have both been deceived, let us stick together.' " [35] But Pepi, too, has an ambition, an idea about the way love, at least, should be: she wants K. to stay with her and with the community of three chambermaids in the cellar of the inn. Come down to the girls, she says. " 'Come to us!' " [36] The simple bovine love that Pepi offers is not accepted by K., whose novelistic adventure ends without his definite acceptance or rejection soon after Pepi's offer. The offer is somewhat attractive to K., but when Pepi, seeing his reluctance, says that he may come to the chambermaids' dormitory only for the winter if he will not come permanently, he asks, " 'How much longer is it till spring?' " [37]

Augie's marriage is not the warm place he had thought it might be; he is, in effect, still a bachelor. He is deprived of both the warmth he expected and of the freedom to seek his self. K. implicitly rejects Pepi's offer of female warmth; he will not be taken from his free path again as he was for Frieda's sake. He remains a true bachelor, ready to act for himself alone. "Sisyphus," Kafka once said, "was a bachelor." [38]

In *Augie March* the theme of the polarity between love and freedom is much enhanced by a conversation about marriage between Augie and Mintouchian, the worldly New York lawyer, a Machiavellian himself but a Machiavellian detached enough to view from some distance the duplicity and deceits of engaged worldliness. Mintouchian spells out for Augie the legends of unintended and intended duplicity immanent in the world, and he sets forth all his legal wisdom on love and marriage. Mintouchian's advice, although it is realistic and grows out of love for Augie, not malice, is re-

miniscent of the Bridge Inn landlady's advice to K. Mintouchian's comments on the conventional customs of love serve
as a supplement to Thea's earlier comments, to Augie's, and
to Stella's. About the same sort of comments, analyses, and
advice in *The Castle,* Nathalie Sarraute says that they are

> minute, subtle analyses that Kafka's characters indulge in with
> impassioned lucidity, as soon as the slightest contact is established
> between them. As, for instance, the skillful dissections of K.'s con-
> duct and sentiments toward Frieda, performed with the keenest
> of blades, first by the landlady, then by Frieda, then by K. him-
> self, and which reveal the complicated interplay of delicate
> wheel-works, a flash of multiple and often contradictory inten-
> tions, impulses, calculations, impressions and presentiments.[39]

If one adds Pepi's final analysis of the love situation in *The
Castle* to Mme Sarraute's list of commentators, the similarities between *The Castle* group and the group in *The Adventures of Augie March* are even more clear. Not only do these
subtle discussions and analyses reveal the "multiple and
often contradictory intentions" of the people involved; they
also take the place of the romantic passionate love which has
disappeared in the Kafkan novel, and almost disappeared in
the recent American novel, from the central narrative.[40]

Passionate love may happen, but it happens involuntarily,
accidentally, and it is more of a distraction to the activist
hero's quest than an event embodied in it. This is even
clearer in Bellow's *Henderson,* in which Frances and Lily,
the two women in Henderson's "normal" American life, are
clearly more hindrances than helps. When Henderson goes to
Africa in quest of his self, he leaves them and all his children
behind. In Africa, the only females of importance to his
quest that he encounters are two: Willatale, the ancient
queen who is considered above male-female distinctions although she, as the ruler of cow-lovers, is clearly an Earth
Mother *par excellence;* and Atti, a lioness.

With the shift in emphasis from the externalized courtship

of a romantic love pattern to the internalized awareness of self, conscious reflection and "minute, subtle analyses" in dialogues between characters become more significant. The level of consciousness—not the level of the subconsciousness or of submerged motivations—remains in the area of awareness, as in the area of action, romantic or otherwise, paramount in the novel of the activist hero. If ironic contradictions occur, they occur on a *conscious* level. The unconscious does not mysteriously intrude itself; rather goals or goods or ideas conflict and oppose one another, and their opposition is exposed through the well-lit surface of conscious awareness and conscious action, not through multilayeredness. The novel of the activist hero is, in its insistence on consciousness, on the exposure and illumination of all events, even those considered dark and mysterious in some quarters, somewhat in the spirit of the epic, although epic patterns are much transmuted by their passage through time and by the accumulated history of literature which erodes and sophisticates them at once.

In his conversation with Augie, Mintouchian comes to the subject of consciousness and the will. After discussing the subject of love and marriage and the worldly intrigue which as a lawyer he sees accruing to them, he says, of human character and of the consciousness of one's own character,

"Mind you, I'm a great admirer of our species. I stand in awe of the genius of the race. But a large part of this genius is devoted to lying and seeming what you are not. We love when this man Ulysses comes back in disguise for his revenge. But suppose he forgot what he came back for and just sat around day in and day out, in the disguise. This happens to many a frail spirit who forgets what the disguises are for, doesn't understand complexity, or how to return to simplicity. From telling different things to everyone, forgets what the case is originally and what he wants himself. How rare is simple thought and pureheartedness!" [41]

Disguises and masks are useful, according to the lawyer Mintouchian, who is also a believer in "secrets," as long as the man who assumes the disguise does not forget himself and the primary purpose behind the mask. Man must remain conscious.

Augie, on the other hand, who insists on his own conscious will toward simplicity and on his own pureheartedness, his lack of hidden motivations,[42] would refuse an out-and-out disguise or mask, even as a temporary device. What he will temporarily assume is not a mask or function, but a job, a role, to find out about life through experience, not to hide or, even temporarily, to lose the true self. Augie, who throughout his process of self-becoming has taken on a variety of experimental jobs, is clearly aware of the danger that playing at roles may usurp the whole life or may be used as a cover for the deep despair of an empty life (a nonexistence). Considering his own insistence on "a fate good enough," for which he has given up and disavowed many obvious, convenient, and easily available social roles and functions, Augie says: " 'And there's even an attitude of mind which finds it almost disgusting to be a person and not a function. Nevertheless I stand by my idea of a fate. For which a function is a substitution of a deeper despair.' "[43] Augie deliberately avoids despair by choosing a sense of life and of himself in it through holding on to his idea of a fate. (In the novels of such writers as John Hawkes, in whose work despair is accepted as a given circumstance of the contemporary condition, the only way a man can live at all is through functions, surrealistically portrayed as symbolic roles which *imitate* life. Hawkes's *Second Skin* is an excellent example of this modernist theme of the acceptance of despair.)

In his conversation with Mintouchian, Augie says a significant thing about his chosen self:

"You will understand, Mr. Mintouchian, if I tell you that I have always tried to become what I am. But it's a frightening thing. Because what if what I am by nature isn't good enough?" I was close to tears as I said it to him. "I suppose I better, anyway, give in and be it. I will never force the hand of fate to create a better Augie March nor change the time to an age of gold."[44]

This passage brings into the verbalized argument all the paradoxes of the manifestations of existential self at once: in it, the natural self, the existentially becoming self, and the willed better, or transcendent, self are all present, and they war with one another, giving to Augie's willed optimism, his antidespair, a note of futility. (Bellow is too honest a writer to insist that willed optimism is an *easy* way out of the existential modern dilemma, as Richard Poirier suggests he does.[45]) Mintouchian underscores this futility by saying, " 'That's exactly right. You take your chance on what you are. And you can't sit still. I know this double poser, that if you make a move you may lose but if you sit still you will decay.' " The end of the conversation leaves Augie in the continuum of choice that he characterizes at the end of the novel in a more random mood as a continuing exploration of the "near-at-hand." According to Max Brod, Kafka intended to conclude *The Castle* with K.'s deathbed scene in which K. would receive a message (yet another unauthenticated message?) from the castle, permitting him to live in the village and to continue his activity there. Transcendence is impossible; only the process of life is, in life, available.

Henderson: An Examination of the Uses of Fantasy

In *Henderson,* the quest for the self starts not with the activist hero's definition of ideality but with a lack of definition. Though Augie's early simplicity may seem akin to Henderson's early emptiness, they are vastly different. (In one respect, this difference may be between Augie's youth and Henderson's middle age.) Henderson, at the beginning of his novel, is in a state of despair in which the meaninglessness and emptiness of his life are manifested by an inner voice that says, "I want. I want. I want." He cannot will a transcendent self since he has lost his natural self and has been unable to recover it through his various experimental roles of pig-farmer, European traveler, husband, lover, and violin player. Through the violin he has attempted to speak to the spirit of his dead violin-playing father. If he could recover his image of his father, thus recovering his past boyhood, he might get in touch with his natural self and its imperatives. The past is, however, not thus available, nor can the past be truly useful in the conscious quest of self. It is the present-to-ward-the-future which is useful.

Henderson does not answer a specific, defined summons. Although he has, at the beginning of the novel, a vague longing to fulfill himself by becoming a doctor of medicine, the longing seems to him, at the age of fifty-five, absurd. His first wife, Frances, laughs at him, a laugh in which her teeth do not show, a death's-head laugh, when he mentions his wish to go to medical school. His second wife, Lily, wants him to do whatever he wishes, and so he goes to Africa. In Africa his concept of ideal being materializes in terms of some sort of community service, such as medicine. He says to Dahfu, an African prince, that ideally "There is some kind of service motivation which keeps after me. I have always admired Doctor Wilfred Grenfill. . . . I would have liked to go on errands of mercy. Not necessarily with a dog team." [46] This service ideal becomes apparent and visible in Africa where he does perform community services, rather as a witch doctor might.

The original summons he answers is the voice of his inner self, which wants without saying what it wants—obviously it wants to be heard and to *be*. Thus he goes to Africa, after a vivid and frightening confrontation with death,[47] as much to escape the voice as to answer its implicit summons or to find out what, what *more,* it wants. What does the inner man want when the social person has all the things which the world deems sufficient for the good life, the life Kierkegaard would call the "aesthetic"—immense wealth, wife, ex-wife, children, physical strength, "ancestoral" home, status, vocation (Henderson's ironic choice of the vocation pig-farming underlines worldly greed and filth), hobbies? He wants more

—more life. But what is more life? Does he want more of the same life? Is he merely piggish and greedy for more of the junk of the world? The "more" for which Henderson yearns is clearly in this novelistic context a yearning for a qualitatively different "more." If all apparently human needs are fulfilled, the "more" must be somehow spiritual. Henderson's quest is more definitive, conceived purely as quest, and is more obviously spiritual than Augie's, though less initially defined by a transcendent goal of "a fate good enough." Purely in quest of his self, which he has completely lost in the business and noise of modern America, he finds in Africa his natural self (a quite Reichian self, as will be seen) and many unexpected fantasy-transcendencies of that found, or redeemed, natural self.

The fantasy-transcendencies, such as Maker of the Burning Bush, Savior of the Cows (an imaged transcendency at which he fails), Strong Man and, ultimately, Rain King, which he discovers as roles for his persona, not the social roles or mere functions of an external scheme, are manifestations of that natural self, lost in America because of the complexities and distractions of modern society and regained in Africa where primitive simplicity reigns. That these fantasy roles all engage his physical strength and engage it toward some community service indicates the way the natural and the ideal may come together, at least in fantasy or dream.

Augie's natural, simple self was recognized by him and sustained, in the midst of complexity, by his construct for ideal being: his dream of the "axial lines" leading to his imaged goal of the foster home. Although Augie does not lose his simple self but willfully keeps it through deliberate pureheartedness, he is in a sense doomed to a futile struggle since his transcendent being always does and, predictably, always will elude him. Only in fantasy, Bellow seems to be saying, may man truly achieve his transcendent being; thus Henderson's adventure, embodied in one of the great seriocomic novels of our time, is affirmative and ironic at once. In this fantasy of the modern self, what are the roles of the persona of the lost and then redeemed natural and concurrently ideal self? They are god roles. Henderson's largeness of physique, his physical strength, his extravagant nature, his abundant emotional energy (everything about Henderson is big and strong), all these are dissipated in the aimlessness of his American life, dissipated in petty anger, in yelling, in pig-farming. In primitive Africa there is a true place for strength and largeheartedness: it is a god's place.

As this activist hero in quest of himself progresses through his African experience, his fantastic roles become more and more grand. There is a progress upward in the novel, an accumulation of African experiences that culminates in Henderson's making of rain (from the dryness of his soul he brings rain to a dry land, and the dry land returns the favor by watering his soul) and in his conversations with Dahfu, the well-educated philosopher-prince of an African tribe.

Rainmaking and these conversations lead to Henderson's *lionheartedness*. Animal symbols emblematically mark his progress: at first, pigs; then an octopus in a French aquarium (which speaks to him of murky death); then cows; frogs; lions (especially the lioness Atti); and a remembered amusement park bear. The bear is out of the past, unremembered till after his acquaintance with the lioness. The lioness Atti, who gives the gift of lionheartedness, or wholeheartedness, to Henderson through his imitation of her, is the crucial animal to which this totemic level of progress in the novel builds. The bear-hugging, almost humanly loving, old bear, remembered affectionately by Henderson as he returns from Africa to America, may be a symbol for him of the way he will have to transmute his lionheartedness of the savage African lion to a bearheartedness of the trained, amusement park bear in his own country.

There is a sense as he flies back to America of his need now to re-evaluate the African experience, a spiritual experience of freedom, simplicity, and self-realization—the independent quest for the self—into terms through which he may share; he must find the way to take the rediscovered and essentially monologic "I" of Africa back to America and convert it into part of an I-Thou dialogue. His inner voice no longer says "I want. I want. I want." Now it says, "He wants. She wants. They want." Henderson befriends a strange dark child, a token symbol of silent but ever present otherness, who sits next to him on the homeward-bound plane. He plans to go, at last, to medical school on his return and to become a real doctor. The personal African discovery, then, is to be used toward some sense of communal value in America as in Africa. The communal value proposed is seen in the various explicit acts and plans of Henderson cited above; it is also embodied, as has been suggested, in his remembrance of the friendly bear and its embrace as he and it once rode a roller coaster together. Animals, throughout, refresh his understanding of human experience. The text intentionally indicates by the euphoria of its ending (which, as has been pointed out in the preceding chapter, seems a somewhat contrived euphoria) that Henderson goes in the direction of new dialogue, and possibly of communal love, as he returns to America. However, since he has realized his transcendent or ideal self in African fantasies, the odds are not entirely in his favor that he will keep that self or effectively employ it in dialogue in the American community.

Though this question is beyond the limits of the novel and somewhat digressive, it might be pointed out here that Tony Tanner, in his article "The Flight from Monologue," discusses the inability of the Bellovian hero in all the novels to achieve dialogue though he seems to wish to do so and seems to wish to fly from monologue and to be loving.[48] My own thought, that for the activist hero, who is constantly in a state of becoming and willfully seeks his own being, relational love, though perhaps wished for, is always secondary, and often a hindrance to the primary goal, has already been given. Through fantasy, Henderson may have regained his own purposeful sense of being; but if one judges from the evidence of the Bellovian hero as type, in America Henderson will remain in the process of becoming, on a pilgrimage in his own country, and will probably find the demands of continuing love, personal and relational or communal, hindering to his individual quest.

Although ideal being may inevitably be still to be sought in American reality, Henderson does bring back to America with him one prize from his African journey into fantasy and possibility: his sense of being or sense of life, his energetic natural self. This he indeed has gained from a series of progressive adventures which start with the Arnewi and the message of Willatale, the old queen of that cow-loving tribe, who tells Henderson "Grum-tu-molani," "Man want to live." She tells him this, although by not killing the frogs in their cows' drinking water and by not allowing the cows to drink from water with strange creatures in it, her people, the Arnewi, have condemned their cows, and probably themselves, to death. Henderson has said to the Arnewi prince, Prince Itelo: " 'Should you preserve yourself, or the cows, or preserve the custom? I would say, yourself. Live,' I said, 'to make another custom.' " [49] (Henderson tries, and fails, to rid the cistern of frogs.) The mutual exchange intended here is a microcosmic picture of the total mutual exchange between Africa and Henderson: water to dryness.

The series of adventures which starts with the Arnewi, the tribe of gentle goodness, and their Queen Willatale culminates with the Wariri, a lion-loving tribe of darker truths, and their king, Dahfu, the dark, philosophical king of many travel books. In a kind of comic free play with literary prototypes, Dahfu is hip as well as mysteriously wise. He is the strange and dark philosopher of another continent in eighteenth-century travel literature as well as the noble savage of that same period's literature: together these two literary prototypes become in Dahfu the Negro hipster of contemporary American literature, "the White Negro" [50] of Norman Mail-

er's Reichian invocation. Although Bellow's African prince
has not the madness—specifically psychopathic, though not
psychotic, according to Mailer—of Mailer's Negro ideal of
freedom and primordial energy, and although Bellow's African prince is an extraordinarily cultivated and educated man
like his eighteenth-century literary prototype, the dark phi-
losopher-advisor, nevertheless his ultimate advice—know the
lioness!—is imagistic Reichianism.

Wilhelm Reich is, perhaps unfortunately, best known for
his invention of the orgone box, which as a mechanical device to explore further his biophysical theories of natural and
human energy brought more disrepute than acclaim to those
theories. The theories themselves, however, have been very
influential on the imagination of modern American writers,
especially on that of Isaac Rosenfeld, Paul Goodman, Saul
Bellow, and Norman Mailer. Reich, starting as a psychologist, worked out his earliest theories in terms of character in
such books as *Character-Analysis*, first written in 1933. To
the third edition of this book, published in 1949, he attached
a preface in which he asserted that since the book's first publication his interest had turned from the psychological study
of character as such to the study of character as biophysical
behavior and to the study of emotions as manifestations of a
"tangible BIO-ENERGY, to the organismic orgone
energy." [51] He says, "In orgone therapy, we proceed bioener-
getically, and no longer psychologically." Although psycholo-
gists and psychoanalysts may continue to analyze character in
older (Freudian) ways, "the discovery of the atmospheric
(cosmic) orgone energy has forced major revisions in our
basic physical as well as psychological concepts." However,
"at present, it is mainly the natural scientist and the natural
philosopher who are being challenged by the disclosure of a
universal primordial energy: orgone energy." [52] Orgone energy, usually interpreted simply as sexual energy, was for
Reich a mysterious, primordial, natural, animal energy without which man could not live. By the end of his life, Reich

had transformed what had started as a biophysical and scientific exploration into man's natural being into a mystical religion.

Such books as Norman O. Brown's *Life Against Death* [53] show the immediate impact of Reich's idea, Dionysian and Nietzschean as it is, on contemporary thought. Karl Shapiro has discussed Wilhelm Reich at length in his *In Defense of Ignorance,* a collection of essays in which Shapiro disavows his past attachment to the literary establishment founded by T. S. Eliot and Ezra Pound and affirms as his heroes Walt Whitman, D. H. Lawrence, Henry Miller, and Wilhelm Reich. Critics frequently speak of the Reichianism in modern literature. Speaking of Isaac Rosenfeld and others, Irving Malin says:

In his last years Rosenfeld had to be certain that he would not lose Transcendence. He had to see it not as some kind of temporary glow but as part of a stable pattern. He sought Fixity—and found it in the "science-mysticism" of Wilhelm Reich.

Of course it is easy to dismiss Reichian psychology as the product of madness. But as a "significant" substitute for religion, it influences Shapiro, Bellow, Paul Goodman; it sanely reaffirms for them, the sense of life. . . . Healthy sex unites the human and the cosmic, body and energy, creating "cosmic consciousness." [54]

Malin, as others do, emphasizes "healthy sex" as the basic principle in Reich's idea. While sex may be basic to Shapiro's and to Mailer's ideological and literary programs, it is not necessarily basic to the Reichian motifs of the others. Indeed, Bellow seems to have set himself the task in *Henderson* of constructing a Reichian fantasy *without* sex. His use of the Reichian notion of primordial energy goes beyond the sexual.

Including the Reichian motif in several works, most strongly in *Henderson,* Bellow reveals an ambivalence toward it. None of his heroes is Reichian. Although Augie's longing for the "axial lines" of his life, for the harmony at the bottom of man's nature, may be termed a Reichian longing for "cosmic consciousness," it is also a longing for a transcendency over the confusions and imprisonments of everyday existence; Augie converts the vision of natural harmony into the ideal goal imaged in the foster home.[55] "Seize the Day," *Henderson the Rain King*, and *Herzog* all have one important character who appears as a Reichian advisor to the hero. In "Seize the Day," Dr. Tamkin, a mad pseudoscientist who claims to be a doctor of psychology, has mystical quasi-religious ideas about the universe and a penchant for expressing them in poetry. He may indeed be a parody of Wilhelm Reich himself. Tamkin is also a kind of surrogate-father for the hero, Tommy Wilhelm.[56] Tommy's own father, a real doctor and a "righteous" man, refuses to love him or to lend him the money which he badly needs. Tamkin advises Tommy in specifically Reichian terms. He gives Tommy a poem as a clue to life's mystery, the first stanza of which is:

> If thee thyself couldst only see
> Thy greatness that is and yet to be,
> Thou would feel joy—beauty—what ecstasy,
> They are at thy feet, earth-moon-sea, the trinity.

And the last stanza:

> Look then right before thee.
> Open thine eyes and see.
> At the foot of Mt. Serenity
> Is thy cradle to eternity.[57]

Tommy does not understand the poem, calls it "claptrap" and a "riddle" which he feels can only mix him up. Tommy, who sees his own bigness as sloppiness and as hippopotamus, not lion, bigness, does at the end recognize that he must seize the day and live, when in that oceanic sorrow of tears and "sea-like music" at the funeral parlor, he finally confronts death—the stranger's, all men's, and his own. But it it not Tamkin's Reichian advice that brings him to an understanding of possible rebirth; rather Tamkin turns out to be, in fact, a *false* father who has duped Tommy out of the small amount of money he had had left.

Tommy Wilhelm is the hero who, in the order of publication of the novels, directly precedes and is the opposite of Henderson. Henderson's Reichian advisor, Dahfu, is not a fraud. Still there is toward Dahfu's Reichian teaching an ambivalence in the novel, manifested by the fact that Dahfu not only lives but also *dies* by the primordial energy of lions and the lion cult which he embraces. By the time Ramona, the Reichian advisor of the last novel, *Herzog*, appears, the Bellovian hero is immune to sermons on the mysterious power of natural energy. Specifically the mysterious is sexual passion, and popular Reichian, in Ramona's case, but her sermonettes are represented as trivial. In *Herzog*, neither sexual energy nor mind can serve as guide to the heart-stricken hero, who feels and wishes to prove himself righteous. *Herzog* is an investigation of the heart, foolish and wise. Dahfu in *Henderson* remains, then, the only strong Bellovian embodiment of the Reichian idea as a possible good.

At the moment that Henderson, sitting next to Dahfu at the Wariri rainmaking ceremony, rises to the African occasion and wishes to exert his physical strength to lift Mummah, the enormous idol representing the Wariri goddess of the clouds—a feat which will bring him the title and role of Sungo, or Rain King—he says, excitedly, to Dafu:

"If I had the mental constitution to live inside the nutshell and think myself the king of infinite space, that would be just fine. But that's not how I am. King, I am a Becomer. Now you see your situation is different. You are a Be-er. I've just got to stop Becoming. Jesus Christ, when am I going to Be? I have waited a hell of a long time. I suppose I should be more patient, but for God's sake, Your Highness, you've got to understand what it's like with me. So I am asking you. You've got to let me out there." [58]

King Dahfu does permit Henderson into the arena to try to lift Mummah; Henderson does lift Mummah; makes rain indeed; becomes the Rain King, Sungo; and, at least in his African dream, *is*. Dahfu, gracing Henderson's urgent wish to be with serious recognition, attempts through philosophical discourse, and finally through his insistence that Henderson know and imitate the lioness Atti, to educate Henderson to a beingness that transcends even the kingly role they have both attained.

Dahfu, described as "virile to a degree that made all worry superfluous" and as "a man [who] takes all he does upon himself," [59] has a "conviction about the connection between insides and outsides. . . . And what he was engrossed by was a belief in the transformation of human material that you could work either way, either from the rind to the core or from the core to the rind; the flesh influencing the mind, and the mind influencing the flesh. . . . The process as he saw it was utterly dynamic." [60] To Henderson, Dahfu's idea of the dynamic flow between mind and body is immediately meaningful, but Henderson is, nevertheless, skeptical. Though through his physical strength he has become a king, attained a fantasy transcendency, he is not certain that King Dahfu's philosophy contains the ultimate possibility. "Thinking of mind and flesh as I knew them, I said, 'Are you really and truly sure it's like that, your Highness?' " Dahfu is "triumphantly sure." [61] And he is intent on converting Henderson. But Dahfu's philosophical discourse fails to convince Henderson, although Henderson understands his points intellectually, saying, "And though I'm no expert I guess he's thinking of mankind as a whole, which is tired of itself and needs a shot in the arm from animal nature." [62] But Dahfu is determined that his friend Henderson learn: "He believed that it was never too late for a man to change, no matter how fully formed. And took me for an instance, and was determined that I should absorb lion qualities from his lion." [63]

Dahfu introduces Henderson to Atti the lioness, an introduction that increases Henderson's skepticism. Looking at Atti, Dahfu points out several lion qualities that will instruct

Henderson in true being if he will literally imitate the movements and noises of the lioness:

"What a Christian might feel in Saint Sophia's church . . . I absorb from lion. When she gives her tail a flex, it strikes against my heart. You ask, what can she do for you? Many things. First, she is unavoidable. Test it, and you will find she is unavoidable. And this is what you need, as you are an avoider. Oh, you have accomplished momentous avoidances. But she will change that. She will make consciousness to shine. She will burnish you. She will force the present moment upon you. Second, lions are experiencers. But not in haste. They experience with deliberate luxury. The poet says, 'The tigers of wrath are wiser than the horses of instruction.' Let us embrace lions also in the same view. Moreover, observe Atti. . . . How does she stride . . . or gaze or rest or breathe? . . . She does not breathe shallow. . . . [She has] vital continuity between her parts. . . . Then there are more subtle things. . . . She has much to teach you." [64]

This mystical awareness of lion-ness, of the way that animal life is completely within the givens of its own nature and truly *is* as a wholeness, is not only Reichian but shares a great deal with all current existentialist psychology.[65] Even after Dahfu's argument has been set forth, Henderson is hesitant about going into the lion's den: the dangers of this psychology are clear when the lion is an actual presence rather than a vague understanding of danger and risk apparent in giving oneself to disembodied primordial energy. Bellow is doing in this presentation of ambivalence in the Reichian idea what he has proposed as a novelistic purpose: showing ideas in opposition to one another and letting them openly push against each other in the context of the novel without necessarily resolving their conflict.

The reluctant Henderson still needs more encouragement from Dahfu (" 'Mr. Henderson! Is this the man who spoke of rising from a grave of solitude? . . . Who wished to end Becoming?' " [66]), but he does finally enter the lion's den in the hope of change, a change toward true being and nobility, fostered by his courage to risk encountering the lion and directly imitating her quality. " 'Be the beast! You will recover humanity later, but for the moment, be it utterly.' " [67] Henderson, in the den, striding and roaring in imitation of Atti's way, makes some progress, but the experiment is left incomplete when, through tribal politics, King Dahfu is forced, by tribal politicians, to perform the traditional ritual feat of capturing Gmilo, a young, wild male lion of the jungle, supposedly embodying the soul of Dahfu's dead father, the former king. Dahfu, who might have avoided this test, will not do so, for he lives by the rule of the lion and is not an avoider. He will break life's meaningless cycle of fear and desire. He asks: " 'What are the generations for, please explain to me? Only to repeat fear and desire without a change? This cannot be what the thing is for. . . . Any good man will try to break the cycle.' " [68]

Dahfu, who courageously accepts his commitment to himself and his own philosophy, is killed by Gmilo. About Dahfu's view of life-and-death in accordance with the primordial force of lion-being in the world of nature, Marcus Klein comments that Henderson's acknowledgment, made after his experiment with Atti, that "inhuman fire is at the center of his humanity too," [69] is not a complete acceptance of Dahfu's extreme way. Klein says:

Henderson is hurried to a further pitch of Reality. Dahfu's lion [Atti] is a pet lioness after all. Henderson is now made to confront the authentic lion [Gmilo]. . . . That lion castrates and kills King Dahfu. The voice of the lion is the voice of death itself. And this Real, far from being an escape from chaos, is chaos and old night itself. To submit to the harmony it offers, on the principle that the lion outside is inside too, would be to accept the inhumanity of the inhuman Real.[70]

My disagreement with Klein's reading is slight but makes, I think, a discernible difference. Klein suggests that Henderson was on the very edge of conversion to Dahfu's lion-cult religion; whereas, it seems to me that Henderson has *always,* even during the experimental process of imitating Atti, remained a skeptic toward lion mysteries, in spite of flashes of intuition, such as Klein cites, which accrue to that process. It is Dahfu whom Henderson has accepted as a person, never his philosophy, and Dahfu through his own imitation of and love for lion kingliness, courage, and wholeness is a complete person. His death by the lion Gmilo is appropriate and establishes a primordial rhythmic pattern in his life and death which breaks the repetitive "cycle of fear and desire," which as a "good man," by his own definition, Dahfu is courageously committed to break. Dahfu is a fulfillment of his own idea; he is transcendent, and most transcendent in his death. Though Henderson embraces Dahfu in love, he is not Dahfu and does not embrace his idea.

Henderson, nevertheless, when he leaves Africa, takes with him something which is relative to, though not the same as, Dahfu's philosophy. He has, after all, come to Africa as part of his quest and the quest of his generation of Americans to learn ("it's the destiny of my generation of Americans to go out in the world and try to find the wisdom of life").[71] If he does not learn a "philosophy," he has absorbed, in somewhat the way that Dahfu's philosophy would dictate, through process and existence in Africa's spiritual geography, what was available to him there. He has discovered the uses of his own lion-like strength and lionheartedness: both are in him and found by him; together they give him a sense of himself, not as transcendent or superlatively primordial being but as living, moving, acting man. Africa has delivered him from "the body of this death." [72] Whether he can take this sense of himself out of Africa and carry it back to America, where the *will,* not the *dream,* prevails, is an unresolved question in a novel of unresolved questions. The novel is one of investigations, immediate and personal (in its focus on Henderson's subjective truths) and universal and American (in its supposition that Henderson's subjective quest relates to his historical time and place). "Millions of Americans have gone forth since the war to redeem the present and discover the future," [73] Henderson says. But he also says, "I don't think the struggles of desire can ever be won. Ages of longing and willing, willing and longing, and how have they ended? In a draw, dust and dust." [74] In spite of this pessimistic recognition, Henderson has made a leap of faith in pursuit of authentic self.

The leap of faith that Augie makes when he chooses his own self originally and when he says of his vision of the "axial lines" that they are "not imaginary stuff . . . because I bring my entire life to the test" [75] is not an earned one, according to Marcus Klein. "The novel does not earn that leap into faith," says Klein.[76] Nor, one wishes to add, does *Henderson* earn Henderson's leap of faith which takes him to Africa to pursue the self and reality, which together will constitute, somehow, he hopes, true beingness. Nor, one wishes to add again, does *The Castle* earn K.'s leap of faith. A leap of faith is not earned in life or in literature. By its very nature it defies "earning"—it is the ultimate existential act in Kierkegaardian terms: the choice that is only because it is. What is strange and special in these novelistic presentations of the spiritual leap of faith is that it does not end striving but seems to intensify and increase it. Here is where novelistic truth parts with philosophical truth, for after the leap of faith, the leaper supposedly rests inside the harmony of a complete faith in God. But when God is absent as a name for the Absolute, the leaper must propose an Absolute for himself and replace the unnamed and absent with another concept of ultimate being or absoluteness; his doing so is to leap into an absolute relation with the Absolute. But it is not a leap into the serenity of harmonious essences. Rather, such a novelistic leap is toward more process of becoming, but a process of becoming that is informed by personal value in relation to ultimate being. Even Kierkegaard, in spite of his philosophical writings, in his own life was unable to do more;

hence he called himself a Knight of Infinite Resignation
rather than a Knight of Faith. The activist hero's leap is a
partial and willful leap then, but a leap nevertheless. To leap
entirely would mean to this hero the embrace of the natural
and the unconscious, the primordial darkness where both the
divine and the diabolical lodge, as has been demonstrated by
the example of Dahfu: better the continuing pursuit of an
absent God.

Paul Goodman defines the psychological structure for this
pursuit in the activist hero of recent novels very well when he
looks at K. and *The Castle:*

Kafka understands that the shut-in consciousness of his *He,* always
interpreting. . . , can never find a truth or a way of life. What
then? Surely the solution is not unconsciousness; nor, if it were,
could one attain unconsciousness by willing it. What is required
is to open a way between the consciousness and the unconsciousness and the world. Not-to-lose-oneself *and* to give in; or at
least not to be afraid to give in to the instincts. This desire, to
combine consciousness and instinct, is K.'s desire, as is shown by
the lyrical day dreams; but his method is disastrous. He *uses* the
instincts, for instance the love of women, in the service of his
idea. . . . Contrariwise, he wants to destroy his idea in order to
give in to his instincts. . . . Kafka well understood that on these
terms no happiness is possible, but he seems not to have conceived any better way out than to reduce the ego to exhaustion by
letting it wreck its constructive will against its hopelessness; ex-
hausted, it has a measure of satisfaction; dead, it will be happy.[77]

Kafka himself, speaking of "pursuit" in his 1922 diary, gives
an account of it in his own life:

This pursuit, originating in the midst of men, carries one in a direction away from them. . . . Where is it leading? The strongest
likelihood is that it may lead to madness; there is nothing more
to say, the pursuit goes right through me and rends me asunder.
Or can I—Can I?—manage to keep my feet somewhat and be carried along in the wild pursuit. Where, then, shall I be brought?
"Pursuit," indeed, is only a metaphor. I can also say "assault on

the last earthly frontier," an assault, moreover, launched from below, from mankind. . . .[78]

If one can manage to keep his feet, not be plunged into madness, he may succeed, if only metaphorically, in making an "assault on the last earthly frontier." Perhaps the leap of faith of the activist hero might better be described as the assault of faith.

Kafka's recognition of this pursuit, its futile hopefulness, which in the end is "hopeless," since death ends the strife and, ironically, brings the sought-after completion, is set in a majestically bare prose. Bellow and his school in recent American fiction give much more flamboyant language to this same quest, making it seem less futile, more filled with lavish promise. Through language and images they enrich the surface of the quest, giving the life process it embodies an exuberance and a feel of hopefulness that is missing in the desperation of *The Castle*. Part of this is the native American optimism of these contemporary writers: abundance, freedom, possibility abound; and if nothing else, there is a larkiness about the pursuit itself though it be doomed inevitably to the same failure as K.'s. The present-toward-the-future is a typically American stance. Perhaps these recent American novelists know the potential despair that they oppose through the activism of their heroes, but they do not know it as a European did—especially as a Jew in Prague in the 1920's must have known it.

The exuberance inherent in the rhetoric of *Augie March* (Bellow has said of that novel that it is "all rhetoric" [79]) is also inherent in the playful symbolism of *Henderson* and in the witty erudition of the many letters that invigorate *Herzog*. *Henderson* eschews rhetoric for its own sake as *Augie March* embraces it. Sometimes *Henderson* even lapses briefly into a clipped, clear, concise prose that suggests a parody of Hemingway.[80] But in a variety of symbols and archetypes, the rich, playful element in this novel as rhetoric is in *Augie March*, Bellow hides the sobriety and manages to convey gracefully that cumbersome thing, a metaphysical quest put into activist terms. But the symbols and the archetypal situations are to be considered as play: Bellow himself warns the reader against deep-reading and symbol-hunting in an essay that appeared at about the same time as the novel.[81] Though Bellow insists that novels be read for their own sake rather than mined for symbolic meaning, and though Henderson's quest is emboldened by, not embodied in, the book's symbols, nevertheless the symbols contribute to the meaning: the lion is as symbolically unavoidable as it is unavoidable in Dahfu's philosophy. None of the symbolism is gratuitous or merely decorative. However, neither is this an allegorical novel in which the symbols may be systematically read.[82] They rather conform to a scheme of no-system, a play scheme, which is one of the comic attributes of the book. And the echoes from *The Odyssey,* from the Bible (Moses and Daniel, especially), from the crusade of Richard the Lionhearted, from *Rasselas,* from Conrad and Hemingway, and from other literature and history, enrich the quest of the present with accentuations from the past, not in Eliot's way in *The Wasteland* or Joyce's way in *Ulysses,* which ways served to show the poverty of the present as it confronts the lost rich traditions of the past, but in its own way, which is to show human possibilities embodied in the past and still, perhaps, there to be rediscovered in all men at any time, even now. These accents from the past, to be sure, are not wholly hopeful, not wholly affirmative; there is a somewhat pessimistic wistfulness in them. Still, there remains the element of the assertion of human possibility. Human nobility may seem to have disappeared, but Bellow appears to ask: Where did it go? Who saw it leave? Perhaps it didn't leave at all. *The Adventures of Augie March* has this same underlying emphasis on past grandeur. Almost every chapter opens with a paragraph or two invoking the past (pastoral, mythic, historic) and making some sort of connection between it and present action which is more than literary decoration.

Herzog: The Hero as Fool

Augie and Henderson stand in the present of their own lives and strive toward the future. Reminders of ancient or merely older patterns of culture do not keep these heroes from determining not to linger in their personal pasts but to pursue their concepts of self in the present, toward the future. Herzog is another story. He is as much a personalist hero as either Augie or Henderson, but he is not an activist. He has made no leap of faith or assault on faith; rather, he is trapped by his own past and forced to make a complete investigation of it before he can free himself from it.[83] Because he is a professor and a student of nineteenth-century intellectual history, his investigation of his personal past includes an investigation of his ideas, especially his ideas about intellectual history. This provides the novel with a wider and more comprehensive past than his own—a past that includes the whole of modern culture. *Herzog* details the investigation that goes toward freedom, is concerned with freedom, but is in no way free.

Herzog, as a literary hero, is not a victim-hero; he is a sufferer, and his kinship is with the fool, the saintly fool of Yiddish stories found in the famous Yiddish story of Isaac Bashevis Singer, "Gimpel the Fool," which Bellow has translated.[84] Herzog's resemblance to Gimpel is minor but important, because Herzog is a unique hero in Bellow's work and has been wrongly criticized when the novel has been evaluated not in literary but in autobiographical terms.[85] *Dangling Man* and *Herzog,* the first and last of Bellow's novels, are reputedly his two most autobiographical fictions. Their form suggests this: *Dangling Man* is a journal and *Herzog* a letter-novel. *Dangling Man,* in spite of its simplicity of form, transmutes the autobiographical material into literature; but the complexity of *Herzog* leaves a wealth of non-transmuted, and therefore curious and somewhat spurious, gestures and actions in the narrative. These raise the question of the novel's success as literature. The critical task, however, is to start not with the autobiographical, and consequently awkward, elements in the novel, but with its authentic literary possibilities.

Herzog must be seen not as Bellow himself but as one of several possible constructs for a novelistic hero: the sufferer, the saintly fool. That the Bellovian hero's progress should begin with the victim-hero construct, proceed through the activist hero, and come to this new hero is an understandable development. The activist hero has been seen as a reaction against the victim-hero and his situation. If, as has been shown, the activist hero's quest is doomed to failure in its most transcendent terms, then the sufferer, the ordinary man of much heart who yearns for more than is possible in the world's terms, or the fool, might well emerge as the dominant hero type in a novelist's work. I would not contend that this is necessarily the case, but it seems a logical progression.

Irving Howe in his introduction to *A Treasury of Yiddish Stories* describes the hero-as-fool, relating the phenomenon to a strong tradition of antiheroism in Yiddish literature:

Dos kleine menschele, the little man, appears again and again at the center of Yiddish fiction: it is he, long-suffering, persistent, lovingly ironic . . . it is the poor but proud householder trying to maintain his status in the Jewish world even as he grows poorer . . . who appeals to [the Yiddish writers'] imagination far more than might an Aeneas or an Ahab. Anyone, they seem to say, can learn to conquer the world, but only a Tevye or a literary descendent of Tevye can learn to live in it. . . .

From this central figure of Yiddish literature—one might call him the Representative Man of the *shtetl*—there emerges a number of significant variations and offshoots. One extreme variation is the wise or sainted fool who has often given up the householder's struggle for dignity and thereby acquired the wry perspective of the man on the outside. . . .

The wise or sainted fool . . . is seen full-face in I. Bashevis Singer's "Gimpel the Fool," where he acquires, with the piling up of his foolishness, a halo of comic sadness, and where, in the end, his foolish innocence triumphs over the wisdom of the world.[86]

This foolish innocent, or saintly fool, is not strong or active but weak and passive; still, he triumphs in his innocence over the power of the world and worldliness. Although Augie as hero is in the activist mode, we remember his foolishness in the eyes of the Machiavellians and his longing for simplicity. But Augie's foolishness and simplicity are only a thematic foreshadowing of Herzog, a hero in another mode.

Moses Herzog is a full-scale Jewish figure as the other Bellovian heroes, all Jewish except for Henderson, are not. This seems to announce Bellow's intention of making something of Jewishness as a significant fact in the world of this novel; and he does. It should not seem, therefore, farfetched to assume some intended relation between this hero and the hero (nonhero or antihero) of a specific Yiddish literary tradition with which Bellow is familiar. Herzog, in his return to his personal past through memory, nostalgically evokes in some of the best sections of the novel his childhood with his Russian-born Jewish mother and father in a ghetto street of Montreal: these rich, imagistic sections of the novel are balanced against the colloquial sections dealing with the present in the streets of Chicago and New York City where modernity reigns and man is dehumanized by machines, noise, busyness, depersonalized mobs of people. The richness of his Jewish past, still kept in Herzog's compassionate, foolish, long-suffering heart, cannot find a place in the modern world, not alone, nor with the help of politicians or philosophers or worldly friends, whose past and present advice Herzog's keen intellect turns over, debates, and rejects in a constant, crucial evaluation that permeates the novel.

The crisis of identity that has made this modern Jewish intellectual aware of the mandates of his heritage and of his heart, which has made a Yiddish "fool" of him, has been initiated by his wife's adultery. (Cf. "Gimpel the Fool" wherein Gimpel's wife's adultery is made the main plot device through which Gimpel's long-suffering and saintly foolishness is shown.) During the course of the novel he undergoes a psychotic episode in which he tries to rediscover his essential self by searching for clues in his own past—his cultural, intellectual, familial, relational, and personal past. No stone is left unturned, and he discovers in himself that comic-ironic Jewish "fool," who in the very process of discovering he seems more to become. Since there is no apparent place in the world suitable for this fool of the heart, as an intellectual like Herzog plainly sees, he comes to the only serenity possible for his fool-persona—a reconciliation with nature, and through nature, with God, when the insoluble dilemma is "concluded" at the end of the novel. The rebirth euphoria at the end of the novel is contrived. It provides a lyrical moment's pause to the suffering of the hero; however, the assumption must be that, given this hero's mode, his suffering will continue as an unending process of self.

Yet Herzog is not a victim of the world: in his personal suffering for his own idea of righteousness there is a spiritual triumph over the world's sordidness, its immorality, its evil, which are ugly realities and not, as some (Camus for one) would have them, absurdities. Herzog throughout the novel claims his suffering as his own, a product of the evil that he can refuse to know but cannot refuse to experience. In his dead father's house, looking at an old photograph of himself, taken when he was grown but still young, the forty-seven-year-old Herzog thinks: "A man in years he then was, but in years only, and in his father's eyes stubbornly un-European, that is, innocent by deliberate choice. Moses refused to know evil. But he could not refuse to experience it." [87] The new sufferer, born from the old saintly fool of European Yiddish literature, is the *deliberately* innocent American.

In pursuit of a truth about the self that only the past, rather than the present-toward-the-future, may reveal, the *Herzog* hero has in common with K., Augie, and Henderson in his quest, which is a reversal of theirs, the impassioned belief that there is a truth, even if it be a subjective one, which is real and may be seized and forced to yield its microcosmic meaning. ("Three thousand million human beings exist, each with some possessions, each a microcosmos, each infinitely precious, each with a peculiar treasure. There is a distant garden where curious objects grow, and there, in a lovely dusk of green, the heart of Moses E. Herzog hangs like a peach." [88]) This sense of a metaphysical quest, whether of the victim-hero, the activist, or the sufferer, in Bellow's work always brings with it two attributes: the *textual* attribute of the play of ideas one against the other, in an open and finally inconclusive opposition, and the *felt* attribute of the existential liveliness of the personal quest for a subjective truth as opposed to an abstract, intellectual, systematized, objective Truth.

5

The Heroes of
Norman Mailer's Novels

K.'s choice is defined by Herbert Tauber in his perceptive study of Kafka's work as between two alternatives. One alternative is complete commitment to earthly matters in the village, to the conventional and traditional, finite and functional goals, "while his connection with the divine would be only an apparent one, that is, without any effect on these arrangements." [1] The other alternative is the total, dependence on the favor of the castle officials—a waiting game but a waiting game that hopes for an authentic connection with the divine (cf. Samuel Beckett's *Waiting for Godot*). As Tauber says, it would be a "waiting for a foundation of a mode of life that results not from accidental, finite, but from absolute conditions." [2]

K.'s alternatives are apparent to him and to the reader of *The Castle;* K. refuses the clear choice, however, disdaining to limit himself to the finite and functional of the conventions of the village, of worldly life, on the one hand, or to wait quietly, patiently, and perhaps one might add sleepily, for the ultimate message from the spiritual Absolute, on the other. Instead, he chooses participation in earthly matters while seeking the spiritual connection at the same time, rather than waiting for divine messages. "The immediacy of life is to reveal to him the possibilities of the way." [3] But his participation in worldly life is dominated by his spiritual goal. This spiritual quest in the secular world is presented most symbolically in Kafka's *The Castle,* most novelistically in Bellow's *Augie March* and *Henderson,* and most ideologically in Mailer's *An American Dream.*[4]

Norman Mailer, whose protagonist, Stephen Rojack, in *An American Dream* represents a radical, or somewhat psychopathic, version of the activist hero, came to this conception by way of several other heroes—specifically, Lovett in *Barbary Shore* (1951), Marion Faye and Sergius O'Shaugnessy in *The Deer Park*[5] (1955). (The latter, Sergius, also appears in a long short story written after *The Deer Park,* "The Time of Her Time."[6]) *The Naked and the Dead*[7] (1948) is a naturalistic collage novel, in the style of Dos Passos' *U.S.A.,* and has no dominating central character as narrator or hero. It is interesting as Mailer's first novel, since it presents his early social and political views, which are still part of his total vision, although that vision is now explicitly directed not to primarily political and social but to spiritual concerns.[8]

Barbary Shore: *The Victim-Hero in a Political Allegory*

Lovett, the pastless amnesiac who is the narrator of Mailer's second novel, *Barbary Shore,* is a victim-hero who nevertheless foreshadows the fully activist hero to come. He has a tentative position, as narrator, in the action of his own story, the most bare and least complex of Mailer's novels. The work is a social-political allegory focused on two other characters, McLeod and Hollingsworth. McLeod, a Marxist and disillusioned Communist, holds the secret of the future's salvation in his keeping, carefully hidden from the F.B.I. agent Hollingsworth, who is a depersonalized, machine-like, efficient seeker after the secret to the future. This secret is embodied in some object or paper that McLeod has found in his Communist past and preserved, hiding himself and it from all potential robbers, whether Communists or F.B.I.

agents, from power-seekers, misusers of human possibility. The object or paper is not defined except in these mysterious and vague terms.

The setting of *Barbary Shore* is a Brooklyn Heights boardinghouse, barren of the bustling of everyday human concerns except in the basement, where the landlady, Mrs. Guinevere, a sluttish, greedy, opportunistic woman, revealed late in the novel as the wife of McLeod, the idealist, keeps a slovenly and unkempt apartment. McLeod lives alone in his own bare, clean quarters on the upper floors. He does not admit that Mrs. Guinevere is his wife until the conclusion of the novel when, shattered by her desertion of him for the F.B.I. agent Hollingsworth, he kills himself, leaving the valuable object, the promise of the future, in the amnesiac-narrator Lovett's safekeeping.

Mrs. Guinevere, it has been suggested, represents the American masses in this allegory of the struggle between the idealist and the depersonalized bureaucrat (the man of the totalitarian state, the Fascist) over the shape of the future. By deserting idealism for bureaucracy, Mrs. Guinevere, as the American masses, slovenly, unthinking, and ruled by animal nature, turns toward Fascism.[9] Mrs. Guinevere may also be seen in terms of a more general allegory, less thoroughly social and political in final intent, as human nature at its most instinctive and basic level, always defeating the rational schemes of abstract and rationalized idealism. King Arthur (McLeod) and Guinevere cannot, finally, live together: Hollingsworth, the F.B.I. agent, is an ironic Lancelot.

Does Lovett fit into these allegorical schemes? As narrator he has a special position: it is his seeing, not his being, that is most involved in the action. He is McLeod's witness and heir. As a narrator he is outside the allegory and partakes of both the victim and activist characteristics found in modern heroes. He is a victim of absurdity in the world by virtue of his trying to understand the world rationally, much as the idealistic McLeod does. On the other hand, Lovett is not so tied to patterns of rationality as McLeod is: Lovett has no pattern inherited from his past; he is, as an amnesiac, truly pastless. He has taken a new name, a new occupation, that of writer, and a new sense of his own becomingness. He is an activist in being toward the future.

Lovett's future is ensnared by McLeod's interpretation of the social-political future, and at the end of the novel he is handed the politically valuable object to protect. Lovett has acquiesced to McLeod's scheme because he has intellectually recognized its validity. He is personally reduced to a function, though a glorious one, when he accepts the task of protecting the social and political future because he rationally accepts the imperatives of that role. In so doing, he gives up his personal freedom and is at the end of the novel about to give himself completely to his absurd task. He is at this point a victim-hero, though he is open, free, and undefined throughout the novel, potentially an activist.

Mailer, at the time of writing *Barbary Shore,* was ambivalent about personal freedom and spiritual activism for the self, as opposed to social and political activism for the community. He was a Marxist by inclination, though, like other American liberals, he disdained Soviet-style Communism as a possible fruition of Marxism. He came of age as a liberal humanist in the style of the thirties, and his despair with society and dislike of what he came to see as its demands for the destruction of the deepest personal imperatives of self were slow to develop. At the beginning of *Barbary Shore* Lovett calls himself an "onanist," suggesting that his freedom of the self is masturbatory; and his wholesome progress is toward community rather than further freedom of the masturbatory self. In spite of his overt intention to suggest that Lovett goes toward social usefulness, a valuable direction, Mailer unintentionally gives the effect of a hero moving toward victimization of the sort which is portrayed by McLeod's situation— alienation, persecution, failure, and suicide. The narrative of *Barbary Shore* may be compared with that of Malamud's

The Assistant. In *The Assistant,* Frank, free to pursue himself, chooses to imitate the life of the Jewish shopkeeper, imprisoned in his shop but ennobled by his performance—more symbolical than factual—of customary duties to the Jewish community and heritage. Malamud says that the Jew is a moral man: he is also the man most imprisoned by the circumstances of his heritage. Frank, a Catholic, elects to be a Jew, a noble choice but a choice that traps him in a victim's life. The irony in Malamud's tale is clearly intended, as it is not, I think, in *Barbary Shore.*

The Deer Park: *Birth of Two Possibilities for an Activist Hero, Sergius O'Shaugnessy and Marion Faye*

If political or social activism inevitably brings the hero into contact with the absurdities of a rationalistic world and makes him ultimately a victim of them, then the hero dedicated to personal freedom must disavow political and social commitments. Hence Marion Faye, the hipster, is born in Mailer's third novel, *The Deer Park;* and Mike Lovett, the pastless, orphaned, free-thinking observer of the world, is more fully realized as a free man, shorn by his own choice of the political and social obligations of the real world where "orphans burn orphans," [10] in Sergius O'Shaugnessy of *The Deer Park.* Sergius, like Mike Lovett, is an orphan and a would-be writer who has come to a place a distance from the concerns of the world. For Sergius this is Desert D'Or (a place probably representing Las Vegas) which has the advantage, in spite of its spiritual and real dryness, of being outside of the realm of routine business, a place of escape. For Lovett, the place of escape was the boardinghouse in Brooklyn Heights. The differences between Lovett and Sergius are significant: Lovett is an amnesiac; Sergius has *chosen* against his past, for his present, and for a better future. The other difference, which stems from this first one, is Sergius' sense of himself and his growing willfulness for that self.

Sergius O'Shaugnessy and Marion Faye are a new breed of men. They share their novel with a third hero, Charles Eitel, who is their mythic father as well as a surrogate-father, a fatherly advisor, to both younger men in the action of the novel. It is Charles Eitel's world which Sergius and Marion have inherited and which they finally eschew. It is the played-out world of politics, power, and enslavement: the world of Washington and Hollywood, of the F.B.I. and the Subversive Activities Committee. Most clearly this world of Charles Eitel, the ex-Communist-sympathizer, is seen in the prevailing metaphors of burning and misused and miscarried flesh that haunt the novel.

All of Mailer's novels are apocalyptic in their underlying war-consciousness. *The Naked and the Dead* is not his only war novel. Lovett is an amnesiac because of the war: either in a tank or in a plane, he cannot recall which, he received the wound, marked by the scar behind his ear. In *The Deer Park*, a sense of war and its destructiveness underlies the several crises of identity which force Sergius O'Shaugnessy to choose a personal fate.

In the early pages of *The Deer Park*, Sergius remembers the Air Force, from which he has come to Desert D'Or. In the Air Force, in the Pacific during the Second World War, Sergius, who had grown up in an orphanage, felt he had at last found a home; the comradeship and community that he had with other men in his group gave him his first feelings of belonging. "There was a feeling for each other. We knew there was nobody like us, and for once in my life I thought I had found a home." But that "home fell apart." [11] The belonging he has briefly felt in the Air Force is destroyed when he, quite suddenly and as if by accident, becomes aware of burned and burning flesh as reality. Although he had dropped his fire bombs on Oriental villages as his part of a group activity and even thought that, seen from the air, "a city in flames is not a bad sight," [12] he is awakened to the meaning of the city in flames when a fifteen-year-old Japanese boy who works in the kitchen of the officers' mess burns his arm on a kettle of soup:

After lunch I took the Jap aside, and asked the cooks for tannic-acid ointment. There wasn't any in the kitchen, and so I told them to boil tea and put compresses on his arm. Suddenly, I realized that two hours ago I had been busy setting fire to a dozen people, or two dozen, or had it been a hundred?

With this flash of recognition, his pleasure in the company of the sociable group of Air Force men wanes, and he thinks: "They were one breed and I was another, they were there and I was a fake." [13]

This recognition of the horror of actual burned flesh and of his personal responsibility for it brings Sergius to his first crisis of identity: he is a "fake," he thinks. He has a nervous breakdown; receives a medical discharge from the Air Force; goes to Desert D'Or to escape the old world and seek himself in a new one. "Built since the Second World War, it is the only place I know which is all new." [14] After this crisis reported at the beginning of the novel, Sergius has two other identity crises: one of love and one of choice. Both of these are imbedded in the burning flesh of the first crisis. In love with Lulu, the film star, Sergius hopes to give a future to the present of their lovemaking, that is, to give meaning to the sexual uses of the body. He asks Lulu to marry him, but Lulu wants to continue as they are, in a random way; she plays and play-acts, thus misusing her flesh with him as she does in films. She has no personal reality or sense of authentic self; and in the scene when this becomes apparent in her implicit but total refusal of Sergius, he is reminded of burning flesh:

What she said made me afraid again, and it was a tangible fear, as if the moment I left her room the burned corpses of half the world would be lying outside the door. We started to make love, and I couldn't think of her or of myself or of anything but flesh, and flesh came into my mind, bursting flesh, rotting flesh, flesh hung on spikes in butcher stalls, flesh burning, flesh gone to blood.[15]

The theme of misused flesh is very clear here; Sergius' impotence after his Air Force breakdown returns, temporarily, at this point in the novel.

The impotence is, of course, important here as an indication of the way misused flesh kills love and spirit. But it is perhaps as important to consider Sergius' capricious potency in *The Deer Park* in contrast with his unfailing and willful potency in the later work, "The Time of Her Time," a long short story intended as a first chapter in Mailer's projected masterpiece, according to his own description a very long, unpublishable novel. In that long short story one sees a Sergius who is more the willful activist and consciously purposeful hero; a hero with varietal and experimental roles in the world; a hero with a transcendent goal of self. He is more Kafkan than the Sergius of *The Deer Park*, who as observer-narrator is somewhat passive since he shares the focus of the novel with Charles Eitel and Marion Faye. Nevertheless, this Sergius does make some significant choices for himself in the Kafkan style. He is not by any means a victim, since he chooses a better destiny for himself and moves toward a self-defined future. But in "The Time of Her Time," Sergius has become even more purposeful and hence more Kafkan; the new Sergius' own definition of K. in *The Castle* might be taken into account.

So often in sex, when the second night wound itself up with nothing better in view than the memory of the first night, I was reminded of Kafka's *Castle*, that tale of the search of a man for his apocalyptic orgasm: in the easy optimism of a young man, he almost captures the castle on the first day, and is never to come so close again.[16]

The Reichian interpretation of *The Castle*, which has been noted in the previous chapter as pertinent to Paul Goodman's analysis of *The Castle*, is clear here. It is relevant that

Sergius' understanding of K.'s purpose is in the terms of "apocalyptic orgasm," for in "The White Negro" Mailer defines the hipster, the new breed of hero, as the man in pursuit of the ultimate orgasm, and he defines good orgasm as primordial spiritual fulfillment, in specifically religious, although Reichian and mystical, terms.

Sergius in *The Deer Park* is, if not the purposeful hero he will become, the neophyte out of which that hero will be born, and the brutality of worldly power is what forces upon him the choice of self. "Burning flesh" urges the initial crisis of identity and informs the crisis of love that occurs just after Sergius' choice of self. Lulu's rejection of Sergius is made specifically in terms of preferring life in the movies to the personal and real life of shared love which they might have; she prefers the world of illusion and social power to his kind of real but uncertain life. This choice of Lulu's comes after Sergius' choice, which marks the high point of his action in the novel. There, too, burning flesh intrudes as Sergius chooses not to sell his "life" for a movie scenario, or himself, as actor, to Hollywood. Hollywood, through its agent Collie Munshin, has offered Sergius two lucrative possibilities. The studio of Mr. Teppis wishes to buy the rights to Sergius' life to make a movie of his Air Force experience, based on the orphan-as-hero idea. Because Sergius is very handsome, Teppis also wishes to use him as the star in the film of his own life. He has consistently said "no" to these two possibilities for selling his life to the Machiavellians of Hollywood. However, he has a moment of practical doubt after Collie Munshin says, " 'Sergius, you've been thinking along the lines that you'd be trading your soul for a bag of loot. You're a child.' " And, " 'This is your opportunity for the real money, kiddo, and dignity and importance,' " [17] After Munshin's talk, Sergius thinks:

I had been tempted more than once to sign the papers Munshin would hand me, but it wasn't stubbornness alone which held me back. I kept thinking of the Japanese K.P. with his arm burned, and I could hear him say, "Am I going to be in the movie? Will they show the scabs and the pus?" The closer I came to wanting the contract, the more he bothered me, and all the while Collie would go on or Lulu would go on, painting my career with words, talking about the marvelous world, the real world, about all the good things which would happen to me, and all the while I was thinking they were wrong, and the real world was underground—a tangle of wild caves where orphans burned orphans.[18]

Finally, Sergius asks his older friend and advisor, Charles Eitel, for advice in making this choice between a Hollywood career and his ambition to become a writer. Eitel helps him to refuse the Hollywood offer and to affirm his transcendent goal, that of becoming a serious writer. Later in the novel, Eitel, representing the older generation, sells out his political integrity (by testifying to the Subversive Activities Committee and naming names of Communist associates of his past) and with it his own sense of himself as an artist. He is only a commercial Hollywood writer, he discovers; he leaves his goal of art behind, passing the torch to Sergius in the final pages of the novel with these contemplative words:

"For you see," he confessed in his mind, "I have lost the final desire of the artist, the desire which tells us that when all else is lost, when love is lost and adventure, pride of self, and pity, there still remains that world we may create, more real to us, more real to others, than the mummery of what happens, passes, and is gone. So, do try, Sergius," he thought, "try for that other world, the real world, where orphans burn orphans and nothing is more difficult to discover than a simple fact. And with the pride of the artist, you must blow against the walls of every power that exists, the small trumpet of your defiance." [19]

There are two real worlds here—the artist's reality and the ultimate ugly reality of brutality in the world: the rest is mummery, appearances, Hollywood films, transient behavior and random sex, superficial happenings, the "whatever is begotten, born, and dies" of Yeats' "Sailing to Byzantium." Eitel, the older-generation Marxist who has sold out to the material world of appearances asks the young artist to seize his personal reality and to pit it, as art, against the ugly, brutal reality of social and political evil. That the artist's reality is personal and is opposed to social-political power is a continuation of the theme Mailer has expounded in *The Naked and the Dead* and *Barbary Shore,* but a continuation in a new key. The theme is stated more metaphorically and less allegorically, though ideology, with its companion allegory, is still present. Also, the theme is now of the individual's quest for the freedom of self so that the self may stand against social evils: the struggle is now not between a social good and a social evil but between the personal, seen as good, and the social, or general, seen as evil.[20]

About the activity of the serious and visionary writer, which he considers himself to be, or trying to be, Mailer has said:

One can even succeed now and again in blowing holes in the line of the world's communications. Sometimes I feel as if there's a vast guerilla war going on for the mind of man, communist against communist, capitalist against capitalist, artist against artist. And the stakes are huge. Will we spoil the best secrets of life or will we help to free a new kind of man? [21]

Two aspects of "a new kind of man" are manifested in Sergius O'Shaugnessy and Marion Faye. Sergius is an orphan. Though he actually had a living father, described as an admirable bum who believed in some better destiny for himself and his son, which he was unable to achieve, Sergius grew up in an orphanage. Faye, too, is a bastard and considers himself an orphan. He is the child of an illegitimate union between Dorothea O'Faye, a nightclub singer, and an unnamed scion of royalty. The name O'Faye was given to him by an ex-lover of his mother's from her vaudeville days, a man who casually married Dorothea to help her out when she was pregnant with Marion.

These two orphans seek to free themselves fully from their

pasts and live only in the present, sometimes simply in the present, sometimes toward the future. They are not activists but are potential activists: they are born, as "beings," [22] in *The Deer Park*. They are two aspects of a new man who will become active in "The Time of Her Time" and in *An American Dream* (which, however, is not the promised successor novel in Mailer's eight-novel plan but an extra novel written, in serialized form, for *Esquire* in 1964 [23]). Sergius in *The Deer Park* has already been discussed here as the intentionally pastless innocent who does come to choose himself and a transcendent fate—that of artist, although the struggle-to-become is not seen in activist terms until he reappears in "The Time of Her Time." Since "The Time of Her Time" is a short story, and thereby committed to a single situation, the hero in process is not completely seen as he would be in a novel; however, the sense of Sergius' activist self is imparted in this story.

Marion Faye represents a more curious and deliberately perverse side of the potential new activist hero born in *The Deer Park:* he is the neophyte hipster that Mailer was later to describe theoretically in his essay "The White Negro." About his emergence in *The Deer Park*, Mailer has said: "The book needed something which wasn't in the first draft, some sort of evil genius. One felt a dark pressure there in the inner horizon of the book." [24] Marion Faye is that—an "evil genius."

Faye chooses evil as his good. His aim is total freedom for himself, and he has a transcendent dream of himself as a saintly sinner who is "the priest who takes the Devil to save the world," the corrupted world of misused and burning flesh, and "must use the Devil to destroy it." [25] He would, apparently, fight fire with fire—save the world by destroying it.

The total personal freedom Faye wills for himself is a freedom of the soul from the body. He thinks "the body and soul are separate, and to be pure one must seek out sin itself, mire the body in offal so the soul may be elevated." [26] It is also a freedom of the personal self from all the snares of the social self—a freedom even from compassion and guilt, attributes of the social self. His struggle to crush his feelings of guilt and compassion for others so that he may become a free soul and the priest who will purify the corrupt world, comprises, with his deliberately evil choices and his acts as a pimp, his part of the novel's action.

Faye's totally rationalistic and "principled" choice of evil as the way toward personal freedom is only partially the premise on which the antisocial, criminal, rebellious freedom of the hipster in "The White Negro" is built. But Faye, unlike the hipster, is a rationalist and a purist. He is against the body, against feeling, against instincts, and against all these in the name of the freedom of the soul and in the name of God. The hipster in "The White Negro" is, like Faye, a violent and sometimes criminal rebel, psychopathically wishing for personal freedom, risking his own death to avoid the social death of routine and conformity, and all this in the name of his own primordial self, or soul, and in the name of the religious mystery, or God. But the hipster of "The White Negro" is not a rationalist—he is rather in search of his sensual self, of the sense of life, of the true feeling he may have of himself and others; [27] and he is, as has been mentioned, on a quest for apocalyptic orgasm, as a way to the center of life's mysteries. He longs, as Stephen Rojack longs in *An American Dream,* to give himself to the "authority of his senses." The hipster and Stephen Rojack do not grow out of Marion Faye's rationalized embracing of evil alone. They grow out of some recognition of the possibilities in the combination of Faye's willful insistence on his soul's freedom and Sergius' innocent, wholesome sensuality.

In *The Deer Park* Mailer cannot come to terms with the dark growth of Marion Faye: he is a dark and unassimilated presence in the novel. Though Mailer has some sympathy with Faye's religious wish for purity of self in a corrupt

world, he allows him to suffer two significant, and ironic, defeats at the hands of the worldly: the criminal worldliness of
syndicated crime and the socialized worldliness of the police.
First Faye realizes that as a pimp he is no longer independent
and free. He is no longer a pimp on principle, but has become routinized—he is a businessman. He keeps books; he
has a system; he has "even caught himself prancing around
one of the executives who ran the syndicate from the capital
to the desert." [28] His second defeat, at the hands of the police and the nice legalities of society, is his imprisonment for
a minor infraction of the rules. For pimping and dope-push-
ing he is never caught or questioned by the police, but accidentally his unlicensed gun is found in the glove compart-
ment of his car and he is put in prison. This minor hero in
the novel, whose quest is for total freedom, is in prison at the
end of the novel—a rebel trapped by the world he would eschew. However, he has been trapped, ironically, for a minor
violation of a legal code, not for his perversity nor for his sti-
fling of all human feeling in himself. The last heard from
Faye in the novel is the postcard he sends to Sergius from
prison: " 'Re: our conversations,' the card read, 'I have the
feeling I'm just getting on to it. Your con friend, Marty.' " [29]

Although Mailer as writer-creator may be ambivalent
about Marion Faye, he manages him deftly in terms of novelistic craft by the employment of this almost cynical irony.
After *The Deer Park,* Mailer becomes less ironic, less craftsmanlike, and more affirmative or prophetic. As his vision of a
new man has become stronger, he has become more prophetic in tone and disavowed the conventionalities of the
craft of fiction. He declares he has done this, purposely, as an
exercise of his courage as a novelist. (Courage is crucial to all
Mailer's heroes whether they are preparing to act or engag-
ing in a process of actions. The courage to act on the imperatives of the self has become primary in Mailer's creed.)
About the narrowness and cowardice of novelistic "craft," he
has said, "By now I'm a bit cynical about craft. I think

there's a natural mystique in the novel which is more important than craft." [30] And, speaking of a fellow novelist who is too craftsmanlike, Mailer damns his reliance on craft to get him out of his novelistic difficulties: "[He has a] terror of confronting a reality which might open into more and more anxiety and so present a deeper and deeper view of the abyss. Craft protects one from facing those endless expanding realities of deterioration and responsibility." [31] Craft, he continues, "is a grab-bag of procedures, tricks, lore, formal gymnastics, symbolic super-structures, methodology in short. It's the compendium of what you've acquired from others. And since the great writers communicate a vision of existence, one can't usually borrow their methods. The method is married to the vision." [32]

This disavowal of craft is relatively new in Mailer. *The Naked and The Dead* is a well-made novel, much admired for its virtues of craft. Mailer has said of it that he pieced it together mechanically with charts on characters and remembered scenes of his war experience much as an engineer might put a building together.[33] *Barbary Shore* is an ideological book, and the craft of ideology is allegory: *Barbary Shore* is a faltering allegory, weak in vision and craft. As Mailer has said of it, his political vision shifted while he was working on *Barbary Shore* from that of "some sort of fellow-traveller" to a "far-flung mutation of Trotskyism." [34] Finally, in *The Deer Park* a personal vision begins to shape itself when the political and social ideology of the older generation fails, as Charles Eitel fails as an ideal father-figure. But the possibilities born with the two new heroes no sooner emerge than the novel ends: the novel is, therefore, not a presentation of a vibrant new vision or new consciousness of possibilities but the presentation of the death of the old social-political alternatives. As such, it is an excellent novel, not as well-made as *The Naked and the Dead,* but full of craftsmanship, announcing its theme through the metaphors of brutalized flesh. In *Deer Park,* ideology does intrude in the

wedding of Hollywood to Washington through the Subversive Activities Committee and the Las Vegas-like desert setting, an environment where all, though new, is dry, and
where nothing is green but the money in the gambling ca-
sinos. However, the realistic and metaphorical triumph over
the merely ideological and allegorical in the novel. A rich
novel on the old corruptions and the new possibilities, it remains Mailer's finest novelistic achievement.

Mailer, who speaks so passionately for the validity of the
novelist's vision, must fight not with his craft but with his ideology to preserve that vision. If his vision is ultimately realized in ideological terms, it will be a philosophical, not a
novelistic vision. As craft, for example, hampers J. D. Salinger's vision until "Seymour: An Introduction," where he
risks all, so ideology now hampers Mailer.

As an indication of the way ideology intrudes in a way that
hampers novelistic vision, one might compare Mailer's use of
environment to Kafka's or Bellow's. (See Chapter 3 of this
study for a discussion of Kafka's and Bellow's environments.)
The difference between the proscribed environment of Desert
D'Or in *The Deer Park* or the surrealistic, closed-off boardinghouse environment of *Barbary Shore* and the more flexible, open environments of *The Castle* and *The Adventures
of Augie March,* which have a symbolic metaphysicality but
are seen subjectively (not objectively, systematically, or ideologically) through the activist heroes and their changing experience, points to a difference between the novelistic vision
of Mailer and that of Kafka or Bellow. Mailer, like Sartre
and Camus, comes to his novel with a preconceived philosophy, worked out in social or political terms (*The Naked and
the Dead, Barbary Shore, The Deer Park*) or in the personal
terms of a new kind of existentialism that he calls American
existentialism. Kafka and Bellow, although they present metaphysical questions, have no answers, solutions, or conclusions
to propose: they allow their hero a process free of preconceived solutions. In *An American Dream,* Mailer's first novel

with a thoroughly fluid hero in a struggle for himself, involved in a process best described as spiritual, Mailer comes closest to what has here been called an activist hero.

An American Dream: *Stephen Rojack as Activist Hero*

Marion Faye of *The Deer Park*, who has chosen evil as his principle of personal freedom, is similar to many embodiments of ambiguous evil in contemporary literature. In American fiction, Mason in William Styron's *Set This House on Fire* [35] and Peter in Herbert Gold's *Salt* [36] come immediately to mind. In these two latter novels, as in *The Deer Park*, the "evil" character is set against another hero, a "good" hero who is also an activist. In *Set This House on Fire* and *Salt*, the dark hero is vanquished by the action of the other, who becomes the clear protagonist. This is not the case in *The Deer Park*, where a subterranean balance is maintained between the two new and equal possibilities for heroic character. Through the expansion of Sergius' character in "The Time of Her Time," Mailer proposes a hero whose sexuality announces his freedom. Finally, through the catalyst of the definition of the ideal American existentialist, the hipster archetypally found in the modern American Negro, he fuses the old Sergius, the new Sergius, and Marion into a single hero who is put into action as Stephen Rojack in *An American Dream*.

What Henderson disavows as the true way when he denies the final validity of the lion cult of Dahfu, what K. disavows by refusing to lapse into the unconscious, Mailer makes the central mystery of his activist's quest for an authentic, better, or transcendent self. Sex, or the unconscious instinctual self—the dark mystery of Reichianism—is that which the Kafkan hero or the Bellovian hero may unwittingly seek on the one hand: the castle connection, the Bürgel episode suggests, only can be received through an unconscious relaxation, not seized through striving, and Augie recognizes that the "axial lines" are there if one is receptive. On the other hand, sex, the unconscious, the relaxation from striving, the dwelling quietly within the "axial lines"—all these threaten the self-as-a-becomingness. In their recognition of this eternal paradox in the quest of the self, Kafka and Bellow surpass Mailer, who seems not to see the paradox or prefers not to acknowledge it. In *An American Dream,* Mailer's ideology again triumphs over existential reality. However, since *An American Dream* is a construct flexible enough to include a personal vision as well as a preconceived ideology, it has an artistry of its own. It is allegoristic but not allegorical as is *Barbary Shore,* and in it Mailer has moved toward symbolism.[37] Certainly the personal visionary element in his philosophy, no matter how much it has been described and predefined in his essays and journalistic pieces (collected in *Advertisements for Myself, The Presidential Papers,* and *Cannibals and Christians*[38]), gives his ideology the intensity of dramatic poetry, metaphor, and symbol in *An American Dream.*

It may, however, be well to look at the definition of this special philosophy, American existentialism, and of the hipster in "The White Negro," before looking at Stephen Rojack in *An American Dream.* That essay starts, as do his novels, with Mailer's war-consciousness:

The Second World War presented a mirror to the human condition which blinded anyone who looked into it. For if tens of millions were killed in concentration camps . . . , one was then obliged also to see that no matter how crippled and perverted an image of man was the society he had created, it was nonetheless his creation, his collective creation (at least his collective creation from the past) and if society was so murderous, then who could ignore the most hideous of questions about his own nature?[39]

Only in this context of the aftermath of the Second World War, a death-in-life context, does Mailer come to his conclusion:

It is on this bleak scene that a phenomenon has appeared: the American existentialist—the hipster, the man who knows that if our collective condition is to live with instant death by atomic war . . . , or with a slow death by conformity with every creative and rebellious instinct stifled . . . , if the fate of twentieth century man is to live with death from adolescence to premature senescence, why then the only life-giving answer is to accept the terms of death, to live with death as immediate danger, to divorce oneself from society, to exist without roots, to set out on that uncharted journey into the rebellious imperatives of self.[40]

This is not obscurely philosophical; it is certainly a conclusion that other writers have come to and have incorporated in their novels: Bellow, Malamud, Salinger, Gold, Roth, all create heroes dedicated to the "imperatives of self," more or less rebelliously. Mailer alone among contemporary American novelists strenuously insists on accepting the terms of death, darkness, and the unconscious and on living with them as immediate personal dangers. He alone persistently maintains that in the quest for selfhood one must include the Evil Impulse. (Including the Evil Impulse is a tenet of the Hasidic view of life as it comes to us through Martin Buber's *Tales of the Hasidim,* which Mailer has elaborated on in a series in *Commentary.*[41])

The religious nature of opposing the single self to the deathlike quality of modern society is made clear in the distinction Mailer makes between American existentialism and French existentialism. In the manifesto language of "The White Negro," he says:

To be an existentialist, one must be able to feel oneself—one must know one's desires, one's rages, one's anguish, one must be aware of the character of one's frustration and know what would satisfy it. . . . To be a real existentialist (Sartre admittedly to the contrary) one must be religious, one must have one's sense of "purpose"—whatever the purpose may be—but a life which is directed by one's faith in the necessity of action is a life committed to the notion that the substratum of existence is the search, the end meaningful but mysterious; it is impossible to live such a life unless one's emotions provide their profound conviction. Only the French, alienated . . . from their unconscious could welcome an existentialist philosophy without ever feeling it at all.[42]

A mystical awareness of death, of sex, and of God is what Mailer goes on to describe as the American existentialist experience. How can mystical awareness be programmatically described, one wonders. It cannot. However, Mailer proposes a creed of activism as an opposing counterpart to a modern European brand of existentialism with its rationalistic, atheistic, pessimistic bias; and though the activistic creed proposed may seem extreme, it is not without its relevance to the American scene, the good and the bad of that scene, the abundance and energy in American life which might go either way—toward perversion, total madness, and collective death, or, through madness and violence, toward new possibilities.

Mysticism—Hasidic or American existentialist—cannot be programmed; it must be imaged, as the Hasidic rabbis, the zaddiks, knew. But Mailer's activistic mysticism cannot be confined in a parable-like short tale or a poem; it is not concerned with the God of the churches, or, for that matter, with an absolute God, but with God in experience, a God who is unconfined and may emerge only through a particular man's experience of Him. In answer to an interviewer of *The Paris Review* who asked if there were a "hidden pattern being worked out in [his] novels," Mailer replied, "I have some obsession with how God exists. Is He an essential god or an existential god; is He all-powerful or is He, too, an embattled existential creature who may succeed or fail in His vision? I think this theme may become more apparent as the novels go on." [43] God known through experience of Him is an expansive theme for which one needs the narrative scope of the novel or the epic poem—lyric poems and short tales may not really encompass it. Yet, even—or especially—in the novel, to speak of God directly has become difficult, the last breach of decorum in the modern literary world. That Mailer undertakes to make of *An American Dream* an exploration of human experience as the field of conflict between God and the devil, as he declared to a reporter of *The New York Times*,[44] and that his metaphysical inquiry finds sex fundamental in describing human experience but does not disavow the realities of God and the devil are, no doubt, intended as revelations of Mailer's "courage." For Mailer, novelwriting, love, and God all require courage. None may be taken easily: not the novel through craft, nor love through passive tenderness, nor God through humble reverence. The difficult way of danger and courage is, according to Mailer's philosophy, the only way.

Sex and God, or sexual experience and spiritual experience, are inextricably joined together, unified as one, in the definitions made in "The White Negro"; and this extreme view must be fully taken into account before the spiritual activism of Mailer's new hero (perhaps more parodied than realized in *An American Dream,* perhaps still to be honestly and completely realized in the promised long novel of the future) can be recognized. Two quotations from "The White Negro" should elucidate this joining of sexual and spiritual experience. If the new hero, the hipster, Mailer says,

moves through his life on a constant search with glimpses of Mecca in many a turn of his experience (Mecca being the apocalyptic orgasm) and if everyone in the civilized world is at least in some small degree a sexual cripple, the hipster lives with the knowledge of how he is sexually crippled and where he is sexually alive, and the faces of experience which life presents to him each day are engaged, dismissed or avoided as his need directs and his lifemanship makes possible.[45]

Sex has become for Mailer an extended metaphor for vitality of spirit. This is not animal or mechanical sex but sex which is the manifestation of the very center of the self. When seen in this enlarged or metaphorical way, the sexual activity of Mailer's hero in pursuit of the transcendent self, to be found, with God, in "apocalyptic orgasm," does not appear as far removed from the activity of the Kafkan hero as it may at first have seemed.

Continuing, Mailer says,

But to be with it is to have grace, is to be closer to the secrets of that inner unconscious life which will nourish you if you can hear it, for you are then nearer to that God which every hipster believes is located in the senses of his body, that trapped, mutilated and nonetheless megalomaniacal God who is It, who is energy, life, sex, force . . . ; God; not the God of the churches but the unachievable whisper of mystery within the sex, the paradise of limitless energy and perception just beyond the next wave of the next orgasm.[46]

In Mailer's recognition that the "unachievable whisper" is just that and that the "paradise," or apocalyptic orgasm, is always beyond the real orgasm is his acknowledgment of the fact that he speaks of pursuit of spiritual fulfillment, through the sexual metaphor, and knows its unavailability in the finite, human world of striving. The Tree of Life is not available through eating from the Tree of Knowledge. Mailer's failure to show through a novelistic hero this paradox in all human striving for spiritual fulfillment is caused by his insistence on the prophetic nature of his task to change modern man's consciousness. The prophet cannot tell the whole truth, or even a whole subjective truth, as the novelist can.[47]

Mailer's existentialist ideas comment, perhaps all too well, on *An American Dream*. But the ideas must be seen as serious and real—the material of his experience to which Mailer is consistently and authentically committed, committed even as a prophet is committed—not as mere psychopathy or exhibitionism before the novel is regarded either with his ideas as a context or without them.

In *An American Dream,* Mailer has made his primary character, Stephen Rojack, the narrator of his own story, a superhero; his settings, political and metaphysical; and his theme, magnificent and large. Stephen Rojack, the superhero as an activist who seeks his identity by following the imperatives of self, is perhaps the first of his kind. One expects of the superhero a certain typicality of character, which is established early and kept unchanged throughout the narrative, like that of Odysseus or James Bond: the fortunes of the superhero may change with his shifting situation and his various adventures, but he himself remains steadfast and true to type. His character is untouched; he does not change or grow. On the other hand, one expects the modern activist hero to learn, change, grow in a constant process of moving and becoming. As his situations change, his experience changes; and responsive to every experience, he feels varieties of hate and love and, in a constant state of flux, he becomes more this or that, more himself, an atypical particular person, an accumulation of his own past moments, but responsible only to the self he finds in the immediate moment of the present and to the transcendent self which is a future goal.

That Stephen Rojack is both superhero and activist establishes the two levels of the novel. The level of the superhero (Harvard graduate, war hero, congressman, husband of an heiress, TV celebrity, writer, existentialist psychologist, and professor) is the political and social, or secular, level. The level of the activist is personal and metaphysical: stripped of his various political and social roles, with nothing but his spirit, mind, and body, the particular person asks the metaphysical questions about his own experience and all human experience. Both levels of the novel are operative throughout the narrative; however, the personal and metaphysical emerge at the expense of the social and political. This is most obvious in Rojack's progressive casting-off, or loss of, worldly roles, the roles or functions which make him a typical role-playing superhero, the roles with which he thunders onto the scene.

Before the time of the novel Rojack is done with Harvard, war, and Congressional careers; he sheds his role as the husband of an heiress by killing his wife and as a consequence of this murder also loses his jobs as TV showman and professor of existentialist psychology. The specific roles are gone, but notoriety and celebrity linger on to hound the personal-meta-physical hero and to keep him involved, off and on, with the social and political world. Existentialist ideas more than linger on, though the course work is done, to help the hero, who endeavors to hold fast to a commitment to the authority of his senses, deal with the worlds of the night club, the police station, Harlem, the Mafia, and the C.I.A. Rojack's own existentialist ideas are peculiarly appropriate to Rojack, a sensual man, for they emphasize dread, fear of death, and magic as the basic primitive components of man's nature. With his sensuality, his dread, his fear, his intense recognition of death, and his intuition of magic, Rojack faces the complexities of the modern world. But Rojack is equipped with more than these fundamentals of primitive man; he has *ideas* about them, and his true power, his ability to will a way toward a better self, ironically lies in those ideas and not in the fundamental attributes of the sensual man.[48]

But if Rojack's power, through his ideas, wins his freedom in the world, the ideas cheat him of the only ameliorative truth achieved through the authority of his senses, his love for Cherry. I do not think that in the dramatic parapet walk of the novel's climax fear overcomes courage, as Mailer intends to suggest, so much as the idea of fear overcomes the idea of courage.

The superhero, the social-political side of Rojack, is also the American dream side of Rojack; as such, he is somewhat of a Pop Art hero. Not only is he similar in many respects to the mass-cult hero of the sex-and-sadism adventure story, the popular hero such as James Bond, but he also has in his guise of half-WASP, half-Jew, intellectual, warrior, something of the aura of Pop Art as it has become stylized in painting and sculpture. Pop Art portrays, without satirizing, the mundane objects of everyday American life and not the superobjects;

however, Pop Art, taken another way, might be said to make superobjects of the objects perceived every day by the modern collective unconscious, to make a wry game of pseudo-archetypes out of the objects of common experience. Rojack's typical, universal, role-playing superhero persona might be seen in this second way. (The best example of a true Pop Art novel is *Candy* [49]—a novel without form or vision, merely the mundane writ large. While it does not have either form or vision or content beyond the trivial and mundane, Pop Art does have a highly cultivated style which is inherent in the ingenious selection of the ordinary object presented and in the manner of presentation—a manner which *pretends* to minimize style and to make the flattest possible presentation.)

Surely the world in which Rojack as the social-political superhero moves is the world of American schemes and dreams, and the situations he encounters, insofar as they touch on the superstructures of the American scene, have their own Pop Art aspects. The Mafia, the C.I.A., the TV station, Big Business, Harlem, the American South, High Society—all of these become stylized institutions in the novel, bigger than life; like an Oldenburg hamburger, they also loom large, or are ubiquitous, in their original forms. But what Mailer seems to be saying about them is that their presence on the American scene is a taken-for-granted, unexamined one, like the hamburger's. Ever present, do they constitute the dream or the reality? Between the dream and the reality is the realistic description, without comment, of the thing, an embracing of what is. Someone has called Pop Art capitalist realism, a counterpart to socialist realism, and that term seems appropriate to the political-social level of Mailer's novel. (In a *Paris Review* interview, Mailer refers to "that godawful *Time* magazine world out there.") Yet this is but one level, and the environment of it—the Mafia, C.I.A., Big Business, et cetera—is only occasionally in the foreground of the novel. More immediate is the New York City street environment, which accommodates the fluidity of the hero's activist persona.

Rojack, nevertheless, must confront the stationary institutions of society, characterized in Pop situations. Caught between the fluid and the stationary are the novel's "others" whom the hero encounters in his thirty-two-hour dark night of the soul, those secondary but important characters, who, as does Rojack, emerge through their roles and ex-roles in the political-social matrix as well as through their personal and metaphysical stances. The three women, Deborah, Ruta, and Cherry, are personifications of High Society, Nazi Germany, and the American South, respectively, but each is engaged in her own personal life and in her own dialogue with God and/ or the devil. (The devil may in fact be Barney Oswald Kelly, who, in the political-social scheme of the novel, represents Big Business, the Mafia, and the C.I.A., all at once.) Rojack murders his wife, High Society, who has lost her soul to the devil and become demonic herself; he buggers his wife's German maid, as a kind of gratuitous peacetime affirmation of his war heroism, the killing of four Nazi soldiers (an event recorded, significantly, on the first page of the novel). In the sexual act with the German maid—a life-denying, anal sexual act embodying hate and death, the devil's sexuality—the Protestant-Jewish Rojack expresses both the American and the Jewish hatred for the Nazi, modern history's manifestation of the devil. Thus, he exorcises death through the murder of High Society, the devil's consort, and hate through a perverse sexual act with Nazi Germany. The grand exorcism of hate, death, and the devil occurs in the crucial acts of killing the Nazi soldiers and murdering his wife with which the novel begins; the sex with the German maid underscores the first two events. Through the violence of the murder of his wife, the hero enters that dark night of the soul out of which it is expected he will be reborn.[50]

The third woman, the American South, poor and incestuous, but growing up to include the otherness of the South, the Negro, through sexual love, is Cherry. Not only is Cherry a representative of the American South, which has had its affair with the devil (Slavery? Barney Oswald Kelly?), finally spurning the devil with the help of her "Angels" and a hipster Negro singer; she is also a blonde (very white), a singer (angelic?), and an eternal virgin (Cherry). Rojack first sees Cherry in the aftermath of his murder and buggering and ultimately joins with her in perfect, wholesome, complete sexuality which proves fertile and promises not only the birth of a child (the wife's inability to have a child with Rojack is specifically important here) but also the birth of love, or the courage to love. (Love is seen in the novel as courageous choice.)

When the characteristics of these three women who share the center of the novel with Rojack are summarized, the difficulty in keeping the social-political level separate from the personal-metaphysical is realized. The two levels are, of course, artistically inseparable; however, they are distinct and their affinity for one another is allegoristic. As the hero strikes against the devil and society's deathlike quality, thus losing his social-political roles and his prestige in the *Time* magazine world, his personal-metaphysical self spiritually ascends, through courage and love, to its point of climactic, full encounter with the devil, or the devil's personification, Barney Oswald Kelly. Courage and love do not survive this encounter: courage fails in the dangerous, risk-taking trial of the parapet walk, and love dies, in Cherry's death, as a consequence of the failure of courage. Still, in this confrontation Rojack stands up to the demonic Kelly and his temptations; and, with the magic help of the umbrella of the Negro singer, Shago, he survives on his own terms, wins, wins himself and his freedom, though he loses love. (Shago's umbrella, which Rojack keeps with him during his confrontation of Kelly, is reminiscent of Aaron's rod, useful to Moses in his confrontation of Pharaoh. The umbrella seems to become a snake in Rojack's hand. Without sentimental exploitation of the idea of the Jew joined with the Negro against the devil of social death, Mailer, through the device of the umbrella, evokes the Jewish-Negro shared consciousness of slavery and freedom.)

Barney Oswald Kelly brings the two levels, the social-political and the personal-metaphysical, together in the climax when it becomes apparent that Big Business, the Mafia, the C.I.A. of the social-political level and the devil of the metaphysical level come together in him. As Kelly had at one time put it to a Jesuit priest, " 'Well, for all we know, I am a solicitor for the Devil.' " [51] Deborah, his child, was conceived through a bargain with Satan, about which he says, " 'You strike a bargain with the Devil, the Devil will collect. That's where Mephisto is found. In the art of collection.' " [52] Kelly defines the devil in businessman's terms, bringing the separate facets of his persona neatly together.

Barney Oswald Kelly is portrayed as a kingly devil, ready to tempt, bribe, and seduce in order to exert control. An expert himself in lust and greed, he knows all the practical and metaphysical angles to make a man conform to his wishes. This is in keeping with his image as the biggest international businessman in America, who has irons in all fires, and with his devil-image. Fire, the devil's element, is also Kelly's. He has received one ominous warning through fire (an ability transferred to Rojack after Rojack's meeting with him), and his talk with Rojack in his tower apartment at the top of the Waldorf Towers is lighted by the blaze of his fireplace, which flares up occasionally when blasts of wind come down the chimney.

The fireplace is in Kelly's den where he sits on a throne, a Venetian antique, surrounded by other antiques. Rojack contemplates the den:

I felt once again as I had felt on entering the Waldorf, that I was in some antechamber of Hell where objects came alive and communicated with one another while I sank with each drink into a condition closer to the objects. There was a presence in the room like the command of a dead pharaoh. Aristocrats, slave owners, manufacturers and popes had coveted these furnishings until the beseechment of prayer had passed into their gold.[53]

In this room Kelly tells the story of his rise to power and affluence; the history of his sexual life; his convenant with the devil at the time of the conception of Deborah, his only child; his diabolical affair with Bess, who was apparently an incestuous Lesbian as well as a heterosexual witch; and his long-lasting incestuous relationship with Deborah. Devoid of all moral vigor, Kelly has led an opportunistic, rich, diabolical life—a match to the room and its accumulated hoard.

It is through Kelly that the three women of the novel—Deborah, Ruta, and Cherry—have known the devil most intimately. Deborah has known him as his child and incestuous partner. Ruta, his servant, spying for and on him, and his partner in perverse sexuality, wishes to marry him, to become voluntarily a member of his family. Deborah, at least, is doomed involuntarily by the fact of her birth; and she did, in her life, struggle against the demonic in herself, although she lost the battle. The wickedness of the Nazi, Ruta, is underlined by her willful ambition to establish a complete and lasting liaison with Kelly. Cherry, through her affair with Kelly, escapes the incestuousness of the provincial South, learns the ways of the world; then, worldly through the help of the devil, she spurns him and his cohorts of the Mafia in order to save herself. She tells Rojack of the way she had decided to leave Las Vegas: " 'I started thinking of that small-town hatred I had always considered beneath me, that envy and spite, and it was now a part of me. I came to the conclusion I'd flip out so far I'd not come back if I stayed in Vegas too long. So I decided it was the year for New York.' " [54] Wishing not to lose her goodness, Cherry chooses to leave the Las Vegas to which Kelly has introduced her. Rid of him, she has been able to rid herself of his ambience—hell.

The sexual life of each of the three women in the novel in-

cludes both Kelly and Rojack, and Kelly in each instance has
preceded Rojack. All Rojack's sex—marital, random, and loving—is doomed or cursed by the priority of the demonic in
the women. Only Cherry, curiously pure, has had the will to
survive her fleshly contact with worldly evil, but she has sur-
vived only as a "spirit," not as a person with a "soul," the latter being a higher form according to her own spiritual hier-
archy. The only way she can maintain herself as a "spirit" is
by loving a person with a "soul"—presumably someone like
Rojack. Cherry's definition of "people with souls" is vague
but seems to include Shago, the Negro singer who was her
lover immediately before Rojack, and Rojack himself. She
says, " 'People with souls are the ones who make the world
move,' " and she adds: " 'If they fail, but honorably, why
then, God, as a mercy, or as a compromise . . . takes their
soul away and makes them a spirit. That's a sad thing to be
because you can't live with other spirits—too sad. So you have
to look for somebody with a soul even if they're mean and
awful.' " [55]

Kelly seems outside of Cherry's definition: there is no specific discussion, but the suggestion is that he is, preternatur-
ally, outside of human categories, even those that deal with
"spirits" and "souls." When Cherry refuses to deny that she
found Kelly not odious but attractive in the past, Rojack
conjectures, "How did one distinguish love from the art of the
Devil?" [56] This would seem to be Rojack's very particular
and personal question; and though he manages to choose to
love Cherry freely and, in spite of dread, courageously, he
does not manage to keep his love safe, and Cherry falls victim to a gang of Harlem hoodlums, while Rojack walks a
parapet railing around the balcony of Kelly's apartment.

This climax occurs in the scene in Kelly's apartment, a
scene that powerfully brings together all the various concerns
of the novel. After this scene, there is only the open road of
Rojack's complete freedom. Rojack, having made a complete
descent politically and socially, must in his confrontation

with Kelly externally establish the fact of his spiritual ascent, resisting all devilish temptations. Kelly, who has through his connections arranged that Rojack not be held for the murder of Deborah, wishes in exchange for this favor Rojack's attendance at Deborah's funeral to indicate to the world of appearance and materiality that the family is united in respectability, unassailable. Rojack refuses; he furthermore confesses to having murdered Deborah and accuses Kelly of a worse crime against her when he says, " 'Yes, I killed her,' " and " 'but I didn't seduce her when she was fifteen, and never leave her alone, and never end the affair.' " [57]

A second temptation, never verbalized but sensually understood by Rojack, is Kelly's proposal to bury murder and incest in lustful violent sexuality—Kelly, Rojack, and Ruta together in the devil's den. Shago's rodlike, magic umbrella slips from Rojack's knee and saves him from this temptation by bringing a telepathic vision of Shago and Cherry together, and an alternate vision of Shago, alone, murdered in Harlem. Rojack bends to pick up the umbrella and receives a parapsychic message that he must walk the parapet or "Cherry is dead."

This magic which is often present in the novel and which takes him away from the second temptation in the climactic scene is a magic which belongs not specifically to God or the devil but to the man who accepts the authority of his senses, augmented by an extra or a sixth sense of supernatural perception. But Rojack, an intellectual, so verbalizes his sensual knowledge that he can never be sure it is guiding him properly. The message, that he must walk the parapet to save Cherry, becomes transmuted, through Rojack's intellectuality, into what might be considered in this scene as the third temptation, to which Rojack succumbs. Though he proves his courage by walking all three sides of the parapet once, he is prompted by an inner temptation to fly while walking the narrow ledge, an archetypal temptation for men of superhuman pride. Though tempted to fly, he does not try, but cautiously completes his walk. Nor does he, when he receives a second message to walk the parapet again, in order to earn his full freedom from Deborah's ghost this time, risk the narrow walk again. He stops his "madness," as he calls it, and goes to Cherry's apartment to find her dying, beaten by Harlem bums who mistakenly thought she had something to do with Shago's death an hour before.

The third temptation, to give in, pridefully, to his own ideas about fear and courage—an inner temptation but one encouraged by Kelly—has defeated the purpose for which the original parapet walk was intended: to save Cherry. If Rojack had followed the simplest authority of his senses and gone to Cherry's apartment sooner, he might have saved her. But his willful, prideful, conceptualized insistence to himself that he must prove his courage by confronting Kelly and, later, by walking the parapet, has lost him Cherry, and true love. However, confronting the devil and walking parapets are dangerous metaphysical and physical games; though he has lost love, he has proved his courage. A predominant theme in the novel, that one must have courage to choose to love and to love, is ironically undermined here by what seems to be a corollary theme, that courage may be incompatible with love.

Through will and courage Rojack ultimately gains his freedom, a total freedom, although possibly not free of ghosts; without community or love, he goes on the road. The spiritual progress of the hero is toward this freedom: the self is reborn at the beginning of the novel through the murder of evil, in the middle of the novel through true orgasm, and at the end of the novel through the loss of love. If one does not necessarily deem these three happenings rebirths, one must nevertheless call Rojack's progress a spiritual ascent coupled with a political-social descent as he loses power, ambition, and roles in the material world. The self has many possibilities, but when it seeks its own imperatives, it finds, it would seem, this nakedness—this total freedom—a kind of purity. For Mailer, the heroic self finally ascends to a nothingness, out of which all is possible and out of which the new, or renewed, hero must constantly redefine himself through personally felt choice, human choice of metaphysical significance to men and of spiritual significance to the existential God or the existential devil.[58]

6

J. D. Salinger's Holden and Seymour and the Spiritual Activist Hero

Mary McCarthy attacks J. D. Salinger's work as sentimental and narcissistic.[1] One expects cool-headedness, tough-mindedness, from Miss McCarthy, and this is of course what she is giving her reader in assailing Salinger's sentimentality; but her view of his narcissism is not tough-minded. To criticize Salinger's work on psychological rather than literary grounds seems to me too arbitrary and simpleminded a method of judging his representation of reality. And it is on psychological grounds that Miss McCarthy's case against Salinger's oral-anal narcissism finally rests. As such it gives us a valid footnote on the Salinger hero but not, I think, a valid or full criticism of him. It would be a narrow psychology which did not make reference to the oral-anal narcissism possible in man; it would be a narrow literature, indeed, which had for its only hero the fully genital hero of Wilhelm Reich and D. H. Lawrence.

On the other hand, other critics of Salinger overemphasize the Freudian validity of his insights. Gwynn and Blotner's book, while useful for its bibliography and general comment, is clumsy in its Freudian analysis of some of the stories. In "DeDaumier-Smith's Blue Period," for example, it does the most shocking job of Freudian analysis possible in its insistence on the castration complex as centrally significant in that story.[2] Blotner, Mary McCarthy, and all those who talk about Salinger's works as if they were case histories forget that we are all post-Freudian: Salinger, too, is post-Freudian, and to analyze him for his readers in Freudian terms is meaningless.

Facile Freudian criticism of modern literature is no longer possible. Perhaps Freud's insights clarify great literary intuitions of the past. We may realize Hamlet's situation to a fuller extent if Hamlet is seen in the light of the Oedipal complex. However, today's literature is post-Freudian: it starts from Freud; it includes Freud; it leaps out of and away from Freud; it opposes itself to Freudian clichés along with a host of other sorts of inherited clichés. The post-Freudian novelist has been given what the post-Freudian critic or reader has been given. I think a modern novelist expects the reader to assume the Freudian ideas with him as part of the general intelligence which he brings to bear on (or which he opposes to) the reality that he presents in his novel.

It is, in fact, on the basis of the recognition that the investigation of heroes with wonderfully varied psyches and an assortment of psychological differences which remain outside Freudian (or other established psychological) categories is possible in literature that I would find fault with much of the favorable and unfavorable criticism of Salinger. Salinger, as many new novelists do, explores possibilities outside normal behavior and outside the usual categories for abnormal behavior. Clearly, today's novelists are not psychological realists in any of the established ways.

However, Salinger may attract critiques based on psychological categorizing from his admirers and detractors because he cheats, especially in his earlier work, on his own vision (a vision of goodness on the edge of madness) in order to structure a story according to external, formalized rules of the storytelling craft. I am not talking of the twenty stories of the apprentice period; these are experiments in storytelling in a number of styles: the styles of F. Scott Fitzgerald, Katherine Mansfield, and a little of the simple surprise-ending stuff of O. Henry. Nor do I find a conflict between vision and form in seven of the *Nine Stories*.[3] All except "Teddy" and "DeDaumier-Smith's Blue Period" are formal studies of love and loneliness; all have *The New Yorker* tone as they make their understatements on the sweet and the sad in modern life. They are, no matter how successful of their kind (in the way, for example, that "For Esme with Love and Squalor" is successful), slight and ephemeral. They are informed by no special vision. "Teddy" and "DeDaumier-Smith" are informed by a mystical vision of madness which provides the way to fullness of being otherwise unavailable in modern life. The vision in these two stories is just beginning to be defined and is, therefore, only contained in some conceptual form within the confines of the craftsmanlike story—the vision is not strong enough to conflict with the form or insist upon a form of its own. In *The Catcher in the Rye* the vision conflicts with the tight formalistic planning; in "Seymour—An Introduction,"[4] the vision insists on finding its own form and thoroughly usurps the Salinger craftsmanship apparent in earlier work.

The vision to which I have been referring should be perhaps more carefully defined before any detailed examination of *The Catcher in the Rye* and "Seymour—An Introduction." The emergent vision in the whole of Salinger's work is one of the potential of the spiritual self, and the elusiveness of that self, which is always ahead of the movement of the particular moment. He sees the inner self as potentially loving, compassionate, in touch with a human goodness that encompasses the mysteries of the world: in this sense, it is a vision of hope and carries with it a celebration of life. However, the full realization of the compassionate inner self is forever out of reach, because, as is seen in "Seymour," the existential facts of life make the inner self one of the ineluctable mysteries. "Seymour" shows the self as unavailable, no matter how seriously sought, in metaphysical terms expressive of the vision at its fullest. *Catcher* shows the self as unavailable in social terms: the corruption and phoniness of society defeat the strivings for personal and spiritual freedom. But the visionary idea in *Catcher* is betrayed as much by the formal craft of storytelling and its rules, to which Salinger became addicted in his earliest work, as Holden is betrayed by society's insistence that he conform to its rules. But Salinger asks for the safety of conformity (as Holden does not) when he writes *The Catcher in the Rye:* perhaps Salinger's inability to risk his vision here may be understood if the vision is seen as an edge-of-madness one which ultimately involves the writer as much as his subject—a curious phenomenon demonstrated in "Seymour," a story in which Buddy Glass, the writer-narrator of the story, becomes temporarily a madman while trying to capture the essence of a ghost's existential madness.

In *The Catcher in the Rye,* Salinger gives us an open, innocent, protean hero who lives, antisocially, on the periphery of conventional sanity—a modern rebel and existential hero, in fact. And he places this hero in a closed, corrupt, highly structured society, the alleys and by-ways of which become the ground of his exploration during his journey of adventure, his dark night of the soul during which he wanders through New York City. We would wish to find out, through the representation of this adventure, what can be existentially discovered in such a situation. It would seem that Salinger, along with other contemporary American novelists, such as Malamud in *A New Life* [5] and Bellow in *Henderson the Rain King,* would somehow wish to show the subjective truths of the particularized but protean hero in an open-ended situation. But the overzealous craftsman in Salinger closes the situation: he makes a structure of Holden's "open" character and puts it against the structure of society, thereby intrinsically denying Holden's inner character, his self, at the same time as he sets it in motion in its primal openness, innocence, and claim to authentic discovery. The closed, literary, prestructured character of Holden is embodied in the archetypal figure of Christ, the incongruously ironic hero who, according to Northrop Frye, appears increasingly innocent the more he is punished by society.[6] He is the innocent victim. The archetypal pattern would not of itself suffice to make Holden a closed, labeled hero; it is the enunciating of this pattern in the details of the story that too tightly restricts the movements of the hero. The significance of Holden's dark wandering, full of temptations encountered; the Christmas season setting; Holden's clearly symbolic wish to be the catcher in the rye (that is, the pastoral Jesus figure, a shepherd in the rye field who would save the innocence and purity of the small children, who make up the Salinger "flock," from the fall, the cliff, the dangers beyond the field). These things overwhelm Holden's becomingness with too rigid a pattern of being, and the being is essentially labeled Jesus. If the suffering in Holden's becomingness merely pointed to an archetypal pattern of the incongruously ironic figure, Holden's particularity would not be restricted by the literary device; but in Salinger's structuring, the archetype rules, and we are given a formula for ideal being rather than an urgent existence. We know the end, and in knowing it, we lose the process.

Holden's definition of ideal being is made in response to Phoebe's demand that he name something he would like to be. " 'Like a scientist. Or a lawyer or something.' "[7] It is at this time that Holden verbalizes his choice, a choice against society, and describes his dream of ideality—his wish to be the catcher in the rye—which he will finally achieve in that concluding moment of the narrative action, when he sees that staying with Phoebe is the meaningful gesture he can make, the gesture which "saves" Phoebe, and, fulfilling the Jesus-pattern, puts him into society's hands to be "crucified." The artistry of this; the sense of wholeness achieved in what appears on the surface to be random observations of an adolescent boy; the final paradox—these things evoke in us an admiration for Salinger's craftsmanship and, more than that, for his ability to create a novel, totally modern in its questions, within the context of older novelistic conventions.

But it is just exactly those modern questions which cannot be answered when they are enclosed in the traditions, novelistic or religious, of the past. Holden's questioning of his society makes an insistent claim to fresh insight; it promises more: it promises to shape, through the process of the hero's adventure, something new, if only a new formulation of the question. It is this claim to modern insight which is forfeited when Salinger fails to take the risks his material demands and to strive for the new forms which might make the material manifest. In his later work, the Glass family stories, and especially in "Seymour," even though he very apparently uses Zen ideas, which are after all also given ideas, I think Salinger is a truer artist and is beginning to take the risks his material demands. Seymour, for example, is allowed to be a hero in process, not one imprisoned by a special given literary, mythic, or social idea. Seymour uses all ideas available to this experience; they do not use him. In so doing he shapes his fictive world; Salinger allows him to do this. And it is a risky business, as is attested by the almost unanimously adverse comment on this story. If "warring impulses of the soul distend the shape of Salinger's fiction," as Ihab Hassan suggests,[8] the distended shape is honest and no charge of literary phoniness may be leveled at it.

"Seymour," a long short story, a plotless narrative, details the events, occasions, and gestures of a unique sort of activist; for Seymour, though a situational man in the world (one who responds to occasions rather than inventing them), is an activist of the spirit. In secular situations, he invents his spirit, but he does not invent the situation for the sake of his spirit, or spiritual self, as one might say spiritual activist heroes of other novels do. Given a situation, he transcends it: he does not reject it or change it. Thus, the story of Seymour depends less on his acts and more on his gestures and words, which become significant as the true outward clues to his inner activity. He is the poet or the saint, as Buddy Glass, the writer-narrator, tells us. But Buddy does not merely tell this, as Salinger tells us Holden is the catcher in the rye: he tries to show this, to prove it. In the process of trying to prove Seymour's saintliness, Buddy is afflicted by delirium, mania, chills, and fever which indicate the strain of the task of making manifest in worldly terms the spiritual activity of a living man, dead at the time of the storytelling, a ghost in fact. Buddy is haunted and, therefore, like the Ancient Mariner, somehow compelled to tell the tale. (There is a Gothic-horror quality about this. Perhaps when Salinger first thought of writing a series of stories about the Glass family, he thought in terms of a modern Gothic tale of a dead brother's ghost. However, Salinger's vision is here more metaphysical than Gothic, and there is, I think, no significant horror for the reader.)

While Seymour is the story's hero, who must finally be isolated and discussed, Buddy as narrator has almost as primary a function in the tale as Seymour; for this is as much a story of the process of storytelling as it is a capturing of the process of a saint's life in New York City. It is as if when Salinger risks himself in telling Seymour's story fully he must tell his own, through Buddy. (I do not think he is being coy or cute, as some critics have suggested, when he gives to Buddy biographical data that belong to himself. Rather I think he is honestly attempting to meet the demands made on him by his tale.) That he must tell his own story as the writer seems very suitable on this occasion when his craft is broken by his vision and he searches for new forms that may encompass the largeness and strangeness of the vision. The story is governed by a sense of breakthrough and experiment.

If significant function in the narrative is equally shared by narrator and hero, the story becomes an exemplification of the relationship between the writer and his material; since it is a story, one might say it is, patently, the relationship between the writer and his material. That is always true; here, however, this truth is overt and functional rather than a simple fact of all storytelling.

The story is prefaced by two comments on the act of writing, one by Kafka, one by Kierkegaard. The quotation from Kafka, used as an epigraph for "Seymour," is:

"The actors by their presence always convince me, to my horror, that most of what I've written about them until now is false. It is false because I write about them with steadfast love (even now, while I write it down, this, too, becomes false) but varying ability, and this varying ability does not hit off the real actors loudly and correctly, but loses itself dully in this love that never will be satisfied with the ability and therefore thinks it is protecting this ability from exercising itself." [9]

Kafka is saying that the characters of a writer, once created, have a presence, a reality, in the world, which belongs to them, not to the writer, and that the writer respects this and protects it even from his own craft, which is perhaps mechanical and falsifies the truth the characters have assumed by their viable presence. Kafka's sense of his characters, created by his art but belonging, once there, to the reality of existence, is illustrated in his own work in which the spiritual and secular levels are inextricably joined, creating a thick unity that has seduced scholars and critics to try to separate the parts in order to see what might make such a substantial yet curiously elusive wholeness. Perhaps Salinger is so seduced, but rather than write a critical essay, he brings his question to his own storytelling. He has, until "Seymour," postponed the question, although one sees him working with it in the three earlier long stories about the Glass family, "Franny," "Zooey," and "Raise High the Roof Beam, Carpenters," [10] in which he has, some of the time, permitted his vision to overwhelm simple storytelling techniques, thus encouraging the personae of his characters to emerge more convincingly than they have in the early stories and *Catcher*.

The epigraph from Kierkegaard reads:

"It is (to describe it figuratively) as if an author were to make a slip of the pen, and as if this clerical error became conscious of being such. Perhaps this was no error but in a far higher sense was an essential part of the whole exposition. It is, then, as if this clerical error were to revolt against the author, out of hatred, for him, were to forbid him to correct it, and were to say, 'No, I will not be erased, I will not be erased, I will stand as a witness against thee, that thou art a very poor writer.' " [11]

Again, this is an enunciation of the writer's creation as having a life of its own, once on the page, once there, even if there by error or accident. Again the material of the work defeats the techniques for its control: a presence once created cannot be dispelled.

The fact of Seymour-as-ghost works as well on this level of the story, which depends upon the dialogue between the writer and his material, as it does on the level of the fictive hero's "simple" story, where saintliness, mysticism, and ghostliness interoperate in a diversity of situation. Seymour, whose death Buddy has depicted in "Perfect Day for Banana Fish," [12] must be confronted as a Kafkan "actor" or a Kierkegaardian "clerical error" that achieves presence as he is acknowledged by his creator, the writer. On the level of the writer's awareness, Seymour's ghostliness is interchangeable with this sort of artistic presence, and Buddy, the writer, struggles with it in chills and fever, reminiscent of Kierkegaard's *Fear and Trembling*. Curiously, Buddy the writer recognizes the urgent reality of his actor as Kierkegaard would have the reader know the immediacy of the Abraham and Isaac story and of all stories. But Salinger makes visible, or conscious, this "immediacy" in his story through his creation of a double for himself, Buddy Glass.

It is possible to say that in some way Seymour is also Buddy's double; he is after all his brother, his sharer of a youth-ful bedroom and of ideas. Buddy is a writer of prose and Sey-mour is a poet. Both strive to catch and hold for a moment the continuum of poetry they sense flowing through all life. Buddy considers Seymour to have been a true poet although he is unable, finally, to say how or why. (Buddy's failure to say how or why Seymour is a true poet seems appropriate: the mystery of Seymour's poetry remains ultimately inexpli-cable.)

Seymour is to Buddy as Buddy is to Salinger. If there is in-deed a series of doubles here, as there seems to be, then the comment on the creative act and on the immediacy of the created actors (the living relationship between writer and fic-tive character) is very special and complex. The comment is also singularly modern in its insistence on the dynamics of the creative act itself, and on the creative juggling of the *is* and *is-not* of the two realities: the world's and the work's. This is the literary juggling of what might in the past have been called reality and appearance—but in the past the ques-tion has been which, indeed, is which. The "Seymour" story does not give us an ironic picture of a reality controverted by a reality. It comes to no ironic conclusions in areas of neces-sity, worked through probabilities and the final exhaustion of all possibilities. The novelty of this story is that it is an in-conclusive presentation of probabilities which remain proba-bilities and of possibilities, always open: the story is without ironic undertones.

In his total willingness to suspend judgments, conclusions, answers, and finalities, ironic or not, Salinger achieves two things with the story: uncompromised openness and an affir-mation of constant flux. He has, furthermore, erased aes-thetic boundaries and aesthetic distance (his own and, with that, the reader's); by determining to recreate experience as experience-in-process and at the same time focusing on the difficulty in the task and the unknowability of reality, he has established spontaneity through seeming chaos (rather than making order out of chaos as is the case in most traditional storytelling). The term "seeming chaos" is used not to suggest that the chaos is accidental but to suggest that the seemingness of this quality is intentionally apparent in the work in which it occurs. A surface chaos is intentional, or, more than that, it is a necessary manifestation on the formal level of the story of the conflict between craft and powerful material. Chaos, never in the history of art and literature considered a formal criterion, becomes in much modern American literature a new dynamic form, reflecting the actual conflict between an outworn traditional form and a new content. The new content, the powerful material, is that of the spirit of man, loosed from its conventional motivations and social modes in literature, art, and religious institutions, but still present to be contended with, accounted for, encountered. If in new literature, madness seems to be the clearer cause for disorder than is spiritual longing, this may be seen as a proof of the struggle with spiritual material that the writer or the hero of the narrative (in the case of "Seymour" both, or all three, if we count the very important Buddy) gives himself to irrationally while half-knowing as he begins that the answers he seeks are by their very nature inaccessible: it is the spiritual adventure that exists in reality which engrosses him; there is no easy conclusion, goal, or answer. The writer knows this and his hero knows this. The task is precipitous since madness is the risk. This risk is clearly indicated in the chaos of such experimental literary work where the destruction of aesthetic limitations, definitions, and aesthetic distance result from the implicit madness (or the choice to live on the edge-of-madness, as Leslie Fiedler has designated the modern spirit-tracking impulse [13]).

Paradoxically, this sort of literature confirms the older aesthetic idea of art as orderly and sane by presenting the reverse of that idea. Perhaps this is the reason that the new activist novel appears to be an anti-art novel, or an anti-novel. In a simpler sense the new novel may be called anti-art be-

cause it tries to come closer to life by imitating its literal surface and also by asking metaphysical questions about what is
below the surface. Literal reality and serious philosophical
questions, combined with the breaking down of aesthetic distance, it may be argued, however, are peculiarly novelistic
since the novel has always been extraliterary; it has func-
tioned since the eighteenth century in England as a place for
direct commentary on life. When it has not been a commentary on life, it has been a comment on manners. However, the
eighteenth or nineteenth century novel contained this commentary within clear aesthetic limits or literary conventions.
The comment in the new American novel is often referen-
tial, unconventional, and uncontained, hence overwhelming,
in the work, to the point that the novel often is philosophical
more than novelistic in its first commitment, and sometimes
prophetic in its final tone.

To weigh an older form against the new, and to call the
old "art" and the new "anti-art" is perhaps a merely con-
fusing and misleading comparison, and surely it is an inap-
propriate stringency. Anti-art is a new form of art; the
anti-novel is a new form of novel. It is only necessary to
take note of the anti-art (or, here specifically, the anti-novel)
idea as such in order to discuss new formalities in the apparent chaos, or "formal discontinuity as a perceptual mode," as
one critic recently put it. And it is an interesting fact that
the most energetic mainstream in art continues by feeding
on all that which traditional art formerly denied. There is
inherent in this the demand for re-evaluation on all levels.

The "formal discontinuity" of Salinger's story "Seymour"
is such a re-evaluation. Its distended form is part of that re-
evaluation, as is the substance of the story dealing with the
narrator's conflict with his material. Because Salinger is very
aware of what he does here, this story becomes important to
the conscious examination of story and novel forms in a way
that William Burroughs' fragmentized novel *Naked
Lunch* [14] does not. *Naked Lunch,* however, participates just

as much in a new formal use of chaos as a constant element as "Seymour" does. It may be more important than "Seymour" because it antedates that story, and in its naturally sprawling, totally undisciplined, drug-addicted way it exists as the ultimate in anti-novel chaos. Yet it is a novel; it is a novel in which the vision of the writer has "destructively" usurped his craft. But the vision is real and powerful; it is so powerful that the serious reader cannot read for any length of time in the book without becoming terrified by the imagery. This, I think, is the reason the book is unreadable. The reason is not the one often given, that is, that the fragmentary pieces of the novel are incoherent to the point of meaninglessness. Incoherent the novel often is, but through this incoherence comes the terrible vision of man's helplessness (man as the naked lunch at the end of the fork) so vivid as to be unreadable, certainly unreadable in any concentrated period of reading time. Burroughs starts where Conrad's "The Heart of Darkness" ends—with the horror. He stays always inside the horror, never at a distance from it. And unlike the suggested Gothic horror of "Seymour," the horror of *Naked Lunch* is felt.

Since, unintentionally or intentionally, Burroughs and Salinger dispose of formal distance and the consequent literary structures for their material in *Naked Lunch* and "Seymour," they make language *qua* language do most of the work in their narratives. One is almost tempted to say that it is all done with language. As if language by itself were the last, as it was the first, instrument of the writer. The vision is the language and the form is the language: there is in these writers a linear, fluid verbal surface, a slangy, inventive, witty argot with its own vitality. Burroughs' nonsense lines are as much a part of this rich verbalism as his sensible lines. Sense and nonsense work together. (Having invented a word, Burroughs will give in parentheses, in a solemn dictionary-like way, its definition. For example, when listing the activities of "adolescent hoodlums . . . of all nations" he says they "throw . . . candiru into swimming pools," and in parentheses he defines the candiru, which is a product of his imagination: "the candiru is a small eel-like fish or worm about one-quarter inch through and two inches long patronizing certain rivers of ill-repute in the Greater Amazon Basin." [15]) Burroughs' words add up; they multiply themselves: they become an inundation, a flow that covers the surface, washing away rational conjectures.

Salinger is not so entirely lost inside his vision or its language as Burroughs is; one must, after all, acknowledge that *Naked Lunch* was largely written when Burroughs was in a drug-addicted state and, therefore, immersed in his private vision and its own language. But that fluid, all-pervasive verbalism, so often noticed in Holden's speech in *The Catcher in the Rye,* expands in "Seymour." Buddy talks and talks: the story is a talkathon. Jokes, witticisms, slang, colloquialisms, aphorisms—the stream of language is torrential. Buddy talks compulsively to the reader as if he might lose the ghost of his hero entirely if he permitted a moment of silence. Through the crack of silence, nothingness might enter.

It has been suggested that the verbal flood in "Seymour" is the ultimate exploration of civilized sound, which marks an attempt to exhaust that sound and come finally to a Zen silence. This judgment seems strained to me because, while Salinger is committed to a Zen idea for the saintly character of Seymour, he does not seem to be so committed for himself as a writer. A modern novelist like Jack Kerouac suggests a Zen ideal for the writer himself when he indulges in automatic writing for its own sake in a way that even Burroughs does not. Certainly Salinger nowhere implies that automatic writing is his aim. Buddy, who is a writer, feels cursed by his inability to cope with his saintly brother as hero. Any seeming automatism in the writing of Buddy, and implicitly of Salinger, is not purposeful but rather imposed by the material. The compulsive and automatic talking of Buddy is artfully viewed as a disease, the artist's disease, a "seizure." Art

—albeit a new art—is Salinger's undeniable aim, not Zen silence.

Buddy's confrontation with the ghost of his saintly brother has two significant themes: Buddy's theme, the writer and his material, deals with the process of storytelling; the other, Seymour's theme, the saint in the material world, explores the process of saintly and "poetic" living. ("Poetic" adds a new dimension which will be taken up later. I might mention here, however, that Seymour-as-poet is more overtly discussed by Buddy than Seymour-as-saint, though poet and saint overlap; their activities would seem to be, in "Seymour," synonymous. The emphasis on Seymour-as-poet in the secondary theme, Seymour's, complements the primary theme, Buddy's.)

I have already investigated the theme of the writer and his material. To look at the story as it exists on its simplest level, the level which embodies Seymour's theme, one must look at the character created as its hero and at the all-but-plotless plot. Who is Seymour? How does he act? What does he do? Is there a semblance of plot through which the character of the hero is revealed in a series of coherently, causally related moves or acts? There would appear to be no true plot in this essayish confession of a writer; however, there are a group of episodes, seemingly disconnected, which exist in a significant relationship to one another under the surface of the work. These are Seymour's episodes; Seymour is the hero after all, and we are in fact introduced to him as it is Salinger's avowed intention in the title of the piece that we be.

The events or episodes which make up the plot are hidden in among Buddy's digressive comments on writing and his descriptions of Seymour. The references to Seymour first emerge subtly (as later the episodes, told in anecdotal form, will come in quietly and unobtrusively) during the course of Buddy's discussion of the Kierkegaard and Kafka quotations which introduce the story. Kierkegaard and Kafka are two of Buddy's four favorite Sick Men and Great Artists. The other two are Van Gogh and Seymour. Thus Seymour gets on the page; then, in quick succession, this hero goes from Sick Man, to Seer, to Muktah (or Mystic), to Saint, to God-seeker, to Fool, to Poet.[16] All these titles or roles given to Seymour are worked into the fabric of Buddy's discourse on writing, the first section of the total work. In the second section of the work, Buddy discusses the poet and his poetry; the poet is Seymour. There are four anecdotes told. These deal with Seymour as a boy of eight, when he brought the right coat for each guest in his parents' living room to the person to whom it belonged without having foreknowledge of the ownership of the coat; as a boy of eleven, when he first discovered poetry books in the library; as a boy of fourteen, when he constantly jotted down poems wherever he was; as an older boy, when he tried to find a poetry form for his "un-Western" vision. There is also mention of his suicide, after which was found one of four poems paraphrased by Buddy. This second section, focusing on the poet and his poetry, ends with a depiction of the literary scene in America, complete with Buddy's amusing concession that critics are not fools because Seymour had said that Christ meant that there were no fools when He said "call no man Fool." In connection with literary gossip, Buddy paraphrases the fourth Seymour poem about a wise old man who, dying, would rather eavesdrop on gossiping in the courtyard than listen to the learned talk in his room.

In the first section we have met Seymour and learned of his several "heroic" roles; in the second section, we have seen him as mystic and poet, heard him talk as saint and poet. In the third section, we have the history of the family which has produced this hero. The family ancestry includes a juggling Polish Jewish clown, an Irish tramp, and Les and Bess, the father and mother who were vaudeville stars. Seymour as poet becomes Seymour as juggler of experience: deep personal experience is balanced with autobiographical experience in his haiku-like poems—that is, while the poems are intensely personal, they are not factually autobiographical: a remarkable feat which Buddy finds a juggling feat.

The fourth section returns to literature, with the emphasis directly on Buddy's writing rather than on Seymour's poetry; however, Seymour is now very much in the piece, and it is on his comments about Buddy's stories that the fourth section concentrates. This section is a new start in a way: at the very beginning of the story we have had Buddy's comments on writing and writers, leading to Seymour's appraisal of him as prose writer. An intricate twist, this return is properly introduced by Buddy's declaration that he has been away from the story and the reader, suffering from acute hepatitis, for nine weeks. He takes us back to the beginning, when he announced his manic happiness to have been an artist's seizure, a compulsion to speak. Perhaps, he says now, he was only liverish; what brings him from his literal sickness now to re-encounter Seymour is an old note of Seymour's, dealing with a 1940 story of Buddy's. The story goes from this note to others until the sum of Seymour's critical thoughts on writing is finally revealed: writing is a religious activity. It is necessary, therefore, to write one's heart out. Writing the heart out is more important, more germinal to the writer, than writing a masterpiece.[17] " 'I want your *loot,*' " not some neat formulized tricks, Seymour tells the young story writer, Buddy.[18] " 'Trust your heart,' " he adds.[19] By way of bolstering these critical insights and dicta of Seymour to Buddy, there are more episodes, anecdotally told, involving Seymour and Buddy as adults. Without the reader's noticing, Seymour has grown up. There are, in the fourth section, fewer tales of his childhood, more tales of his mature activity and thought. However, childlikeness pervades his personality. Adulthood does not change the nature of his innocence.

The last and most important section of the story might be called Seymour as corporeal being. Since this story is about Seymour, who was almost all spirit in life, and is literally all spirit at the time of writing, this fifth and last section, which takes more than one-third of the story's 137 pages, is an attempt on Buddy's part to keep Seymour on the page, to give him material being, in "life" and in literature, the dual task of Buddy the brother and Buddy the writer. As Buddy goes through the specifics of describing Seymour's earthly appearance, there is a paradoxical intensifying of Seymour's otherworldliness. The random list, a device of many contemporary American novelists,[20] makes its appearance in this section as an element of structure. Nose, wrists, hair, hands, teeth—all of these fall into line, but without apparent order. One physical aspect grows out of a story about another. The organization is linear, not Gestalt, and Buddy makes a special point of repudiating Cubist theories of art that might be applied to his attempt to see the parts of Seymour at the same time that he sees the whole of Seymour, to see a point in time in Seymour's life at the same time that he sees all of Seymour's life. Buddy says, always keeping his focus on Seymour and Seymour's thoughts, even while discussing his own ideas of prose writing:

It wouldn't worry [Seymour] a very great deal, I think, if after due consultation with my instincts I elected to use some sort of literary Cubism to present his face. For that matter, it wouldn't worry him at all if I wrote the rest of this exclusively in lowercase letters—if my instincts advised it. I wouldn't *mind* some form of Cubism here, but every last one of my instincts tells me to put up a good, lower-middle-class fight against it.[21]

Buddy, as usual, puts down the literary label, whether Freudian or Cubist or other, before it comes up. He is being, above all else, honest, as Seymour would have him be. (Alfred Chester notes *Salinger's* honesty in writing this story; he calls it "courageous" and suggests its honesty be compared to the dishonesty of earlier Salinger stories.[22] Salinger, through Buddy, keeps his effort at honesty in the foreground.)

Sticking to his linear organization of this final section, Salinger allows Buddy to leap from physical feature to physical feature until he lands in the description of the essence of Seymour's physicality—Seymour's inexplicable athletic prowess —based on a formlessness which for anyone but Seymour would have led to a loss of control in games such as tennis, ping-pong, stoop ball, pocket pool, and curb marbles. The curb marbles anecdote, set in a time-suspended moment on a New York City sidewalk, is the appropriate climax of the whole story; it is not a climax in the usual sense of the culmination and coming together of several strands of action in a story but rather in the sense of the high moment (perhaps to be compared to Joyce's epiphany, although epiphany, as Joyce defines and exploits it, is even more a mysteriously poetic, organic, and final revelatory moment) when the reader feels that he at last has "the loot"—Salinger's loot, Buddy's loot, and Seymour's loot: the metaphysical loot of the story which goes beyond the story.[23] And the reader gets to his point not with a sense of consummation and conclusion but with a sense of a meaningful respite in a continuum that extends outside the story and past its final sentences.

The curb marbles episode is, again, anecdotal and tells of a ten-year old Seymour, a figure coming into the field of marble-playing through the shadows of a city dusk ("his face shadowed, dimmed out" [24]—that physical face which Buddy has just gone to great trouble to capture, pin down on the page, piece by piece, returns for this scene to immateriality); he sees the game that Buddy, a boy of eight, is playing with a friend, and advises Buddy on his playing. Two things Seymour says at this time stand out particularly: " 'Could you try not aiming so much?' " and " 'If you hit him when you aim, it'll just be luck.' "[25] Seymour walks toward the two marble players; and Buddy quickly breaks up the game. Several pages later, just before the last pages of the story, Buddy interprets Seymour's advice:

When he was coaching me, from the curbstone across the street, to quit aiming my marble at Ira Yankauer's—and he was ten, please remember—I believe he was instinctively getting at something very close in spirit to the sort of instructions a master archer in Japan will give when he forbids a willful new student to aim his arrows at the target; that is, when the archery master permits, as it were, Aiming but no aiming.[26]

Buddy goes on from here to disclaim the wish to make a one-to-one relationship between Seymour's instruction and Zen instruction. He insists that he himself is Zenless though interested in the classical Zen writings; that Zen is in disrepute because it has been dirtied by popularizers who make of Zen detachment "an invitation to spiritual disinterestedness"; [27] that pure Zen will survive however. But the comparison between Seymour and the Zen archery teacher stands, and Seymour's Zenfulness, as opposed to Buddy's Zenlessness, stands. The heart of the curb marbles anecdote is the sense of formlessness as value; deliberate formal aiming corrupts because it betokens a belief that one may or may not hit his target. Formlessness assumes that one naturally, intuitively, instinctively hits the target. The arrow is made for the bull's eye, the thrown marble for the stationary marble. The man attuned to the game, the true player, stands between the two—arrow and bull's eye, marble and marble. He can best be an intermediary by shunning formal, external, given rules or forms for the game, by simply playing.

In life, as in games, the Seymour-hero goes, without method, rule, or external form, from "one little piece of Holy Ground to the next." [28] In life, which is a meta-game, formlessness is still the rule (or nonrule). (In spite of Buddy's insistence on his own Zenlessness, he has adopted Seymour's nonrule formlessness for this story, the implication being that he must since Seymour is its hero and the story shapes itself in acquiescence to the hero and his gestures and acts.) It is because Seymour makes of life a meta-game that excludes worldly social and ethical rules of conduct and depends instead upon a formlessness in responses which are dictated by an awareness and "feel" for any particular situation that I call him a spiritual hero.

Since Salinger, through the narration of Buddy, explores

possible formula types, or archetypes, for Seymour (Sick Man, Poet, Mystic, Saint) and is forced always beyond each of these by the nature of his hero, he is finally committed to a description of Seymour's existential being, unformulated and loose, as it confronts the thick and secular world. The question posed (more posed than answered) by Seymour's behavior is the question of what is spirit in the modern world, on the street, released from religious institutions? How does the spirit function, act, and move? Seymour's existential being is to be understood as a cipher for spirituality. (The initial S. is sometimes used by Buddy to stand for Seymour and seems more of an indication of the nature of the hero as cipher than it does a mere abbreviation of the name.) Buddy's strenuous effort to capture the material substance of his brother Seymour is an inverse way of showing us that this is impossible and of proving Seymour's existence to have been almost wholly a matter of spirituality, not physicality. Seymour does not live in a secular world but redefines the world of things in his own terms so that he goes from one piece of holy ground to the next. It is not necessary for him to rebel against the secular as it is found in the community (the village in *The Castle*), for he does not recognize the community. He sees only individuals and he sees only one group, the family group. The family is so thoroughly released from everyday concerns (in spite of the Glass parents' concern when Waker gives away his new Davega bicycle) and its members are so much more spiritual descendants of clowns and hoboes than they are New Yorkers that Seymour's willing and intimate involvement with them puts no strain on his secularly ignorant spirituality.

As has been said, Seymour makes of life a spiritual metagame, in which the only code is formlessness.[29] The object of the game seems to be that the man be an intermediary between one concreteness and another for the sake of an undefined but absolute spirit. In the guise of poet, for example, Seymour, writing his own brand of double haiku, brings the

red balloon, or the old wise man, or the widower to language. He makes himself a passive connection between the
thing-in-life and the language. The double haiku, invented
by Seymour, represents the loosening of an already "formless" form, the Japanese haiku, which restrains the poem
only in number of lines and syllables. The only reason he
looks for a form at all is so that he may write poems that will
be understood by his favorite librarian. He does need a form
in order to communicate, but he finds only a tenuous one, as
a gesture of love. In the passive, innocent, mediating role
that Seymour plays as a primary stance in his life meta-game
(the corollary roles to this total one are those of mystic, poet,
teacher, et cetera), love is not a commitment but a natural,
effortless gesture. Seymour overcomes alienation and nothingness, those twin curses of modern life, by turning alienation
into the necessary solitary independence of the saintly and
spiritual man and by turning nothingness into a formlessness
to be celebrated. The modern traumas are grist for his particular mill.

"To unlearn the illusory differences: this is what for Salinger it means *to be as a child*. And the Glasses, we remember,
are in this sense children, holy innocents still at twenty or
thirty or forty." [30] If Seymour is in the serene state of being
of a child, free of the illusory differences of worldliness, he is
in a state of lyrical freedom which K. partially achieves in
what Paul Goodman calls "manic responses in abnormal
states of consciousness" [31] and finds in four particular lyrical
passages in *The Castle:* the walk through the snowy night
with Barnabas; the encounter with Frieda under the bar; the
wait for Klamm in the snow; the bedroom scene with the castle official, Bürgel. Goodman also speaks of the "turmoil of
conflicting plots" in *The Castle:* "[The conflicting plots] are
in two sets: K.'s purpose and the high authorities; and the
village, Frieda . . . —and this turmoil is so managed and so
kept in motion by the protagonist's character . . . that it
can never come to an end." [32] But, he says, the lyrical pas-

sages interrupt the turmoil and hold the possibility of a resolution. The protagonist is "watchful, willful, and stubborn,"
and Goodman contends that the "pattern of the book . . . is
to exhaust him and carry him away with the satisfaction that
comes with finally giving in." He adds: "We must envisage a
resolution passage in the ending not unlike the four just
quoted, but with one important difference: it is not
manic. . . . it is an open-eyed view of the actual scene and
therefore spontaneous and unwilled." [33] This finding from
an analysis of the structure of *The Castle* is very ingenious,
but I do not think the abnormal lyric passages necessarily
point to a consummation in the grace of a lyrical resolution.
Grace, through access to the castle, may be that toward which
K. strives, but his existence as hero depends upon the process
of striving; he is watchful and willful, aware and active.
That his story ends without resolution, without a true conclusion, seems appropriate to the full realization of his character, his existence. Seymour, on the other hand, is constantly
in this state of formless lyrical freedom and grace and not ab-
normally or manically so. He is never so because he is drunk,
sleepy, or involved in sexual fantasy, as is K. in the lyrical
passages Goodman cites. The striving for the castle is Buddy's. Buddy becomes the Kafkan hero, and Seymour is his
castle. Shall we ask ourselves of Seymour, as we do of the castle, is he diabolic or divine? And does it matter? To the story
qua story I think it does not matter. The definition of spirit
lies as much in the process of attempting its capture in language as it does in the description of Seymour which finally
evolves, and the twofold structure of the "Seymour" story
rests on the process of description as well as on the ultimate
description.

Spirit may be diabolic or divine in the modern world. It is
sought for itself. It would seem not to matter very much in
which direction the spiritual activist goes in the modern
world, up, down, sideways, in circles, so long as he goes,
moves. Erich Heller, after discussing the modern loss of "the

relation between mundane and transcendental reality," with the transcendental, or spiritual, losing its validity in a positivistic-scientific time and the mundane "becoming more 'really' real than before," [34] says that by Kafka's time "reality has been all but completely sealed off against any transcendental intrusion" and that, therefore, in Kafka's world the "heroes struggle in vain for spiritual survival." [35] He continues, "Thus [Kafka's] creations are symbolic, for they are infused with . . . negative transcendence." [36] It is because K. does *not* gain the castle (or finally give in to the lyrical state of consciousness which Goodman speaks of) and because Buddy remains Zenless and cannot firmly capture the essential nature of Seymour's existence that K. and Buddy both seem to be literary heroes created in the terms of the most honest modernist vision of the spiritual quest, and its inevitable failure.

Minor American Novelists
in the Activist Mode

The School of Saul Bellow

The structural pattern and spiritual commitments of the contemporary activist novel are most obviously embodied in the fiction of Saul Bellow and of Norman Mailer (and, softened and sentimentalized, in the work of J. D. Salinger). Other novelists of the fifties and sixties are also of great significance, however, if one is to hope to understand the nature of modern American fiction. Bernard Malamud, Herbert Gold, and Philip Roth, for example, have certainly moved toward the activist mode. Malamud, in his third novel, *A New Life,* falls into this category, seemingly through a process of novelistic realization on his own part rather than through imitation. Herbert Gold and Philip Roth, younger men, seem more imitative in their adaptations of the activist mode to their own writings; they seem influenced by Bellow, and perhaps by Mailer or Malamud also. That they are genuinely concerned with the problems of modern man's freedom and spirit, which the device of the activist hero has given them the opportunity to explore, does not lessen their indebtedness to Bellow for the first powerful presentation of such a hero in recent American fiction. George P. Elliott, who is also a novelist, acknowledges this, and makes acknowledgment for Philip Roth, when he says, in a review of Irving Malin's *Jews and Americans:*

It was in 1943 that I first came upon Saul Bellow when *PR* [*Partisan Review*] printed a section of *Dangling Man,* and it did not seem to me that Joseph's former Jewishness had much more to do with his plight than my former Quakerishness had to do with mine, which was quite similar to his—mostly American. My gratitude to Bellow was complex and deep: he helped define my situation at the time, and also showed me that out of my ordinary experience as a young intellectual, lively and intelligent fiction was possible. I was astonished, therefore, when four years ago I heard Philip Roth say that Bellow's fiction had had a great releasing effect upon him, in good part *because* Bellow was *Jewish.* I demurred, saying that it had affected me similarly without my having any notion that Bellow was a Jew and that I would not have cared if I had known. Roth at first looked surprised by what I said, and then relieved.[1]

Bellow's definition of the situation of the young intellectual in his characterization of Joseph and later his definition of a possible answer—at least a literary answer—to the dilemma of that situation in his characterization of Augie March changes the whole course of American fiction. Bellow affected a whole generation of younger novelists to whom the stylized sensitivity of the novels of the twenties and the somewhat naive social realism of the novels of the thirties seemed no longer adequate after the holocaust and the terror of the Second World War. Hemingway's approach to the world had lost its abilty to persuade. It seemed no longer sufficient to say that man is lost. Playing manly games, in sweet lostness and ineffectuality, without investigating either the nature of the loss or the nature of the man lost, was to take the frightening, terrifying facts of a darkened world like a man, perhaps. But, finally, as in *Across the River and Into the Trees,* it was to be only soft and sentimental and too stylized about one's own hard-boiledness.

On the first page of Bellow's *Dangling Man,* which is the first page of Joseph's journal, Bellow effectively repudiates Hemingway's position:

Today the code of the athlete, of the tough boy—an American inheritance, I believe, from the English gentleman—that curious mixture of striving, asceticism, and rigor, the origins of which some trace back to Alexander the Great—is stronger than ever. Do you have feelings? There are correct and incorrect ways of indicating them. Do you have an inner life? It is nobody's business but your own. . . . To a degree, everyone obeys this code. And it does admit of a limited kind of candor, a closemouthed straightforwardness. But on the truest candor, it has an inhibitory effect. Most serious matters are closed to the hard-boiled. They are unpracticed in introspection, and therefore badly equipped to deal with opponents whom they cannot shoot like big game or outdo in daring.

If you have difficulties, grapple with them silently, goes one of their commandments. To hell with that! I intend to talk about mine, and if I had as many mouths as Siva has arms and kept them going all the time, I still could not do myself justice.[2]

This passage marks the moment in contemporary literature that opened the floodgates through which the words of what some consider to be a prose renaissance have flowed.

If Hemingway and his style were rejected on the grounds of aloofness and disengagement, the social realists were rejected on the grounds of a mistaken engagement with social and political schemes rather than with the personal questions of existence. In *Dangling Man,* the old Joseph, rationalist and humanist, had been a Trotskyist, as Bellow himself had once been. The new Joseph, the journal-keeper, the dangling man, rejects the old Joseph's hopes for a social utopia as an external ideal scheme which evades the inner man in search of his authentic self as much as does the external money-making scheme of the Machiavellian majority. In rejecting society and its purposes for his own personal questions, the new hero rejects not only the crass materialism of the society but also its ideal dreams of utopia. However, in the history of the American novel, the line from Dreiser through Dos Passos, Steinbeck, and Farrell to the activist novelists of the present is a clearer line than is the one from Hemingway to these recent writers. The representation of the yearning for the utopian completion of society is transformed into that of the personal yearning for true being—both representations, at their best, reveal the weaknesses and the struggles without glamorizing them. Hemingway and his school glamorize.

Writing of the fiction of the fifties, Herbert Gold acknowledges the debt of the novelist of his own generation to Saul Bellow:

Saul Bellow, an exemplary writer of this generation, expresses most clearly the philosophical and religious quest necessarily contained within an abiding sense for passing things. All his work seems to ask the question, "Why am I here?" And answers in his comic mood: "Because I'm here—that's enough!" But his intensely lyrical and dramatic, onflowing participation in the life of his Chicago, his Africa, his universe, makes the underlying metaphysical question possible; and so his deepest answer seems to be: "Why? Because we are all here together on earth. It is both enough and not enough."

That is probably the only permanent answer to a question which never remains the same.[3]

Gold's interpretation of Bellow's work, while recognizing the debt of recent novelists, including himself, to Bellow and while defining Bellow's picture of a spiritual activism in a temporal setting very accurately, reveals his own great sense of "passing things." Gold's love for the concrete, tangible things of his temporal settings seduces his fiction away from his intended focus on the spiritual quest of his activist heroes in *The Man Who Wasn't With It*,[4] *The Optimist*,[5] and *Salt*, three of his most recent novels.

However, before discussing Herbert Gold and Philip Roth as the two most prominent among the younger novelists who inherit Bellow's vision, who perhaps admire it too much, and who are overshadowed by its depth and immensity in their imitation of it, I wish to talk of Bernard Malamud, an innovator in his own right and one whose pattern in novel writing is Kafkan: the movement from the vision of the absurd novel, *The Trial,* in which the hero is ultimately defeated by accepting the guilt of his past (a guilt defined by circumstance and precedent and accepted by a character who stays within the dictates of circumstances and customs in order to prove himself "innocent"; a guilt which makes the hero incapable of walking through a door which is his), toward the vision of the activist novel, *The Castle,* in which the hero denies the past and wills his own fate by living in the present toward a privately defined transcendent, future self.

Malamud's first novel, *The Natural,*[6] is a fable built on the myth of the American baseball game. Roy Hobbs, the hero of this fable, the savior of the game and creator of his own immortality (a place in the Hall of Records), equipped with his miraculous bat, Wonderboy, is given heroic proportions. He is a hero outside of the Kafkan schemes described above; however, his similarities to *Amerika*'s Karl Rossmann are unmistakable: he is an innocent victim in an open society where villains lurk. It is not the acceptance of his past as a kind of guilty burden that keeps Roy Hobbs from being the ultimate champion he intends to become; it is his innocence, through which he is seduced to his downfall.

It is in this, and in his wandering over a timeless, placeless countryside—a wandering spotted with surreal episodes as the country is with surreal baseball parks, woods, locker rooms, and offices—a countryside called America, that Roy Hobbs resembles Karl Rossmann. However, Roy's fable is too calculatedly mythopoeic in its own terms as well as in the story's paralleling of the Grail myth [7] to be said to share the style of Karl's innocent quest for identity, which, however much it may seem to be informed by the perception of the mythic homeless wanderer, is not constructed as a myth or on a myth.

The Natural is constructed both as a myth and on a myth. The myth on which it is constructed is the Grail myth of a heroic and pure quest; as a myth, the surface fable makes the game of baseball a metaphor for the game of life in a completely overt way. Roy Hobbs comes out of his pastoral childhood (which is described in recurring images—child, dog, woods—as a remembered past throughout the story) into the world, unequipped except for his wondrous, handmade bat, and announces his intention of becoming a hero; he is almost immediately shot in the stomach by a hero-killing witch. Fifteen years later, he comes out of an undescribed retreat to resume his quest for heroism in the game of life-baseball. He joins the Knights, a team of baseball players in a bad slump, and through his miraculous batting pulls them up to the top of their league. He meets during this time of renewed quest, two women: Memo, a more worldly seducer of heroes than Harriet Bird, the hero-hater who shot him in the stomach, and Iris, the wearer of the white flower, who loves heroes and knows what they are good for. " 'Without heroes,' " Iris says, " 'we're all plain people and don't know how far we can go.' " [8] Heroes are those men who create new forms for and expand the possibilities of life. Iris is true love; but Roy falls instead for the seductive Memo, takes a bribe to throw an important game for the Knights, and then falls not into love but out of grace. His end is in defeat, for the Knights and for himself. The mythic quality is sustained throughout, and the underlying myth of the Grail evokes nothing that is not obvious. However, the surface story, which embodies a modern quest for the ultimate transcendent self, the heroic one, is charming in its naturalness and innocence, while the literary undertones supplied by the gratuitous existence of the Grail myth on a second level are decorative, contributing wit and erudition. *The Natural* is an accomplished literary performance.

More serious—or more completely engaged with questions of a metaphysical nature—are Malamud's two other novels, *The Assistant* and *A New Life. The Assistant*, the second of Malamud's novels, avoids the obviously mythic for an ironic-absurd emphasis in the story of Morris Bober, the poor Jewish grocer, and Frank Alpine, a poor Catholic boy. Alpine's Catholicism (his wish to become like St. Francis and his preoccupation with sin-guilt-redemption) leads him, ironically, to adopt the Jew (a simple honest man whose poverty and suffering are unrelieved by his respect for the Jewish Law, the Talmud and the Torah) as a father-image and to become himself a Jew—not only a Jew but a Jew in the style of Morris Bober, a man enclosed in an impoverished, small store in a Gentile, or alien, slum neighborhood, a man without alternatives. Although Malamud thinks of the Jew as a moral man, a *mensch,* and his suffering as ennobled by his dignity and patience, it is not Morris who occupies the center of the story. It is Frank who, at the center of the novel, enacts an absurd role in a surreal situation and is, however unwittingly, the victim of his own spiritual wish to become St. Francis—a wish he realizes by becoming a Jew.

Frank, who originally offers himself to Morris Bober as an assistant in penitence for the crime of having masked himself and, with a friend, robbed and beaten the grocery store owner, falls in love with Bober's daughter, Helen. However, driven by lust at the very moment when Helen might love him, he rapes her. At the end of the novel, after Bober has died, Frank continues Bober's roles of Jew, father, and shopkeeper. This assumption of Bober's roles are for the assistant a continued penitence through suffering, a Catholic motif; however, there is the sense of spiritual rebirth accompanying Frank's self-imposed imprisonment inside these roles. This joining of the imprisonment and rebirth themes makes a final irony, heightened by the fact that the rebirth is suggested in the spiritual terms of the Catholic Church although it is presented as an actual conversion to Judaism. The last two paragraphs of the novel read:

As [Frank] was reading he had this pleasant thought. He saw St. Francis come dancing out of the woods in his brown rags, a couple of scrawny birds flying around over his head. St. F. stopped in front of the grocery, and reaching into the garbage can, plucked the wooden rose out of it. He tossed it into the air and it turned into a real flower that he caught in his hand. With a bow he gave it to Helen, who had just come out of the house. "Little sister, here is your little sister the rose." From him she took it, although it was with the love and best wishes of Frank Alpine.

One day in April Frank went to the hospital and had himself circumcised. For a couple of days he dragged himself around with a pain between his legs. The pain enraged and inspired him. After Passover he became a Jew.[9]

The irony at the end of the story, when Frank is reborn into his ideal St. Francis-like identity and converts to Judaism, is intensified by the invocation of Passover in the last line— Passover, close to Easter, the Christian festival of rebirth, is a festival celebration of freedom from slavery. But by becoming the Jew Morris Bober, Frank, though reborn, has in effect chosen to be a sufferer for the Law and a slave to the store.

Following the pattern of many modern novelists, Malamud leaps in his third novel away from the enclosed and ironic mode of his stories[10] and novels of innocent victims and guilty victims to the openness of the activist hero who pursues his fate, outside of games and stores, in the promised new land of freedom, the American West. S. Levin in *A New Life* chooses his life and chooses his self; discards his past (as an alcoholic in New York City); and pursues his present and his future through a series of events presented in a manner reminiscent of the style of a picaresque novel although *A New Life* is not the tale of a picaro. Jonathan Baumbach has remarked:

A New Life is to Malamud's career what *The Adventures of Augie March* on a larger scale was to Bellow's, a breaking away from the airlessness and intensity of his two earlier novels, an attempt to extend the range of his concerns beyond the impulse of his talent.[11]

Baumbach's phrase "an attempt to extend his concerns beyond the impulse of his talent" might be used to define the progress of many recent novelists from the closed, inevitably ironic view of life, which attention to the formal perfection of a tight literary construct seems to impose on the content of the novel, to a more affirmative view of the possibilities in life which the open, experimental form of the new activist novel permits. Malamud's shift from the closed form to the open is paradigmatic.

The accompanying shift—from passive hero, victim of events in an absurd world, to an active hero with a commitment to his own fate—has been discussed in this study relative to the heroes of Kafka's novels and to the idea of a spiritual quest. David Stevenson, in a recent critical article, describes and defines the emerging new form and its hero in recent American novels without reference, however, to Kafka or spiritual concerns. Of the heroes of this new American novel form, he says:

> Its Augie Marches (Bellow's *The Adventures of Augie March*), its Burr Fullers (Gold's *The Optimist*), its S. Levins (Malamud's *A New Life*) are ontologists all, avid investigators into the essential qualities of the events and the human relationships that chance their way. Unlike Hemingway's Robert Jordan or Faulkner's Joe Christmas, who finally surrender to fates imposed by the conditions of society, the new activist hero remains to the end an intrepid opportunist of the self. He is an eager, insatiable explorer of his own private experience, always on the alert, in Augie March's phrase, for "a fate good enough" to vindicate the energy spent on the exploration.[12]

Stevenson's emphasis on what he considers to be the essentially secular nature of the quest of the hero in the activist novel can be seen in the preceding quotation as well as his observation that "the activist hero sustains himself by a commitment to a sense of the transient. He inhabits a very real modern world, quite cold, beyond comedy, beyond tragedy." [13]

Malamud's *A New Life*, as well as the activist novels of Gold and Roth, is more clearly involved with a sense of the transient than are the novels of Bellow, Mailer, and Salinger, which, in spite of their rich descriptions of the transient details of the passing temporal scene, seem to me to defy secular-realist categories. And I do not think it is the intention of Malamud, Gold, and Roth to stay clearly inside these categories; they are, as writers, simply more intensely absorbed in the world of factual detail than they are in the quests of their heroes. They love detail to such an extent that, even when they attempt to satirize the evils of worldly things, they produce vivid and exciting—often witty and comic—representations of cocktail parties, nightclubs, carnivals, state-grant colleges, et cetera, which beguile the reader rather than suggest to him that these things are the representatives of a transience the self must overcome in order to survive in its own purposes. The expressed commitment of their heroes, nevertheless, is never to a sense of the transient world but to a sense of self. That self inhabits a cold and absurd modern world composed of things and events which possess no externally meaningful structure, quite beyond comedy and tragedy, as Stevenson says. The hero himself, through himself, may recognize the comic or the tragic, or both, in his situation, but at his best he is above them both, existing in the realm of possibility. And his insistence on his freedom and his possibilities in the face of either an indifferent or a deterministic universe may often seem comic and tragic at once.

In *A New Life* it is the comic that prevails. S. Levin, the *schlemiel*-as-activist, assumes, sometimes intentionally and sometimes unintentionally, the role of the clown in the university environment of Cascadia College in the Pacific Northwest, to which he has come, shunning his alcoholic past in New York City, to make a new life as a professor of English. He finds Cascadia College a provincial outpost of sterile academia and the chairman of the Cascadia English department, Gilley, a man who has, as his wife, Pauline Gilley, says, "no seeds at all." [14] S. Levin, whose initial for a first name is reminiscent of Kafka's K., reveals on the last page of the novel that his family always called him "Sam," although the other characters of the novel have called him "Sy" throughout the story. Clearly he is a cipher for alienation, for random identity. This semianonymous hero takes Pauline Gilley as his mistress after a series of romantic, pseudo-pastoral episodes with other women and a woodland encounter with Pauline that results in their liaison. Levin has been preceded at Cascadia in the English department and in the heart of the adulterous Pauline by Leo Duffy, an Irishman who was committed to a progressive Leftist political ideology and who committed suicide some time after he was publicly fired from Cascadia. Levin has Duffy's office, literally and symbolically, in the English department. Levin does have an assortment of fragmentary liberal-humanist political-social ideas which he fences with now and then, but he is not committed to an ideology, only to life, his own primarily. Nevertheless, Duffy and Duffy's failure at Cascadia and subsequent suicide haunt Levin; Duffy as a ghostly double for Levin becomes a foil for the Levin of the present. Though Levin seems to fail, we see his real success through the character of Duffy used as foil. Duffy is political; Levin is not. Levin's spiritual vitality carries him alive, if not triumphant, through his Cascadia experiences and away from Cascadia to start *another* new life with Pauline, who becomes his wife at the end of the novel.

Levin's spiritual vitality lies in his guiltlessness, acquired through giving up his past (the pastlessness emphasized by the initial rather than the full first name); his insistence on himself in his present situation; his natural, impulsive, vital choices. His choices and actions destroy his dream of being a college teacher but make him that which he may in fact more existentially be and yet that which may also be the essence of the true teacher, a lover—specifically Pauline's lover; but from the details of that affair we may read his more general lovingness. Love, here, triumphs over personal freedom as it does, or threatens to do, in *The Castle* and *The Adventures of Augie March*, as well as in other novels in the activist mode; but love, here, is a good and, furthermore, has virtues as a moral position. Though Levin has fallen out of love with Pauline when he takes her, pregnant with his child, away from Cascadia, he assumes responsibility for her. He assumes this responsibility, even though he does not have to, because, as he says, he *can*.[15] He gives up freedom of the self; chooses love; does what he can; is moral.

When Levin goes to ask Gerald Gilley for the custody of Gilley's and Pauline's two adopted children, Gilley is astonished that Levin would take on the burden of Pauline, whose many faults he enumerates, and the two children. When Levin says he will because he can (and because Pauline, a free agent, whom he loved once, wishes to marry him), Gilley elaborates his intended revenge: he will make it impossible for Levin ever to teach at the college level again. (Gilley says, " 'You'd do less harm in high school. You're not fit to teach at the college level.' " [16]) Still Levin persists in morally assuming the burden of Pauline. Here the concept of the Jew-as-moral-man, uniquely Malamud's among recent American novelists, asserts itself.

In discussing Malamud's short stories collected in *Idiots First,* F. W. Dupee makes a major point in his critique of Malamud's emphasis on Jewishness as a pervasive, felt morality and on the Old World Eastern European quality of that Jewishness. Dupee quotes Norman Podhoretz to support his idea: "To Malamud, Mr. Podhoretz says, 'The Jew is humanity seen under the twin aspects of suffering and moral aspiration. Therefore any man who suffers greatly, and also longs to be better than he is, can be called a Jew.' " [17] This vision of the Jew is most clearly seen in *The Assistant* and in the short stories. Among the stories there are, however, three Arthur Fidelman stories, one in *The Magic Barrel* and two in *Idiots First,* which suggest an experimentation with freer form dictated by the activist hero's quest outside and beyond the burdens of Jewish suffering and point toward *A New Life.* In *A New Life,* the burden-assuming, suffering nature of the Jew comes up almost as an afterthought, a comic after-thought; it in no way encloses the whole story, nor is the whole story confined within its ironic conclusions.

The Jewish "suffering" in Levin's final predicament—the moral assumption of the burdensome Pauline—is made clear in the scene between Levin and Pauline, which follows the interview between Levin and Gilley. Now Pauline tells Levin how it was that Gilley had originally picked him to fill the opening on the staff of the English department at Cascadia; she herself had picked Levin's application out of many applications that her husband had considered and discarded.

> Afterwards Levin asked her why she had picked his application out of the pile Gilley had discarded.
> "You had attached a photograph," Pauline said, "although you weren't asked to."
> "It was an old picture. I wanted them to know what I looked like."
> "You looked as though you needed a friend."
> "Was that the reason?"
> "I needed one. Your picture reminded me of a Jewish boy I knew in college who was very kind to me during a trying time in my life."
> "So I was chosen," Levin said.[18]

This, the first mention of Jewishness, comes late in the novel, and is linked with the concept of being chosen rather than choosing. Malamud is playing with the concept of the Jews as the Chosen People. This late scene ties Levin to his heritage as Jew, to a prescribed destiny of moral suffering that he can usually evade but not entirely avoid. But while this comic-ironic note in Levin's pilgrimage of the self makes the final situation in the novel more complex, it does not circumscribe the whole novel. It was through a photograph, an illusory image on film, that he was chosen; the real Levin, introduced through the longer narrative, still makes his own choices. And, as the real Levin and Pauline drive through the college community on their way out of town, on their way, unplanned and risky, toward another new life, there is another reference to the illusory image of a man which may be caught while the actual man travels on.

Two tin-hatted workmen, with chain saws were in the maple tree in front of Humanities Hall, cutting it down limb by limb, to make room for a heat tunnel. On the Student Union side of the street, Gilley was aiming a camera at the operation. When he saw Levin's Hudson approaching he swung the camera around and snapped. As they drove by, he tore a rectangle of paper from the back of the camera and waved it aloft.

"Got your picture!" [19]

These are the last words of the book. All Gilley has, however, is a picture of Levin, while Levin, unimpeded by the mechanistic devices and illusions of the material world represented by Cascadia and Gilley, remains, in spite of some new, but self-chosen, limitations on his freedom, spiritually active, ever alert to new possibilities and a better fate—heading for an open road.

The similarities between the Kafkan hero K. and S. Levin are self-evident: the mixtures of irony with affirmation and of wordly defeat with the continuing, freed spiritual hope for the self are present in *A New Life* by virtue of the nature of its hero.

The activist novels of Herbert Gold and Philip Roth, who seem more within the school of Saul Bellow than original novelists or pioneers in the mode, are *The Optimist, The Man Who Was Not With It,* and *Salt* (Gold) and *Letting Go* (Roth). These novels present a special problem. Clearly Gold and Roth, in these specific works, intend the mixture of irony and affirmation which Bellow, Mailer, and Malamud achieve; they are, however, unsuccessful in sustaining that mixture. On the basis of the Kafkan prototypal pattern, and a failure to achieve it, I do not wish to find fault with these writers: it would be arbitrary to use as the ground for aesthetic judgment an idea which is the focus for a discussion of modern fiction, not a critical tenet for the evaluation of literary excellence in any ultimate sense. However, certainly Herbert Gold, through his theoretical essays and fictional practice, and, to a somewhat lesser extent, Philip Roth, through the novelistic procedure adopted for *Letting Go,* have shown their intention of writing metaphysical novels in the activist mode; and if the metaphysical activist novel indeed has a uniqueness—a spiritual emphasis suggested by K.'s quest in *The Castle*—which defines its peculiar excellences, then Gold and Roth produce inferior work in that mode.

The world is, perhaps, too much with them, and they, like their heroes, seem to cherish experience for its own sake. Burr Fuller, the hero of Gold's *The Optimist,* at the end of the novel, after romantic, school, army, marital, extramarital, and political adventures, wants more of life, even though his adventures have shown him the imperfections of life in the modern world and led always to new questions.

> Let the man who knows perfection rest in it. Burr could only ask for more.
> Burr Fuller was not thirty-five years and had two sons. Eyes clouded by longing, he reached out to take a cloud in his arms.
> More. More. More! More! More! [20]

This "more" is quantitative, not qualitative, the "more" of the strength and power of a private life-force, but a private life-force passionately felt in its effect in the present moment in the world, a life-force which culminates in experience in the present. *The Optimist* satisfies David Stevenson's proposition about the activist novel.

> [It] consists in portraying the temporary results of encounters between the average, intellectual man, an Augie, and his random assortment of experiences, sexual or otherwise. The experiences themselves are conceived as occurring in an endless moment-to-moment discontinuity. [21]

But *The Optimist*, in spite of its intention to do so, does not convincingly go beyond this, as Stevenson, partly quoting Gold, suggests the activist novel intentionally does:

Once we step outside the easy patterns of contemporary living, defined most eloquently by the society pages of our newspapers, once we leave the safe arena where, in Gold's words, women are "getting brightly married to well-brushed men," we enter a new level of concern for the human condition. It is this level which is exploited in activist fiction. It is one in which the bareness, the strangeness, uncomfortableness of existence is seen to be part of an ineradicable conviction of the nearly comical, nearly intolerable limits which reality imposes on an individual's inner urge to exercise his will, his feelings of agency.[22]

We can tell from the surface of Gold's novels, by the philosophical interjections and dialogues which he supplies, that Gold intends to give us in *The Optimist* and in *Salt* the presentation of a metaphysical quest beyond the limits of the worldly environment which his hero—usually a well-brushed lawyer, like Burr Fuller in *The Optimist*, or a well-brushed advertising man, like Dan Berman in *Salt*—inhabits; but we cannot tell this from a level other than the surface. *The Optimist*, Gold's first novel in the activist mode, and *Salt*, a more recent novel, also in this mode, are not informed by Bellow's hero's urgent sense of self or separation (not necessarily alienation) of self from the masses.

Gold's Burr Fuller wants more of worldly experience; he loves life; he does not separate himself from this experience or from its worldly patterns. Although Gold satirizes ordinary middle-class life and ordinary sophisticated life, the comforts and the evils of the corrupt world from which the hero would disengage himself, nevertheless there is always the nagging suspicion that Gold is forced to satirize the world to keep himself, and his hero, from embracing it. Ordinary life is not nearly unpleasant enough, as Augie, too, knows; it is pleasant; it is seductive. The life of what Kierkegaard calls the aesthetic realm, the sensual life of sex, domestic comforts, and art, is in itself neither good nor evil although it may be a temptation to the man who has moved beyond it to the ethical realm and a hindrance to the man who has moved beyond that to the spiritual realm. Augie knows the delights of the aesthetic life, and he knows that these are found in the world of ordinary events and ordinary men. Augie enjoys the world —Bellow's descriptive and comic gifts do not seem satirical—and Augie finds it necessary to say "no" to its schemes for his own comfort because he has a personal, serious, transcendent idea of a better fate which becomes defined in the process of his quest for it. His better fate is not Burr Fuller's "more," the "more" of life-force muscle-flexing, nor is it the fate found in the resolution of Dan Berman's quest, which is marriage to Barbara, the mature, attractive, loving young woman who reads seed catalogues and represents the one fertile spot in the salted, destroyed, dead place that is urban modernity. Burr's and Dan's wish finally is for the comforts and pleasures which they see spoiled in the carryings-on of *lesser* ordinary men. Burr and Dan wish something special for themselves, a refined sensuality, which is beyond the sordidness of the commonplace and above the absurdities of vulgar triteness.

It is enough, and yet not enough. It is enough for life, perhaps, but not enough for the novel. Each novel needs to define itself structurally, whether the structure be traditional or antitraditional and activist; and part of structural definition lies in theme. The theme of becoming in the successful activist novel demands a basically open structure to reveal the hero-in-process, but there must be something besides this openness to make the structure complex and to give it its narrative significance: some conflict, opposition, or tension is necessary. The process of becoming posed against a personal concept of ideal being, the existential fact against the awareness of possibilities, especially the transcendent possibility of the self—must be dramatized if the narrative of the activist hero's adventures is to be considered as more than picaresque, as a new pattern for modern man's metaphysical and spiritual investigation. K. is always a surveyor of the castle's land, never the Land-Surveyor. A continuing frustration of the will to ideality is coupled with an ironic realization of his ideal self in the process of his existence: this duality is at the root of the art of the activist novel. It is this duality which Gold does not achieve.

Philip Roth, in his first novel, *Letting Go,* written after his contained and craftsmanly first longer fiction, a novella called "Goodbye, Columbus," [23] attempts a narrative in Bellow's style as Gold has done. *Letting Go* is looser and freer than "Goodbye, Columbus," which is a poignant look at first love in a satirized suburban setting. (Roth's true gift is for the comic and satirical. When he is being satirical he is not ambivalent, as Gold seems to be, about the subject of his satire.) However, *Letting Go,* the history of an activist hero, Gabe Wallach, fails as an activist novel for the same reasons that Gold's activist novels fail; it fails to present dramatically inside the narrative action the conflict between the existential reality and the ideal possibility. Gabe Wallach, even more than Burr Fuller or Dan Berman, fails as a figure of spiritual activism since his quest bogs down in Freudian ponderings. Gold keeps his hero's quest pure and conscious and directly in relation to the fictive life in the moment, in the present: Roth's Gabe Wallach, on the other hand, does not desert his past for the sake of the present but uses it as an integral part of his investigation into the meaning of his life. He does not come to terms with that past and its psychological implications for his present; and his habit of looking backward while supposing himself to be moving forward has a curious effect, making of Gabe a whining and ineffectual hero with whom the reader is supposed to sympathize in spite of his unattractiveness.

Binx Bolling, in Walker Percy's *The Moviegoer,*[24] is a more successful example of the activist hero in a minor mode; his looking backward into his past for clues is purposeful, clear to Binx and clear to Binx's creator. The use of the past is enunciated in the novel's own terms. Binx's quest is not forward-moving, but is a search for the self involving a series of researches into both his past and present simultaneously, a vertical and horizontal investigation. His new forms for his experience in the present, however, always very consciously involve an awareness of and stylized use of the past. For his quest into his life's meaning, he invents forms he calls "repetitions," "circumlocutions," and "duplications" —these are researches, part of what Binx calls the "vertical search" of the laboratory. Although he attempts a horizontal search in his existential wandering, he never really seems to move forward, only sideways. Through his researches and his extraordinary devotion to self-awareness he avoids despair, but he never moves beyond the brink of despair where he is precariously perched throughout the novel.

The Moviegoer is reminiscent of *Nausea*. Sartre the philosopher talks of man actively making himself, but when Sartre the novelist pictures the human predicament in *Nausea*, it is a picture, like that in *The Moviegoer,* of man grounded in malaise, of man in the process of recording and thus discarding his past without finding or making vital new forms for his present experience and without inventing possibilities which might break through the limitations in his given psychological situation. Roquentin of *Nausea* is intensely aware but he is not an activist.

At the end of *The Moviegoer* Binx's marriage to the passive Kate, who is so extremely lacking in a sense of herself that she does not feel she exists unless her existence is witnessed, unless someone is watching her, maintains the tenuous, hovering, just-beyond-despair which Binx has managed in his life through his researches. Gabe Wallach is afflicted by encroaching despair and inability to move forward as Binx is, but Binx knows it while Gabe, as well as Roth, seems not to know it. *The Moviegoer* is self-defining and all of a piece as Roth's *Letting Go* is not. At the conclusion of *Letting Go*

the reader is bewildered by what seems the arbitrary assertion that Gabe has acted, made a choice, done a significantly
life-changing thing when he melodramatically attempts a violent action in recovering the adopted child of Libby, the
wife of his friend, and a woman with whom he is half in love.
Gabe has throughout the book insisted upon the possibility
of meaningful choice while drifting intellectually and emo-
tionally through his days, half in love with Libby, a charac-
terless, self-pitying woman, and half in love with Martha, a
divorcee and careless housekeeper. Like S. Levin's, Gabe's
story is set in an academic atmosphere, but the university is
urban (Chicago) and serves more as background than as an
opposing force in the foreground as Cascadia College does in
A New Life. Hence, the university environment in *Letting
Go* emphasizes the intellectual drift of the hero. The emotional and intellectual drift might have been redeemed if
Gabe, with his climactic choice near the end of the novel,
really thrust himself out of drift, into action and autonomy.
The intention to do this is not realized: the presentation of
Gabe's weak character prevails and overwhelms the reader's
sense of him as he undertakes his only, and very belated, significant act. The climax of the novel thus seems arbitrary
and melodramatic. And when Gabe says, in a letter to Libby,
that he has to "make some sense of the larger hook [he's]
on," [25] it seems that his statement is contrived to give metaphysical depth to a really quite ordinary problem of a basically dull modern man caught in the meaningless drift of our
time.

It may be useful to quote more of the letter that is Gabe's
final statement:

"I can't bring myself yet to ask forgiveness for that night. If
you've lived for a long while as an indecisive man, you can't simply forget, obliterate, bury, your one decisive moment. I can't—in
the name of the future, perhaps—accept forgiveness, forgiveness
for my time of strength, even if that time was so very brief, and
was followed so quickly and humiliatingly by the dissolution of

character, of everything. Others—you may see my decisiveness—my doing something—anything—that—as born only of desperation, and therefore without value. I, nevertheless, have to wonder about it a little more. You see, I thought at the time that I was sacrificing myself. Whatever broken explanations I offered to others in the days that followed, whatever—I find I cannot finish this sentence.

. . . It is only kind of you, Libby, to feel that I would want to know that I am off the hook. But I'm not, I can't be, I don't even want to be—not until I make some sense of the larger hook I'm on." [26]

There are neither ironies nor earned affirmations here. There is nothing but Gabe's verbal justification through which Roth attempts to redeem the novel from a very loose presentation of assorted, somewhat related episodes in the life of an ineffectual man. Roth uses the openness of the activist novel without the justification of an activist hero, even such a minor-mode activist as Binx Bolling.

Roth, however, is magnificently expert at describing the individual scenes and situations of the world; it is only in the creating of the tension necessary as novelistic ingredient in the activist hero's total situation that he fails. As the notion of the contraception diaphragm as a proof of love seems devised (if not devised, then surely pitched too low to say very much about the nature of love, even in an absurd modern time) in "Goodbye, Columbus," so the single act—and that single act without reference to a clearly envisioned better self—seems devised when considered as a proof of self in *Letting Go*. One might argue that Roth's novel in its inability to create viable alternatives to the nihilism which informs modern life is existentially faithful to the way-it-is. But in Gabe's protests we inevitably read a larger (finer) intention—the intention to show the pitting of the choosing self against the caging of his past and the determinism of his environment—which is not realized.

*Other Schools in the Activist Mode: The Negro Novelists
and the Paulinist-Christian Novelists*

A special context created by a particular vision of man and
his world different from the Kafkan vision employed in the
activist novels so far surveyed—which have been novels written by Jews—inevitably conditions the possibilities open to
the hero. Two prevailing views of the world which affect the
activist novel in America call for special notice: the view of
the American Negro and a view which I will call Paulinist-
Christian. Both views have difficulty seeing the self as a
particular with the available choice of a willed and *self-*
defined, free, and finally transcendent relationship, or dialogue, with the Absolute. Neither view sees the individual as
the maker of his own better fate. The subjectivity of the
Negro self or the Christian self is necessarily limited by a set
of very strong *a priori* givens: unavoidable social circumstances for the Negro and *a priori* religious beliefs, especially
the belief in the fallen nature of man and in the concept
of Original Sin, for the Paulinist-Christian. Neither the Negro
nor the Christian can be the agent of his own salvation:
the Negro, of course, *may* be, though he has not had very
much success so far. However, the possibility for Negro will
in the definition of self brings the Negro activist hero's
existential struggle for true being in the present and toward
an envisioned future, as novelistically described in James
Baldwin's *Another Country* [27] and Ralph Ellison's *Invisible
Man*,[28] closer to the Kafkan mode than the struggles toward
true being of the activist heroes in, for example, William Styron's *Set This House on Fire* and R. V. Cassill's *Clem
Anderson*.[29]

Of James Baldwin's *Another Country*, David Stevenson
says:

. . . [it] is in structure, in substance, in point of view, still another somewhat individualized version of this new fiction. Be-

cause it concerns Negro and white racial problems in New York, *Another Country* gives the appearance of being one more sociological novel, a post-war *Grapes of Wrath*. But the heart of the novel is the battle between the active, eager self, Negro or white, and its environment. Baldwin, indeed, follows closely the pattern initiated by Bellow, except that he is insistently more grim in his own look at the caging of the conscious self.[30]

In *Another Country* the "active, eager self" is not only Negro or white, it is also heterosexual or homosexual; hence not only the social circumstances of being Negro in white America but also the social and psychological circumstances of being homosexual in a heterosexual community impinge on the free willing of the active self in contest with the materiality of its environment. Interestingly enough, of the three heroes who share the center of *Another Country*, Rufus, Vivaldo, and Eric, it is Vivaldo, the white heterosexual man, who fares least well in his pursuit of a better fate. Baldwin seems to be saying that Rufus, the Negro, has an authentic self as a given, not as a transcendent ideal, and that Eric, the homosexual, has within his homosexuality a possibility denied the "normal" man—the possibility for greater, wider, more varied love. Rufus finds his authentic self too difficult to live with in a white society, and so discovers his purest act in suicide. Rufus' story makes up Part One of the novel; in Part Two and Part Three, Vivaldo and Eric, friends of Rufus, become central. It is finally Eric, the homosexual, who consummates (sexually) all the possible relationships set in motion by the narrative; and it is Eric who becomes what he is and has been, most fully recognizing his own truth, his own truth being that *eros* can become *caritas* and most surely so through homosexuality. He is a heroic hero about whom Cass, the woman with whom Eric has had a tender heterosexual love affair, thinks:

He would use everything life had given him, or taken from him, in his work—*that* would be his life. He was too proud to use her, or anyone, as a haven, too proud to accept any resolution of his sorrow not by his own hands. And she could not be bitter about this, or even sorrowful, for this was precisely why she loved him. Or, if not why, the *why* of such matters being securely locked away from human perception, it was this quality in him which she most admired, and which she knew he could not live without. Most men could—did: this was why she was so menaced.[31]

In spite of the fact that Cass' love and admiration are given to Eric because of his independence of spirit, it is love, not freedom, that is his forte; and when he decides to keep his relationship and *ménage* with Yves, his French boy-lover, he exercises a capacity for love, spiritual in its widest implications, but not for the spiritual freedom of a K. It is as if *The Castle* were to conclude with K.'s reconciliation with Frieda and, implicitly, with the whole community of the village.

Ellison's *Invisible Man* presents the theme of the individual activist quest for spiritual freedom in a purer, more abstract form than Baldwin. Ellison's narrative does not compromise with its theme: there are no resolutions in love. The invisible man, the Southern Negro narrator, elects to call himself only "invisible man." This anonymous Negro thrusts again and again, in a series of episodes, parallel and repetitive more than sequential and developing, against the walls of his environment. That he does not prevail against the environment does not lessen the dramatically-perceived nature of his quest: the search for an authentic identity beyond the labels the world would give him. Frustration is everywhere, and he finds the group with which he most identifies, the Negro group, most susceptible to the world's labels for it, most confined, and most self-defeating in its pursuing of group purposes.

In electing to be an invisible man, the narrator elects to be free of all labels, white or Negro, for himself; he elects to lose his group identity and to live alone, alienated and free. The choice of invisibility (by living underground) as freedom is the end-choice, after the above-ground struggles of the novel, which are told in a reminiscence. The Prologue and the Epilogue of the book deal with the idea of invisibility, giving a surreal context and emphasis to many of the realistically described scenes inside the main narrative. Ironically, anonymous is what the Negro is in a white society: by electing this condition for himself, as a defense against white society's labels for him, which he has found set him and his brothers against one another, he makes the only free choice which remains available to him. Living underground in a hole, full of light from 1,369 lights lit by voltage stolen from the Monopolated Light and Power Company, and full of sound (Louis Armstrong playing and singing "What Did I Do to Be So Black and Blue?"), he feels he truly lives at last. "I myself, after existing some twenty years did not become alive until I discovered my invisibility," [32] he says.

The invisible man is both the victim hero trapped in an absurd world and the activist hero. In the Epilogue to the novel, he says, "All life seen from the hole of invisibility is absurd," [33] and he has experienced throughout his adventures above ground a cruel victimization from the absurdities, black and white, of the world. Yet he has acted; he has sought himself and finally found himself in the ironic recognition of his own invisibility. While in the underground retreat which he considers only a place of temporary freedom before he embarks on another active phase in the absurdities of the world above ground, he can say:

But live you must, and you can either make passive love to your sickness or burn it out and go on to the next conflicting phase.
    Yes, but what *is* the next phase? How often have I tried to find it! Over and over again I've gone up above to seek it out. For, like almost everyone else in our country, I started out with my share of optimism. I believed in hard work and progress and action, but now, after first being "for" society and then "against" it, I can assign myself no rank or any limit, and such an attitude is very much against the trend of the times. But my world has become one of infinite possibilities. What a phrase—still it's a good

phrase and a good view of life; that much I've earned underground.[34]

In an essay, "Black Boys and Native Sons," [35] Irving Howe has attacked Baldwin and Ellison for having deserted what he considers to be the authentic tradition of Negro writing, the social protest novel best characterized by the work of Richard Wright. One of his complaints against Ellison is his making the narrator-hero of *Invisible Man* speak of his life as one of "infinite possibilities" at the time that he is living in a hole in the ground. Ellison, in answering Howe's essay, accuses Howe of having missed the irony in this.[36] Not only does Howe, a social literary critic, miss the irony, it seems to me he also misses the specific evasion of social considerations in the quest for personal and spiritual freedom proposed here by a Negro writer whose concept of his own novel is that

it's a novel about innocence and human error, a struggle through illusion to reality. Each section begins with a sheet of paper; each piece of paper is exchanged for another and contains a definition of his identity, or the social role he is to play as defined for him by others. But all say essentially the same thing, "Keep this nigger boy running." Before he could have some voice in his own destiny he had to discard these old identities and illusions; his enlightenment couldn't come until then. Once he recognizes the hole of darkness into which these papers put him, he has to burn them.[37]

The hole is twofold: the ultimate trap and the freely chosen place where he may burn the old papers and roles behind him before going to his next activist phase above ground.

While the main theme is uncompromisingly one of identity and freedom in *Invisible Man*, Ellison, like Baldwin, finds it necessary to invoke love. Ellison, however, does not culminate his hero's quest in the conclusive and resolved terms which love, as the final truth, gives to *Another Country;* he rather sees that the freedom of a Negro person may evaporate in hate, and love becomes necessary to supply a balance that enables progress toward freedom of the self. The narrator says: "In order to get some of it down I *have* to love. I sell you no phony forgiveness, I'm a desperate man— but too much of your life will be lost, its meaning lost, unless you approach it as much through love as through hate." [38]

Love—the ability to love, the need to love, the discovery of the self through love, or the loss of the self in love—is a central Christian concern in the novels of Baldwin, Ellison and in William Styron's *Set This House on Fire*. Love, beauty, grace (grace in the religious sense) are the attributes of the activist's quest for true being in *Set This House on Fire* and Cassill's *Clem Anderson,* the two novels I would take as only two of several possible examples of a special kind of spiritual activist novel that are Paulinist-Christian in temperament. Freedom, will, and infinite possibility are not the spiritual proposals of the hero-in-process of these novels: the hero, though still a hero-in-process and still an activist in quest of a transcendent self, seeks the wholeness of grace, more clearly than he does freedom or inner authenticity of the self. This hero appears to feel mortally wounded, inadequate, a partial man as a consequence of his consciousness of Original Sin. He lives in a fallen world, having been redeemed (by Christ) without feeling redeemed, and hoping for wholeness through grace, not searching for it through his own will. However, God is missing—absent or hidden. The activist hero with a Paulinist-Christian orientation is as much in pursuit of a hidden God—a pursuit spelled out in the terms of a personal quest for a transcendent self—as are the other activist heroes. In the Christian context, however, there is more true despair than there is in the Kafkan context.

A useful theological note may be provided here by Martin Buber's essay, "Kafka and Judaism." Buber discusses what he calls the Paulinism of modern times in relation to the Christian and to the Jew, and says:

The periods of Christian history can be classified according to the degree in which they are dominated by Paulinism, by which we mean, of course, not just a system of thought, but a mode of seeing and being which dwells in the life itself. In the human life of our day, compared with earlier epochs, Christianity is receding, but the Pauline view and attitude is gaining the mastery in many circles outside that of Christianity. There is a Paulinism of the unredeemed—one, that is, from which the abode of grace is eliminated: like Paul, man experiences the world as one given into the hands of inevitable forces, and only the manifest will to redemption from above, only Christ, is missing. The Christian Paulinism of our time is a result of the same fundamental view, although it softens down or removes that aspect of demonocracy of the world: it sees, nevertheless, existence divided into an unrestricted rule of wrath and a sphere of reconciliation. . . .[39]

Atheistic Paulinism—the world seen as an "abyss covered now by nothing but impenetrable darkness" [40]—is easily recognized as characteristic of many modern novels, especially many French novels: one thinks of Genet's *Our Lady of the Flowers*.[41] Such novels are pervaded by an abiding pessimism. Christian Paulinism is the modern Christian view which dominates the work of novelists such as William Styron: *Set This House on Fire* is pervaded by a sense of incompleteness, a longing for true being while trapped in a world of "wrath," deprived of "reconciliation."

Cass Kinsolving is the activist hero in quest of being in *Set This House on Fire*. Peter, the narrator, and Mason, the evil, almost demonic, antagonist, share the center of the novel with Cass; they also may be said to be on their own quests for being. Cass considers himself as fallen, incomplete, and somehow innately evil: he is, as a consequence of this view of himself, obsessively self-destructive. David Stevenson interprets Cass' self-destructive alcoholism as "his means of evading his terror of the meaninglessness of his own existence." [42] Terrified of meaninglessness in himself and the world, he intensifies that meaninglessness through his own act of choosing to stay inebriated; thus, if nothing else, he controls his terror while waiting for a miracle of grace. The miracle of grace and reconciliation is promised in two alcoholic, manic visions of mysterious beauty and in one idyllic, pastoral love episode with a young Italian peasant girl. The miracle, in fact, occurs: in great anger, Cass acts against Mason Flagg, the evil antagonist who has enraged him by raping the young Italian girl of his pastorale. In his anger, Cass accidentally kills Mason. The trauma of anger and the violent act "set [his] house on fire," bringing him to himself and to a reconciliation with his life, with his beingness, seen as achieved at the conclusion of the novel.

That Styron intends Cass' story to be a modern spiritual parallel to the Christian story of earlier epochs is suggested by his quoting, as an introduction to his book, from John Donne's sermon, "To the Earle of Carlile, and his Company, at Sion." Part of this selection from Donne reads:

". . . that that God, who, when he could not get into one by standing, and knocking, by his ordinary meanes of entring, by his Word, his mercies, hath applied his judgments, and shaked the house, this body, with agues and palsies, and set this house on fire, with fevers and calentures, and frightened the Master of the house, my soule, with horrors, and heavy apprehensions, and so made entrance into me; That that God should frustrate all his owne purposes and practices upon me, and leave me, and cast me away, as though I had cost him nothing, that this God at last, should let this soule goe away, as a smoake, as a vapour, as a bubble, and that then this soule cannot be a smoake, a vapour, nor a bubble but must lie down in darknesse, as long as the Lord of light is light it selfe, and never sparke of that light reach to my soule; What Tophet is not Paradise, what Brimstone is not Amber, what gnashing is not a comfort, what gnawing of the worme is not a tickling, what torment is not a marriage bed to this damnation, to be secluded eternally, eternally, eternally from the sight of God?" [43]

Donne's picture of God as hidden from man and of man's soul, unable to respond to a hidden God, as lying down in darkness, from which it may be awakened to God only by the horrors of God's wrath, which may "set this house on fire," exemplifies an extreme of the Paulinism described by Buber.

Buber contrasts Paulinism, Christian or atheist, to Kafka's Judaism. Two implicit premises in Judaism differ significantly from two implicit premises in Christian Paulinism: in Judaism the Creation is more important than the Fall; and in Judaism, the Jew awaits the coming of the messianic age; he is not in a supposedly redeemed or saved state. Allegorical interpretations of *The Castle,* such as Edwin Muir's, read Joseph K.'s struggle in *The Trial* as a quest for justice and K.'s struggle in *The Castle* as a quest for grace. However, the Christian concept of grace is alien to Judaism, and K.'s struggle is toward a clear connection with the Absolute, a connection he has himself subjectively envisioned, not toward a theologically defined grace. If his "messianic" struggle resembles a going toward grace, the quest must nevertheless be seen as presalvation, not postsalvation; as Jewish, not Christian. Grace is not promised; not known; not available. There is no possible redeemer of the self but the self.

There is a curious hopefulness, a kind of ironic optimism inherent in *The Castle.* Underneath K.'s desperation, his apparent despair, there lurks a Jewish knowledge which keeps him from Paulinist despair, even though Kafka is the "Pauline painter of the foreground-hell," according to Buber.[44] Buber says:

He describes, from innermost awareness, the actual course of the world, he describes most exactly the rule of the foul devilry which fills the foreground; and on the edge of the description he scratches the sentence: "Test yourself on humanity. It makes the doubter doubt, the man of belief believe." His unexpressed, everpresent theme is the remoteness of the judge, the remoteness of the lord of the castle, the hiddenness, the eclipse, the darkness; and therefore, he observes: "He who believes can experience no miracle. During the day one does not see any stars." This is the nature of the Jew's security in the dark, one which is essentially different from that of the Christian. It allows no rest, for as long as you live, you must live with the sparrow and not with the dove, who avoids your hand; but, being without illusion, it is consistent with the foreground course of the world, and so nothing can harm you. For from beyond, from the darkness of heaven the dark ray comes actively into the heart, without any appearance of immediacy. "We are created to live in Paradise, Paradise was appointed to serve us. Our destiny has been changed; that this also happened with the appointment of Paradise is not said." So, gently and shyly, anti-Paulinism speaks from this Pauline painter of the foreground-hell: Paradise is still there, and it benefits us. It is there, and that means that it is also here where the dark ray meets the tormented heart. Are the unredeemed in need of salvation? They suffer from the unredeemed state of the world. . . . The unredeemed soul refuses to give up the evidence of the unredeemed world from which it suffers, to exchange it for the soul's own salvation. It is able to refuse, for it is safe.[45]

The security and safety of the unredeemed soul are in the fact that it believes in God without miracle, without mysterious intervention, but directly, even though the directness may be difficult to sustain in the darkness of an unredeemed world to which a messiah has not come and which does not will God as the unredeemed soul does. Without miracle, salvation, and grace, man suffers, but through his very suffering he may better contrive a way to God in a seemingly godless world. Buber's interpretation of Kafka's Judaism and of Christian Paulinism makes clear a distinction between the spiritual activism of the Kafkan hero and the spiritual activism of the Christian novelistic hero.

From the evidence of Styron's *Set This House on Fire* and Cassill's *Clem Anderson,* for example, one concludes that spiritual activism in the modern Christian context represents an even more desperate and hopeless struggle than K.'s does and is a struggle marked by a self-destructiveness which indicates that the path away from meaninglessness in the world and toward grace is the way which destroys, not willfully asserts, the self.

Clem Anderson, Cassill's hero, a novelist and poet, a man whose life is validated by language, writes a novel about his own history; this autobiographical novel is then incorporated into the total action of *Clem Anderson*. Experience has to become past before it can become art, and once it is made into art, it is no longer life. This is a way for Clem to lose his personal experience at the same time that he transcends it by making it art. This illustrates the transcendence of self through the loss of self in the artist. Two good ways to lose the self are through art and alcohol: Clem Anderson uses both. Cass Kinsolving does not really use his painting (he is an artist also) for self-destruction (or a kind of self-transcendence); Cass uses only alcohol.[46]

But the spiritual quest of man *qua* man may not be equated simply with the quest of the artist, as Cassill shows when in *Clem Anderson* the artist dies with the man. True vocation is not true being. It is the mark of the novels by the American-Jewish writers here discussed that the metaphysical investigation insists on knowing man not as a social or political creature, nor yet as an artist, but as man, the existential human thing that moves toward purely human distinctions and connections and in that very movement asserts the self in relation to the Absolute.

While the Kafkan hero asserts a transcendent self, the modern Christian hero, as simple man, actually appears to wish to transcend the self, to come to true being by becoming one with the divine will, enacted through Christ's coming and the salvation of man. In the modern world, when God and Christ, his intermediary in the world, are hidden, the attempt to save the soul, or transcend the self, may take on the characteristics of a self-destruction of the worldly body, the vesse! of universal sin, and of worldly consciousness. Clem Anderson, like Cass Kinsolving, is an alcoholic, but Clem, unlike Cass, commits suicide. Cass is "saved" from total self-destruction through the "miracle" of his traumatic anger, his accidental murder of Mason Flagg, the antagonist, and his consequent awakening to his own beingness. Cass is a more interesting example of this phenomenon than Clem, since Styron has clearly pointed to his intention by allowing his characters to make philosophical statements on the problem of ontology throughout the novel. At the end of the narrative, Cass, engaged in wholesome family life with his wife and children, and painting,[47] in a comfortable, easy-going South Carolinian setting, confides in Peter, the narrator, that he has come to this conclusion, after his salvation:

". . . to be truthful, you see, I can only tell you this: that as for being and nothingness, the one thing I did know was that to choose between them was simply to choose being, not for the sake of being, or even the love of being, much less the desire to be forever—but in the hope of being what I could be for a time. This would be an ecstasy. God knows, it would." [48]

Cass, through grace, comes to a pause, a rest, a cessation of striving, which for him has been a self-destructive process, through a miracle. He accepts his human incompleteness and *is*. This resolution includes Cass' earlier recognition in the novel that to desire to destroy the self was a sickness. To become one with the fallen world of appearances—with meaninglessness and nothingness—was not to transcend the hated worldly self but to destroy simple being. Before the occurrence of his miraculous salvation, which makes his choice of being clear, he has said:

"What I was really sick from was from despair and self-loathing and greed and selfishness and spite. I was sick with a paralysis of the soul, and with self, and with flabbiness. I was sick with whatever sickness men get in prisons, or on desert islands, or any place where the days stretch forward gray and sunless into flat-assed infinitude, and no one ever comes with the key or answer. I was very nearly sick unto death, and I guess my sickness, if you really want to know, was the sickness of deprivation, and the deprivation was my own doing, because though I didn't know it then I had deprived myself of all belief in the good in myself. The good which is very close to God. That's the bleeding truth." [49]

The Christian Paulinist longing for an answer which re-
solves the question of existence and which, when not forth-
coming, produces self-hate, self-destruction, and paralysis, is
not the longing of the Kafkan spiritual activist. In his unredeemed state he has a kind of freedom—a dreadful freedom,
but a freedom nevertheless. His subjective assertion of his
particularity in absolute relation to the Absolute can only be
pushed forward in this state of freedom. The willful choice
of self is a free choice; the choice of one's own fate is a free
choice; the proposal of a transcendent self as "a fate good
enough" must be made in freedom from divine will, freedom
from prejudgments, divine or human, and freedom from the
concept of grace as already given, which is a confinement.
The quest is a free one, in the form of a question, and the
answer is never given, nor really, according to the definition
of the quest, essentially wished for. How can it be when freedom is the key? In uncertainty and doubt, as K. fully knows,
lie his hope and main chance.

Isaac Rosenfeld, whose interpretation of Kafka's work is
different from that presented here, since it rules out the apprehension of the Absolute as primary, finds "freedom as a
final cause" in Kafka's art. He says:

It is to freedom as a final cause that the whole of Kafka's art has
been moving. . . . Without it, his whole vision of the world, almost magical, almost mad, in its sense of identities, is as yet incomplete. Without acknowledgment of at least the possibility of
freedom, his whole effort in its extreme suffering and understanding, is not yet done. It is a freedom in spite of the world, in spite
of the ultimate struggle, for which man has no capacity, in spite
of the Law, which is incomprehensible, and God, who cannot be
known.

Rosenfeld concludes:

Kafka begins where he ends, with an understanding of the lim-
itation of human freedom, and an effort to transcend that limita-
tion to the achievement of as much peace as one can reach in
mankind.[50]

However much Kafka's art may enact the exploration of freedom as a human cause, the work is inconclusive, "not yet done." Freedom is not the final cause, as Rosenfeld contends; but it is the necessary single ingredient for the spiritual quest, the "ultimate struggle." Though God cannot be known, He may be perceived, dimly and darkly, through the darkness. The ultimate struggle toward the Absolute may be a continuing one, doomed to incompletion; but it is all there is. The freedom of Kafka's K. is presented as a freedom to choose what is—the endless struggle toward what we demand *be*.

NOTES

Preface

1. Alfred Kazin, "Bellow's Purgatory," *The New York Review of Books,* X (March 28, 1968), 32.
2. F. R. Tennant, *The Sources of the Doctrines of the Fall and Original Sin* (New York: Schocken Books, 1968), *passim.*
3. Leslie Fiedler, *Waiting for the End* (New York: Dell Publishing Co., 1965), p. 65.
4. Quoted by Norman Podhoretz in *Making It* (New York: Random House, 1968).

Chapter 1. *Amerika* and *The Trial:* Preliminary Studies in Innocence and Guilt

1. Max Brod's postscript to the 1925 edition of *The Trial,* reprinted in Franz Kafka, *The Trial* (New York: The Modern Library, n.d.). The republication of the definitive edition of *The Trial,* translated from the German by Willa and Edwin Muir and published by Alfred A. Knopf in 1937 and 1956, is the source for my references to *The Trial* throughout this study.
2. Franz Kafka, *Amerika,* trans. Edwin Muir (New York: New Directions, 1946). This edition is the source for my references to *Amerika* throughout this study.
3. Franz Kafka, *The Castle,* trans. Willa and Edwin Muir (New York: Alfred A. Knopf, 1961). This edition is the source for my references to *The Castle* throughout this study.
4. Franz Kafka, *Diaries,* ed. Max Brod (2 vols.; New York: Schocken Books, 1948, 1949), II, 232.
5. Introduction to *Selected Short Stories of Franz Kafka,* trans.

Willa and Edwin Muir (New York: The Modern Library, n.d.),
p. xxi. This collection of short stories, published originally in
America by Schocken Books, 1946, contains the short stories referred to throughout this study, except for "The Stoker," which
is intact as the first chapter of *Amerika*.

6. "Today I got Kierkegaard's *Buch des Richters*. As I sus-
pected, his case, despite essential differences, is very similar to
mine, at least he is on the same side of the world. He bears me
out like a friend" (Kafka, *Diaries*, I, 298). Kafka's reference here
is to the problem of courtship, by which he was troubled in 1913,
the date of the cited entry in the diaries.

7. *Ibid.*, II, 188.

8. Kafka, *Amerika*, p. 34.

9. *Ibid.*

10. Kafka, *Diaries*, II, 132.

11. Kafka, *Amerika*, p. 276. This footnote refers to Brod's
Afterword in the New Directions edition cited above.

12. *Ibid.*, p. 252.

13. Kafka, *Diaries*, II, 188.

14. Kafka, *Amerika*, p. 252.

15. Thought of in this way, Kafka's three novels may be seen
as a Hegelian trilogy of innocence, guilt, and the combination
of the two in a synthesis which is mystery. The novels conceived
of in this manner are reminiscent of William Blake's poems of innocence, poems of experience, and the final mystical poems.

16. Kafka, *The Trial*, pp. 267 ff. The tale the priest in the
Cathedral tells Joseph K. is a parable complete in itself. It is the
story of a stern doorkeeper who guards the door to the Law and
of the man who comes to the door seeking the Law. The man sits
beside the door all his life, and only at the moment before his
death does the doorkeeper say to him: " 'No one but you could
gain admittance through this door, since this door was intended
for you. I am now going to shut it.' "

17. I use the concept of the absurd world which Albert Camus
has described in *The Myth of Sisyphus* (New York: Vintage
Books, 1960). His concept of the absurd depends upon the perception of rationalistic man as existing in an irrational, indifferent, mysterious (and, for Camus, totally meaningless) universe
into which the ordinary man insists on reaching some reasonable,

or ideal, meaning and order. The victim in this absurd world is trapped, as the best of the theater of the absurd has illustrated, in repetitive farce. (Camus' alternative to the ordinary man who is victimized is a hero who refuses to be victimized by this existential situation; he is the man who acts, who subjectively thrusts himself into self-defined secular human activity, although it may or may not be ultimately meaningful. He heroically puts himself against what any reasonable, passive man experiences as absurdity. Sisyphus is thus the prototype for Camus' hero.)

18. Albert Cook, *The Dark Voyage and the Golden Mean* (Cambridge: Harvard University Press, 1949).

19. Alfred Camus, *The Stranger*, trans. Stuart Gilbert (New York: Alfred A. Knopf, 1946).

20. Jean-Paul Sartre, *Nausea*, trans. Lloyd Alexander (London: New Directions, 1949).

21. Saul Bellow, *The Victim* (New York: The Vanguard Press, 1947). Bellow has himself commented on *The Victim*, "I think that realistic literature from the first has been a victim literature. Pit any ordinary individual—and realistic literature concerns itself with ordinary individuals—against the external world and the external world will conquer him, of course. Everything that people believed in the nineteenth century about determinism, about man's place in nature, about the power of productive forces in society, made it inevitable that the hero of the realistic novel should not be a hero but a sufferer who is eventually overcome. So I was doing nothing very original by writing another realistic novel about a common man and calling it *The Victim*" (interview with Saul Bellow in "The Art of Fiction, XXXVII," *The Paris Review*, IX [Winter, 1966], 61).

22. Saul Bellow, *Dangling Man* (New York: Meridian Fiction, 1960). The first edition of this novel, generally unavailable now, even in libraries, was published in New York by The Vanguard Press, 1944.

23. B. J. Friedman, *Stern* (New York: Simon and Schuster, 1962).

24. Bernard Malamud, *The Assistant* (New York: Farrar, Straus and Cudahy, 1957).

25. Norman Mailer, *Barbary Shore* (New York: Rinehart and Co., 1951).

26. J. D. Salinger, *The Catcher in the Rye* (Boston: Little, Brown and Co., 1951).

27. Thomas Pynchon, *V.* (Philadelphia: J. B. Lippincott Company, 1963).

28. John Hawkes, *The Cannibal* (New York: New Directions, 1949).

29. John Hawkes, *Second Skin* (New York: New Directions, 1964).

30. John Barth, *The End of the Road* (New York: Doubleday and Company, 1958).

31. John Barth, *The Sot-Weed Factor* (New York: Doubleday and Company, 1960).

32. John Barth, *Giles Goat-Boy* (New York: Doubleday and Company, 1966).

33. Joseph Heller, *Catch-22* (New York: Simon and Schuster, 1961). Holden Caulfield, the hero of *The Catcher in the Rye,* and Yossarian, the hero of *Catch-22,* might be called victim-activists. They are not, as is usually the case with victim-heroes, passive in their situations though they are nonetheless trapped by those situations. They do protest and insist on their own madness as preferable to the world's. The wish to be mad in one's own way becomes in these novels a kind of sanity—or, at least, a healthy passion—posed against the world's absurdities. What these novelists suggest, however, is that personal madness, necessary to live at all in the world, is true madness. The world has forced this upon Holden and Yossarian, and in their acceptance of the world's terms—in their mad, "comic," acting-out of that which has been imposed upon them, they seem more deluded, deceived, and defeated than bold in a quest of a better self.

34. In discussing his shift from the victim-hero of his two early novels to the activist hero of his later novels, Saul Bellow, in the interview cited in note 21, speaks not only of his own early work but of the work of other writers who insist on examining the world from an intellectual-philosophical position: his imagery reminds us of *The Trial*'s parable of the Law. "It seems to me they can't know enough about it [life] for confident denial. The mystery is too great. So when they knock on the door of mystery with knuckles of cognition it is quite right that the door should open and some mysterious power squirt them in the eye."

The turning is away from the cognitive victim-hero in a world unavailable to reasonable minds, toward the activist hero, the seeker open to all life-mysteries.

35. Camus, "Hope and the Absurd in the Work of Franz Kafka," *The Myth of Sisyphus*, p. 96 ff.

36. Saul Bellow, "Notes of a Dangling Man," *Partisan Review*, X (September–October, 1943), 402–409, 429–438.

Chapter 2. The Kafkan Hero K. of *The Castle:*
Prototype for a Modern Spiritual Activist Hero

1. Albert Cook, *The Meaning of Fiction* (Detroit: Wayne State University Press, 1960), p. 248.

2. Aphorism 109 of Franz Kafka's series of aphorisms entitled "Reflections on Sin, Suffering, Hope and the True Way," in Franz Kafka, *Dearest Father, Stories and Other Writings,* trans. Ernst Kaiser and Eithne Wilkins (New York: Schocken Books, 1954).

3. Saul Bellow, "Where Do We Go from Here: The Future of Fiction," *Michigan Quarterly Review*, I (January, 1962), 27.

4. Søren Kierkegaard, *Fear and Trembling and The Sickness Unto Death,* trans. Walter Lowrie (New York: Doubleday Anchor Books, n.d.), p. 36.

5. Max Brod, *Franz Kafka: A Biography,* trans. G. Humphreys Roberts (New York: Schocken Books, 1947), p. 194.

6. The concept of the particular person who in faith places himself—purposely, and according to his own subjective truth—into vital and absolute relation with the Absolute, as the Kierkegaardian Knight of Faith, Abraham, does, is developed in *Fear and Trembling.*

7. Kafka, *The Castle,* p. 95.

8. Aphorism 89 of "Reflections on Sin" in *Dearest Father.*

9. Kierkegaard, p. 70.

10. *Ibid.,* p. 71.

11. Kafka, *The Castle,* p. 96.

12. Kierkegaard, p. 71.

13. Kafka, *The Castle,* p. 63.

14. *Ibid.,* p. 113.

15. *Ibid.,* pp. 72–73.

16. Aphorism 62 in 'Reflections on Sin" in *Dearest Father*.

17. Kafka, *The Castle*, p. 21.

18. *Ibid.*, p. 73.

19. *Ibid.*, p. 207.

20. *Ibid.*

21. *Ibid.*, p. 206.

22. *Ibid.*, pp. 199–200.

23. *Ibid.*, p. 199.

24. *Ibid.*, pp. 74–75.

25. *Ibid.*, p. 75.

26. *Ibid.*, p. 139.

27. *Ibid.*, p. 197.

28. *Ibid.*, p. 140.

29. *Ibid.*, p. 251.

30. Paul Goodman, *Kafka's Prayer* (New York: The Vanguard Press, 1947).

Chapter 3. Kafka and Bellow: Comparisons and Further Definitions

1. Kafka, *The Castle*, p. 422.

2. *Ibid.*, pp. 425–426.

3. Thomas Mann in his "Homage," which serves as a preface to the 1961 definitive American edition of *The Castle*, uses the term *grace* and categorizes the castle as God, the village as the normal world of ordinary life, and Kafka as a "religious humorist" (*ibid.*, p. x).

4. Saul Bellow, *The Adventures of Augie March* (New York: Viking Press, 1953), p. 519.

5. "The Good Guy," *Time*, September 25, 1964, p. 105.

6. Robert Gutwillig, "Talk with Saul Bellow," *The New York Times Book Review*, September 20, 1964, pp. 40–41.

7. Bellow risks it and partially fails in *Herzog*, which is somewhat boring, as Thomas Meehan has pointed out in a parody of *Herzog* ("Claus," *The New Yorker*, January 9, 1965, pp. 26–27). This is because *Herzog* as the story of the inner experience of a personal life is not fictively transvalued as it is in *The Adventures of Augie March* and *Henderson the Rain King*. In *Herzog*,

Bellow does not "bring it out." This may be because *Herzog* is, in fact, very close to autobiography.

8. Saul Bellow, "A Comment on 'Form and Despair,' " *Location,* I (Summer, 1964), 10–12.

9. Nathalie Sarraute, the particular French *nouveau roman* novelist whose work Bellow calls boring in his *Location* article, has herself written illuminatingly on the novel in *The Age of Suspicion: Essays on the Novel* (New York: George Braziller, 1963). Although she sees herself in a continuing literary tradition which, interestingly enough, starts with the Kafkan novel, the novel "in situation," as opposed to the psychological novel, she does not write literature about literature. What Bellow means perhaps is that she is excessively self-conscious about her place as writer in a continuing literary tradition, the newest phase of which is, in France and to some extent America, the anti-traditional novel, or the anti-novel as Sartre has called it. Bellow finds such discussion as Mme Sarraute's superfluous to writing. About his place and the place of other writers in history, culture, and literary tradition, he has said: "Who was Babel [Isaac Babel]? Where did he come from? He was an accident. We are all such accidents. We do not make up history and culture. We simply appear, not by our own choice. We make what we can of our condition with the means available. We must accept the mixture as we find it—the impurity of it, the tragedy of it, the hope of it" (Saul Bellow [ed.], *Great Jewish Short Stories* [New York: Dell Publishing Co., 1963], p. 16).

10. Goodman, *Kafka's Prayer,* p. 207.

11. Kafka, *Selected Short Stories,* p. ix.

12. *Ibid.,* p. viii.

13. Kafka, *Diaries,* I, 285.

14. Saul Bellow, "Distractions of a Fiction Writer," *The Living Novel,* ed. Granville Hicks (New York: Collier Books, 1962), pp. 13–31.

15. *Ibid.,* pp. 30–31.

16. Goodman, *Kafka's Prayer,* p. 207.

17. Saul Bellow, "The Writer as Moralist," *The Atlantic,* CCXI (March, 1963), 58–62.

18. *Ibid.,* pp. 58–59. Cf. "We have to begin somewhere. Touch

me, he said, and you touch a man. I am not different from others; they are not different from me." This is Bellow defining Whitman's position in "Distractions of a Fiction Writer," in the *Living Novel,* p. 23. Cf. Schlossberg, a character in *The Victim,* who is one of the few of Bellow's sages characterized unambivalently, as an energetic and dignified man, and who is a Yiddish writer. Another character in *The Victim* says of him, " 'Take Schlossberg, for example. . . . With him it's a case of "touch me and you touch a man," and these days you can't always be sure what you're touching' " (Bellow, *The Victim,* p. 260). Bellow's apparent affection for this idea of writers, and especially of Whitman, who teaches by making a *new* archetypal man of himself and by making representations of himself through the cosmic "I" of his poetry, suggests the way Bellow himself would consider the writer as moralist or teacher even now, though he calls the Whitman way "Romantic" in his *Atlantic* essay, and Schlossberg in *The Victim* is also a representative, as a Yiddish writer, of an older, more Romantic type.

19. Bellow, *The Atlantic,* p. 62.

20. However, I doubt that Bellow means even that, when he considers poetry, since (1) he seems to prefer Whitman to more formal poets, and (2) I would suspect his disposition in all forms of writing to be similar to that of his friend Karl Shapiro, who has recently attacked formal poetry as childlike playing with words in order to imprison them, tyrannically, in forms (see *In Defense of Ignorance* [New York: Random House, 1960]). Shapiro's view of the moral obligation of the poet is much like Bellow's view of the moral obligation of the novelist. Shapiro, too, admires Whitman most highly among American poets.

21. Bellow, *The Atlantic,* p. 62.

22. Bellow, *The Living Novel,* p. 30.

23. Bellow, *The Atlantic,* p. 62.

24. *Ibid.*

25. He makes a particular reference to Camus and Camus' vision of "a self devoid of depths" in *The Stranger.*

26. Saul Bellow, "Some Notes on Recent American Fiction," *Encounter,* XXI (November, 1963), 22–29.

27. *Ibid.*

28. Kafka, *Diaries.*

29. Goodman, *Kafka's Prayer*, p. 241.

30. Kafka, *Diaries*, I, 300.

31. In Chapter 2, I have discussed K. in *The Castle* as a Kierkegaardian Knight of Faith who has put himself, a particular, into absolute relation with the Absolute. This is a spiritual position, even though the nature of the Absolute remains unknown: Is the castle divine or diabolical? One does not know. Paul Goodman would call the castle the soul and the soul the unconscious. Is the unconscious the reward or the threat? But Goodman's investigation, in *Kafka's Prayer*, is on another level from mine, since his best insights derive from a very searching psychological analysis of Kafka's personality as revealed in his writing.

32. Bellow, "The Writer as Moralist," *The Atlantic*, p. 62.

33. *Ibid.*

34. Saul Bellow, *Henderson the Rain King* (New York: The Viking Press, 1959).

35. Eliseo Vivas, *Creation and Discovery: Essays in Criticism and Aesthetics* (New York: The Noonday Press, 1955), p. 45.

36. *Ibid.*, p. 42.

37. Bellow, *Dangling Man*, pp. 24–25.

38. Saul Bellow, *Herzog* (New York: The Viking Press, 1964).

39. Tony Tanner, "Saul Bellow: The Flight from Monologue," *Encounter*, XXIV (February, 1965), 62.

40. Saul Bellow, *Seize the Day* (New York: The Viking Press, 1956). This original edition includes the novella "Seize the Day," three short stories, and one one-act play.

41. *Ibid.*, p. 147.

42. See Kafka, *Diaries*, *passim*. Snow: Kafka's diaries contain his accounts of weariness and fatigue while walking through the snowy streets of Prague. The effort was made more intense for him by his illness.

43. As defined by Paul Goodman, these four lyric interludes are sex with Frieda under the bar; the drinking of Klamm's brandy; the walk with Barnabas; and the sleepy conversation with Bürgel in the bedroom in the inn (*The Structure of Literature* [Chicago: University of Chicago Press, 1954], pp. 173–183).

44. Bellow, *Augie March*, p. 175. For other references to darkness, see pp. 201, 212, 229, 273, 281, 291, 401, 429, 468, and 482.

45. This passage, incidentally, is a fine example of the rich texture of Bellow's style, a contrast to Kafka's bareness. The passage is a proliferation of images which become part of the basic metaphor of darkness for a deterministic force in nature.

46. Joseph Wood Krutch, "In Back of Man, A World of Nature," *A Quarto of Modern Literature*, ed. Leonard Brown (New York: Charles Scribner's Sons, 1964).

47. Bellow, *Augie March*, p. 536.

48. In *Henderson*, the African landscape is dry and barren—a nature similar to that comprehended, underneath surface variety, as "a darkness" in *Augie March*. It is interesting to note that the American seeker-after-self is the Rain King in Africa's dryness. Here the act is as symbolic as the background for it.

49. Bellow, *Henderson*, pp. 340–341.

50. Bellow, *Herzog*, pp. 325–326.

Chapter 4. The Heroes of Saul Bellow's Novels

1. Bellow, *Dangling Man*, pp. 140–141.

2. *Ibid.*, p. 191.

3. *Ibid.*, pp. 153–154.

4. These terms, *being-in-the-world* and *being-in-the-midst-of-the-world* are Jean-Paul Sartre's terms to oppose energetic active being to vegetable being. His full elaboration of what he specifically means by the terms is found in *Being and Nothingness*, trans. Hazel E. Barnes (New York: Philosophical Library, 1956).

5. Perhaps the similarity between Joseph in *Dangling Man* and the Underground Man in Dostoievski's *Notes from the Underground* should be remarked. Several critics have noted this similarity. Cf. Ihab H. Hassan, "Saul Bellow: Five Faces of a Hero," *Critique*, III (Summer, 1960), 28–36.

The Victim is regarded by some as Bellow's best novel in the tradition of the well-made novel. It is also highly regarded by critics most interested in the dark novels of contemporary American literature. Jonathan Baumbach in a series of studies of what he calls American "nightmare novels" concludes that Bellow "has written the best of our nightmare novels" in *The Victim* (Jonathan Baumbach, *The Landscape of Nightmare: Studies in* the *American Novel* [New York: New York University Press, 1965], p. 35).

6. Bellow, *Augie March*, p. 536.

7. Herbert Gold, "The Discovered Self," *Nation*, CLXXXIII (November 17, 1956), 435–436.

8. Martin Buber, *I and Thou* (New York: Charles Scribner's Sons, 1958); *Tales of the Hasidim: Early Masters* and *Tales of the Hasidim: Late Masters* (New York: Schocken Books, 1961).

9. Malcolm L. Diamond, *Martin Buber, Jewish Existentialist* (New York: Oxford University Press, 1960).

10. Buber, *Tales of the Hasidim: Early Masters*, p. 251.

11. See "The Vocal Group" from the *Times Literary Supplement*, reprinted in *The American Imagination* (Middletown, Connecticut: Special "Our Times" Edition, 1960), pp. 173 ff.

12. Bellow, *Seize the Day*, p. 118.

13. Bellow, *Augie March*, p. 515.

14. Frederick J. Hoffman, *The Mortal No* (Princeton: Princeton University Press, 1964).

15. *Ibid.*, p. 319.

16. *Ibid.*, pp. 321–322.

17. Martin Buber, "Teaching and Deed," *Israel and the World* (New York: Schocken Books, 1948).

18. *Augie March* starts with a long section devoted to Augie's childhood and early youth in a Chicago slum. The first chapter of this section and of the novel was published under the title "From the Life of Augie March," *Partisan Review*, XVI (November, 1949), 1077–1089. The unfinished novel's title was then announced as *Life Among the Machiavellians*.

19. Augie says, "You know, I did admire Georgie for the way he took his fate. I wished I had one that was more evident, and that I could quit this pilgrimage of mine" (Bellow, *Augie March*, p. 424).

20. *Ibid.*, p. 454.

21. "Gimpel the Fool," translated by Bellow, is the title story in a collection of I. Bashevis Singer's stories, *Gimpel the Fool and Other Stories* (New York: The Noonday Press, 1957).

22. Bellow, *Augie March*, p. 456.

23. *Ibid.*, p. 457.

24. *Ibid.*, p. 527.

25. *Ibid.*, p. 401.

26. *Ibid.*, p. 154.

27. Notice that Augie feels ugly and guileful, just as the land-lady and Frieda tell K. he is, because of this conflict. Both Augie and K. are trying to be as honest as they can; they feel innocent, but the fact of their singular purpose, "an independent fate," makes them unintentionally guileful in communal and relational events.

28. *Ibid.*, p. 402.

29. *Ibid.*, p. 403.

30. *Ibid.*, p. 424.

31. *Ibid.*, p. 458. This prophecy is included, implicitly, in all of Kafka's works, as Nathalie Sarraute points out in her essay on Kafka in *The Age of Suspicion*. Only in K. do we find a Kafkan hero in opposition to that portended future. *The Trial* contains an ominously clear picture of this condition in which "Obedience [is] God, and freedom the Devil." "In the Penal Colony" contains a similar adumbration. K.'s actions in *The Castle* suggest a remedy to such legalized, or sanctified, uniformity.

32. Kafka, *The Castle*, p. 378.

33. Bellow, *Augie March*, p. 384.

34. *Ibid.*, p. 523.

35. Kafka, *The Castle*, p. 401.

36. *Ibid.*, p. 405.

37. *Ibid.*, p. 407.

38. Kafka, *Diaries*, II, 205.

39. Sarraute, *The Age of Suspicion*, p. 43.

40. The disappearance of romantic love (or European courtly love) is considered as culminating in *The Castle* by Erich Heller, in "The World of Franz Kafka," *The Disinherited Mind* (New York: Meridian Books, 1959). See especially pp. 221 ff., starting with the paragraph "In K.'s relationship to Frieda the European story of romantic love has found its epilogue."

The absence of romantic, passionate love between a man and a woman as a central theme in American literature, old and new, is heavily documented by Leslie Fiedler in *Love and Death in the American Novel* (Cleveland and New York: The World Publishing Co., 1962). Fiedler does not see Bellow's male-female relationships as yet another epilogue to romantic love, but he might have done so. He comments: ". . . the whole of Bellow's work is singularly lacking in real or vivid female characters; where women are introduced, they appear as nympholeptic fantasies, peculiarly unconvincing" (p. 360). The same sort of thing might be said of the work of Mailer, Malamud, Salinger, and Gold—women, not just passionate love, have begun to lose their human significance in the story of the activist hero's quest, and they appear, when they do, with "spiritual" significance to this quest. They are often emblematic or fantastic types. One thinks immediately of Malamud's *The Natural* and Bellow's *Henderson* as containing the clearest exemplifications of this.

41. Bellow, *Augie March,* pp. 484–485.

42. Although Augie believes that true innocence is unavailable in the modern mechanized world, still he feels that one can will a kind of pseudo-innocence, intend simplicity and clarity of purpose without impure (and possible malevolent) motivations arising unwanted from the subconscious. He says to his psychologist friend, Clem, "You can always find bad motives, . . . There are always bad motives. So all I can say is I don't want to have them" (*ibid.,* p. 457).

43. *Ibid.,* p. 516.

44. *Ibid.,* p. 485.

45. Richard Poirier, "Bellows to Herzog," *Partisan Review,* XXXII (Spring, 1965), 264–271.

46. Bellow, *Henderson,* p. 189.

47. Henderson finds Mrs. Lenox, his housekeeper, dead in the kitchen pantry; in this scene his awareness of his own wasted, empty life, his own living death, is heightened. "And I thought, 'Oh, shame, shame! . . . How can we? Why do we allow ourselves? What are we doing? The last little room of dirt is waiting. Without windows. So for God's sake make a move, Henderson, put forth effort. You too will die of this pestilence. Death will annihilate you and nothing will remain, and there will be nothing left but junk. Because nothing will have been and so nothing will be left. While something still is—now!'" (*ibid.,* p. 40).

48. See Tony Tanner, "The Flight from Monologue," *Encounter,* XXIV (February, 1965), 58–70, for an excellent summary of the hero's metaphysical quest in Bellow's works. About

Henderson's return to America and the possibility of his achieving communal or relational love there, Tanner says: "Henderson, like other characters in Bellow's work, wants to find out how a man can properly *submit* to reality . . . and at the same time *transcend* himself and slough off hampering limitations. . . . There are many Nietzschean echoes in the book, and indeed the motto of the prolonged metaphysical quest . . . could be Zarathustra's contention that 'Man is a thing to be surmounted.' Henderson desperately wants to find a new hope, a new nobility in life . . . but though he learns many new ideas it is hard to feel, at the end, as he returns to his wife with the intention of entering medical school, that his ebullient and tormenting individualism will ever be really surmounted or transformed. What he says at the start—'Society is what beats me. Alone I can be pretty good'—is scarcely modified at the end (like Augie, he talks of 'love' but seldom manifests it). There seems to be no obvious way in which he can apply the lessons he learnt from his strange African quest. . . ." (pp. 60–61).

49. Bellow, *Henderson*, p. 62.

50. See Mailer's essay "The White Negro," in his *Advertisements for Myself* (New York: G. P. Putnam's Sons, 1959).

51. Wilhelm Reich, *Character-Analysis* (New York: The Noonday Press, 1949), pp. ix–xi.

52. *Ibid.*

53. Norman O. Brown, *Life Against Death: The Psychoanalytical Meaning of History* (London: Routledge and K. Paul, 1959).

54. Irving Malin, *Jews and Americans* (Carbondale: South Illinois University Press, 1965), p. 111.

55. See Paul Goodman, who speculates, in *Kafka's Prayer,* that the castle, psychologically analyzed, may be seen as the successfully completed orgasm, which is divine and diabolical at once, since it brings joyous harmony but also the loss of self and the consequent threat of darkness and chaos. Castle-belonging as the ideal construct for this longed-for transcendence and harmony, however, changes the nature of the original desire.

56. Bellow may be playing on the name Wilhelm.

57. Bellow, *Seize the Day,* p. 75.

58. Bellow, *Henderson,* p. 191.

59. *Ibid.,* p. 174.

60. *Ibid.,* p. 236.

61. *Ibid.*

62. *Ibid.,* p. 251.

63. *Ibid.,* p. 254.

64. *Ibid.,* p. 260.

65. See Rollo May (ed.), *Existential Psychology* (New York: Random House, 1961).

66. Bellow, *Henderson,* p. 265.

67. *Ibid.,* p. 267.

68. *Ibid.,* p. 297.

69. Marcus Klein, *After Alienation: American Novels in Mid-Century* (Cleveland and New York: The World Publishing Co., 1964), p. 55.

70. *Ibid.,* p. 56.

71. Bellow, *Henderson,* p. 277.

72. *Ibid.,* p. 182.

73. *Ibid.,* p. 276.

74. *Ibid.,* p. 285.

75. Bellow, *Augie March,* p. 455.

76. Klein, *After Alienation,* p. 53.

77. Goodman, *Kafka's Prayer,* p. 219.

78. Kafka, *Diaries,* II, 202.

79. Robert Gutwillig, "Talk with Saul Bellow," *New York Times₁ Book Review,* September 20, 1964, p. 40.

80. That a Hemingway parody is incorporated into *Henderson* not only through the somewhat barer nature of much of its language but also through its hero's bigness, his "lost generation" adventures in Paris early in the novel, his African trip, his association with lions, and the initials of his name, Eugene Henderson, is an amusing bow, on Bellow's part, to his American literary heritage. His disenchantment with Hemingway's "hard-boiledness," however, is made clear in the opening lines of *Dangling Man.* Mailer, on the other hand, has always admired Hemingway and the cult of virility, as he makes evident in his essays in *Advertisements for Myself.*

81. Saul Bellow, "Deep Readers of the World, Beware!" *The New York Times Book Review,* February 15, 1959, pp. 1 and 34.

82. *Henderson,* more than any other of Bellow's novels, appears to be an allegoristic interpretation of experience. However,

an allegory of one-to-one relationships never takes shape. Instead there is a kind of pseudo-allegoristic playfulness, seemingly parodying archetypes and archetypal situations for the fun of it, for the exercise of wit and imagination.

83. The investigation involves *Herzog* in Joycean patterns of mixed presentation of consciousness (peripheral and focused) and subconsciousness (random and motivational). Moses Herzog's very name comes from the "jewmerchant" of the Cyclops chapter of *Ulysses*, indicating an intended reference to Joyce. It has been suggested (by a student of literature in Israel) that *Herzog*, which embodies a Diaspora Jew who seeks the meaning of his lost roots while wandering, alienated, in modern urbanity, is Bellow's answer to Joyce. More precisely, the answer is in the person of Moses Herzog, whose quest is different from Leopold Bloom's in that it concentrates on his Jewishness. Bellow seems to be saying to Joyce that the modern Jew is too busy looking for his own particular truths to be a light unto the Gentiles as Bloom might wish to be and is indeed made to be by the father-son theme in *Ulysses*.

84. Norman Mailer, who does not like the character Herzog, says of him: "Herzog was an unoriginal man, Herzog was a fool —not an attractive God-anointed fool like Gimpel the Fool, his direct progenitor, but a sodden fool, over-educated and inept, unable to fight, able to love only when love presented itself as a gift" ("Modes and Mutations: Quick Comments on the Modern American Novel," *Commentary*, XLI [March, 1966], 37–40).

85. Bellow is severely criticized by Richard Poirier for not making clear enough the distinction between his hero's mind and his own in *Herzog*. I think this criticism unwarranted, but some of Poirier's other critical insights into the novel are very worthwhile, especially his view that Bellow states an optimistic point of view, against modern metaphysical pessimism, that he is unable finally to sustain novelistically (Poirier, *Partisan Review*).

86. Irving Howe and Eliezer Greenberg, eds., *A Treasury of Yiddish Stories* (Cleveland and New York: Meridian Books, 1961), pp. 40–41.

87. Bellow, *Herzog*, p. 245.

88. *Ibid.*, p. 175.

Chapter 5. The Heroes of
Norman Mailer's Novels

1. Herbert Tauber, *Franz Kafka* (New Haven: Yale University Press, 1948), p. 137.

2. *Ibid.*

3. *Ibid.,* pp. 137–138.

4. Norman Mailer, *An American Dream* (New York: The Dial Press, 1965).

5. Norman Mailer, *The Deer Park* (New York: G. P. Putnam's Sons, 1955).

6. "The Time of Her Time" is reprinted in *Advertisements for Myself.*

7. Norman Mailer, *The Naked and the Dead* (New York: Rinehart and Company, 1948).

8. For a thorough discussion of the social and political views expressed, through the device of allegory, in *The Naked and The Dead* as well as in *Barbary Shore* and *The Deer Park,* see Diana Trilling, "Norman Mailer," *Encounter,* XIX (November, 1962), 45–56.

9. Trilling, *Encounter,* p. 49.

10. Mailer, *The Deer Park,* p. 224.

11. *Ibid.,* p. 45.

12. *Ibid.,* p. 46.

13. *Ibid.*

14. *Ibid.,* p. 1.

15. *Ibid.,* p. 229.

16. Mailer, *Advertisements for Myself,* p. 495.

17. Mailer, *The Deer Park,* p. 221.

18. *Ibid.,* p. 224.

19. *Ibid.,* p. 374. Words similar to these remained in the 1967 production of the play Mailer made from *Deer Park.* But the spirit of them was lost with the theme of misused flesh—the theme and its imagery were trampled in the stage business which transformed the narrative into a Pop spectacle. *An American Dream,* Mailer's 1965 novel, used some forms borrowed from Pop Art to investigate American experience, but these were legitimately used as novelistic manifestations of Mailer's initial

vision. In the off-Broadway play of *The Deer Park* Pop Art devices superimposed on the original insights hid rather than revealed those insights.

20. The war-consciousness in Mailer, which made him first a war novelist and political ideologist, then led him to see the total political-social milieu as the evil, regardless of the party or the platform, and finally led him to personal and spiritual affirmations of the self against all social deaths, is also present in *An American Dream* in the early pages of which the Second World War contest between four Nazi soldiers and the hero, Stephen Rojack, is described in terms of brutality, hell, and anality. War-is-hell anality becomes a prevalent metaphor in the story of this hero's quest for his spiritual self. See Richard Poirier's explication of the war scene and the anality metaphor for the evil of the devil in "Morbid-Mindedness," *Commentary*, XXXIX (June, 1965), 91–94.

21. Norman Mailer, "The Art of Fiction XXXII," *The Paris Review*, VIII (Winter–Spring, 1964), 58

22. Mailer prefers to think of his major characters in *The Deer Park* as "beings," not "characters." His distinction between the two types of novelistic actors is defined thus: "A character is someone you can grasp as a whole, you can have a clear idea of him, but a being is someone whose nature keeps shifting" (*ibid.*, p. 48).

23. Mailer first conceived of *The Deer Park* as one part of a long novel, or series of novels, a major work of eight parts. Prologue to the eight novels, of which *The Deer Park* was first, was to have been the short story, "The Man Who Studied Yoga," which may be found in *Advertisements for Myself*. "The Time of Her Time" would be the first chapter of the second novel in this series.

24. Mailer, *The Paris Review*, pp. 48–49.

25. *Ibid.*, pp. 329–330.

26. *Ibid.*, p. 329.

27. To what extremes the hipster may go not only for a sense of himself but out of a compassion for others (distinctly disavowed by Faye in *The Deer Park*) Mailer makes clear in this reply to an interviewer (quoted by Diana Trilling, *Encounter*, p. 54): " 'Now if the brute does it and at the last moment likes

the man he is extinguishing then perhaps the victim did not die in vain. If there is an eternity with souls in that eternity, if one is able to be born again, the victim may get his reward. At least it seems possible that the quality of one being passes into the other, and this altogether hate-filled human, grinding his boot into the face of someone . . . in the act of killing, in this terribly private moment, the brute feels a moment of tenderness, for the first time perhaps in all of his experience. What has happened is that the killer is becoming a little more possible, a little bit more ready to love someone.' " Mailer later greatly modified this statement.

28. Mailer, *The Deer Park*, p. 328.

29. *Ibid.*, p. 347.

30. Mailer, *The Paris Review*, pp. 51–52.

31. *Ibid.*, p. 52.

32. *Ibid.*, p. 54.

33. *Ibid.*, p. 38.

34. *Ibid.*, p. 39.

35. William Styron, *Set This House on Fire* (New York: Random House, 1960).

36. Herbert Gold, *Salt* (New York: Dial Press, 1963).

37. Austin Warren explains allegory and the deviations from pure allegory that the writer's vision may take: "An allegory is a series of concepts provided with a narrative or a narrative accompanied by a conceptual parallel. Strictly, it is a philosophical sequence which systematically works itself out in images. But allegory is rarely as pure as *Pilgrim's Progress* or *The Romance of the Rose:* it deviates from purity in two directions—by losing its systematic character, becoming a series of intermittent symbolisms; or by keeping its system but abstaining from offering a conceptual key to its parable." Warren continues with a comment on Kafka, of some interest here. "The novels of Kafka are not . . . allegorical. . . . that they are 'metaphysical' novels we should surely have discerned without aid. . . . it is their special richness that they have much particularity untranslatable into generality" (Austin Warren, "Franz Kafka," *Kafka: A Collection of Critical Essays*, ed. Ronald Gray [Englewood Cliffs: Prentice-Hall, Inc., 1962], p. 130.

38. Norman Mailer, *The Presidential Papers* (New York: G. P.

Putnam's Sons, 1963); *Cannibals and Christians* (New York: The
Dial Press, 1966).

39. Mailer, *Advertisements for Myself*, p. 338.

40. *Ibid.*, p. 339.

41. Mailer's series of comments on the Hasidic tales, originally
published in *Commentary*, is included in his *The Presidential
Papers*, pp. 152–157 and 190–198.

42. Mailer, *Advertisements for Myself*, p. 341.

43. Mailer, *The Paris Review*, p. 50.

44. "Authors Discuss Sick-Book Trend," *The New York Times*
(March 10, 1965), p. 34.

45. Mailer, *Advertisements for Myself*, p. 349.

46. *Ibid.*, p. 351.

47. The urgency Mailer feels in undertaking his prophetic
task is illustrated by his own acting out in his life the principles
of his philosophy. About this, Diana Trilling has said, "But
Mailer's impulse to break the metaphor-barrier and himself act
out, or ask that we act out, his ideas would now appear to have
another, much deeper source than his impatience with the ability
of art to achieve its tangible miracle of renovation. Intense as
his literary dedication unquestionably is, his religious mission is
now infinitely more compelling. Just as he writes in order to
preach the word of God, by whatever thorny path. And when he
invites us to follow his example he literally means us to join a
religious crusade" (Trilling, *Encounter*, p. 55).

48. This is not D. H. Lawrence's story—that straight, serious
story of the efficacy of the genital life. Mailer's idea, as embodied
in Rojack, is more complex than Lawrence's. *An American
Dream* is the post-Lawrence novel *par excellence*. As has been
suggested, all the sex in the novel is a kind of metaphor for
spirit.

49. Terry Southern and Mason Hoffenberg, *Candy* (New York:
G. P. Putnam's Sons, 1964).

50. However, the act of murder itself *may* be considered as the
moment of rebirth, as Rojack indicates when he says, "Well, if
Deborah's dying had given me a new life, I must be all of eight
hours old by now" (Mailer, *An American Dream*, p. 93).

51. *Ibid.*, p. 236.

52. *Ibid.*, p. 241.

53. *Ibid.*, p. 235.

54. *Ibid.*, pp. 173–174.

55. *Ibid.*, p. 174.

56. *Ibid.*, p. 176.

57. *Ibid.*, p. 253.

58. If, as A. Alvarez critically suggests in an unfavorable review of the English edition of the novel (*Spectator*, May 7, 1965, p. 603), the devil seems to occupy most of Rojack's time, one need only think of Milton's *Paradise Lost* and consider the obvious attractiveness of the devil to the poet to understand the concentration on the hero's metaphysical awareness of the devil-in-the-world. God is not so easily pinned down in materiality or language, which may, or may not, be to God's advantage.

Chapter 6. J. D. Salinger's Holden and Seymour and the Spiritual Activist Hero

1. Mary McCarthy, "J. D. Salinger's Closed Circuit," *Harper's Magazine*, CCV (October, 1962), 46–48.

2. Frederick L. Gwynn and Joseph L. Blotner, *The Fiction of J. D. Salinger* (Pittsburgh: Pittsburgh University Press, 1958).

3. J. D. Salinger, *Nine Stories* (Boston: Little, Brown and Company, 1953).

4. "Seymour—An Introduction," in J. D. Salinger, *Raise High the Roof Beam, Carpenters and Seymour—An Introduction* (Boston: Little, Brown and Co., 1959).

5. Bernard Malamud, *A New Life* (New York: Farrar, Straus, and Cudahy, 1961).

6. Northrop Frye, *Anatomy of Criticism: Four Essays* (Princeton: Princeton University Press, 1957).

7. Salinger, *The Catcher in the Rye*, p. 223.

8. Ihab Hassan, "The Rare Quixotic Gesture," in Henry A. Grunwald, editor, *Salinger: A Critical and Personal Portrait* (New York: Harper and Brothers, 1962), p. 162.

9. Salinger, *Raise High*, p. 111.

10. "Franny" and "Zooey" are in J. D. Salinger, *Franny and Zooey* (Boston: Little, Brown and Company, 1961). "Raise High the Roof Beam, Carpenters," is in *Raise High*, cited above.

11. Salinger, *Raise High*, pp. 111–112.

12. "Perfect Day for Banana Fish" is in *Nine Stories*.

13. Leslie Fiedler, "Up from Adolescence," in Grunwald, *Salinger*, p. 56.

14. William Burroughs, *Naked Lunch* (New York: Grove Press, Inc., 1959).

15. *Ibid.*, p. 44.

16. Salinger, *Raise High,* pp. 121 ff.

17. *Ibid.*, pp. 178–187.

18. *Ibid.*, p. 180.

19. *Ibid.*, p. 187.

20. A study might be made of the lists and catalogues of American writers from Walt Whitman to the present: the list for its own sake would seem to be a thrust into the density of the material world.

21. Salinger, *Raise High,* p. 199.

22. Alfred Chester, "Salinger: How to Love Without Love," *Commentary,* XXXV (June, 1963), 474.

23. I hesitate to call this "climax" in the story a literary representation of *satori*, but as a notation, I would call attention to Salinger's genuine though eclectic interest in Zen Buddhism, obvious and apparent throughout his late stories, the Glass stories, and very significant in "Seymour," and to *satori* as the moment of "pure consciousness," of nonintellectual enlightenment, of the awakening (see William A. Briggs [ed.], *Anthology of Zen* [New York: Grove Press, Inc., 1961]).

24. Salinger, *Raise High,* p. 235.

25. *Ibid.*, p. 236.

26. *Ibid.*, pp. 241–242.

27. *Ibid.*, p. 242.

28. *Ibid.*, p. 248.

29. Robert Penn Warren, and others, have observed of Hemingway's work that in it, after confronting nihilism in the world, he gives to dangerous games with their rules and codes, through which manliness and virtue may be attained and sustained, the meaningful place of focus. Salinger seems to operate in a similar way, though he arrives at a very different formulation. Finding the codes and rules of the world and its games meaningless, he has his hero ignore social forms, deny all rules, and make of the whole of life a meta-game in which formlessness is of value.

30. Fiedler, *Salinger*, pp. 61–62.
31. Goodman, *The Structure of Literature*, p. 177.
32. *Ibid.*, p. 182.
33. *Ibid.*, p. 183.
34. Heller, *The Disinherited Mind*, p. 211.
35. *Ibid.*, p. 213.
36. *Ibid.*, p. 215.

Chapter 7. Minor American Novelists
in the Activist Mode

1. George P. Elliott, "A Surfeit of Talk," *Commentary*, XXXIX (June, 1965), 98.
2. Bellow, *Dangling Man*, p. 9
3. Herbert Gold (ed.), *Fiction of the Fifties* (Garden City, New York: Dolphin Books, Doubleday & Co., Inc., 1961), pp. 11–12.
4. Herbert Gold, *The Man Who Wasn't With It* (Boston: Little, Brown and Company, 1956).
5. Herbert Gold, *The Optimist* (Boston: Little, Brown and Company, 1959).
6. Bernard Malamud, *The Natural* (New York: Farrar, Straus and Cudahy, 1952).
7. The Grail Myth, as it underlies the also mythic surface of *The Natural*, is neatly explicated by Jonathan Baumbach in his chapter on Malamud in *The Landscape of Nightmare: Studies in the Contemporary American Novel* (New York: New York University Press, 1965).
8. Malamud, *The Natural*, p. 154.
9. Malamud, *The Assistant*, pp. 245–246.
10. Bernard Malamud's short stories are to be found in two collections: *The Magic Barrel* (New York: Farrar, Straus and Cudahy, 1960), and *Idiots First* (New York: Farrar, Straus and Cudahy, 1960).
11. Baumbach, *The Landscape of Nightmare*, p. 102.
12. David L. Stevenson, "The Activists," *Daedalus*, XCII (Spring, 1963), 238.
13. *Ibid.*, p. 249.
14. Malamud, *A New Life*, p. 193.
15. *Ibid.*, p. 360.

16. *Ibid.,* p. 357.

17. F. W. Dupee, "The Power of Positive Sex," *Partisan Review,* XXXI (Summer, 1964), p. 429.

18. Malamud, *A New Life,* p. 361.

19. *Ibid.,* p. 367.

20. Gold, *The Optimist,* p. 395.

21. Stevenson, *Daedalus,* p. 249.

22. *Ibid.*

23. The novella "Goodbye, Columbus" appears in a collection of stories by Philip Roth, *Goodbye, Columbus* (New York: Houghton Mifflin Company, 1959).

24. Walker Percy, *The Moviegoer* (New York: Alfred A. Knopf, Inc., 1961).

25. Roth, *Letting Go,* p. 630.

26. *Ibid.*

27. James Baldwin, *Another Country* (New York: Dial Press, 1962). I have chosen to write about *Another Country* rather than about other novels or essays by James Baldwin because it is the novel of his which was written in the early sixties, around the same time as the other major novels discussed here, and which best participates in the activist form of the novel. However, in connection with Baldwin's work generally and with the work of the other American Negro writer that I discuss in this chapter, Ralph Ellison, I think I should add some comments on the categories I have made in separating the Kafkan mode of the activist novel from a Paulinist-Christian mode and a Negro mode.

American Negro novelists are of course Christian novelists, and Baldwin and Ellison share some of the characteristics of what I describe in this chapter as the Paulinist-Christian temperament; for example, they tend to see their nobler heroes engaged in self-destructive activities (cf. my discussion of Rufus, and his suicide, in the novel *Another Country,* in the main text of this chapter) and to regard love as graced with exceptional power—a regard I consider throughout Chapter 7 as a reflection of love as divine love, as the theological concept of divine love, as the *caritas* and the *agape* which are church formulations.

On the other hand, American Negroes seem to have a heightened sense of the Hebrew Bible that goes beyond the usual sense of the Old Testament in white Fundamentalist Christianity; this is true because of the experience of slavery in an alien land and the longing for freedom common to the ancient Hebrew and the American Negro. Jews still feel deeply about and celebrate in their most important holiday, the Passover, the deliverance from the slavery of Egypt; and the Hebraic messianic strain is understood as a movement always toward a future of deliverance from all slaveries, for all people.

James Baldwin in "The Harlem Ghetto," an essay in *Notes of a Native Son* (Boston: The Beacon Press, 1955), confirms the mixed sources of Negro spirituality when he says:

Here, too, can be seen one aspect of the Negro's ambivalent relation to the Jew. To begin with, though the traditional Christian accusation that the Jews killed Christ is neither questioned nor doubted, the term "Jew" actually operates in this initial context to include all infidels of white skin who have failed to accept the Savior. No real distinction is made: the preacher begins by accusing the Jews of having refused the light and proceeds from there to a catalog of their subsequent sins and the suffering visited on them by a wrathful God. Though the notion of the suffering is based on the image of the wandering, exiled Jew, the context changes imperceptibly, to become a fairly obvious reminder of the trials of the Negro, while the sins recounted are the sins of the American republic.

At this point, the Negro identifies himself almost wholly with the Jew. The more devout Negro considers that he *is* a Jew, in bondage to a hard taskmaster and waiting for a Moses to lead him out of Egypt. The hymns, the texts, and the most favored legends of the devout Negro are all Old Testament and therefore Jewish in origin: the flight from Egypt, the Hebrew children in the fiery furnace, the terrible jubilee songs of deliverance. . . . The images of the suffering Jew and the suffering Christ are wedded with the image of the suffering slave, and they are one: the people that walked in darkness have seen a great light.

But if the Negro has bought his salvation with pain and the New Testament is used to prove, as it were, the validity of the transformation, it is the Old Testament which is clung to and most frequently preached from, which provides the emotional fire and anatomizes the path of bondage; and which promises vengeance and assures the chosen of their place in Zion. The favorite text of my father, among the most earnest of ministers, was not "Father, forgive them, for they know not what they do," but "How can I sing the Lord's song in a strange land?" (*Notes of a Native Son*, pp. 66–68).

In another essay, "Everybody's Protest Novel," Baldwin attacks the white gentility of Harriet Beecher Stowe's Paulinist-Christianity when he says:

[Uncle Tom's] triumph is metaphysical, unearthly; since he is black, born without the light, it is only through humility, the incessant mortification of the flesh, that he can enter into communion with God or man. The virtuous rage of Mrs. Stowe is motivated by nothing so temporal as a concern for the relationship of men to one another—or, even, as she would have claimed, by a concern for their relationship to God—but merely by a panic of being hurled into the flames, of being caught in traffic with the devil. . . . Here black equates with evil and white with grace; if, being mindful of the necessity of good works, she could not cast out the blacks—a wretched, huddled mass, apparently, claiming, like an obsession, her inner eye— she could not embrace them either without purifying them of sin. She must cover their intimidating nakedness, robe them in white, the garments of salvation; only thus could she herself be delivered from ever-present sin, only thus could she bury, as St. Paul demanded, "the carnal man, the man of the flesh." Tom, therefore, her only black man, has been robbed of his humanity and divested of his sex. It is the price for that darkness with which he has been branded (*Notes of a Native Son*, pp. 17–18).

Thus, the social circumstances of the Negro impinge on his spiritual awareness in such a way as to locate his religion, and the motifs he takes from it and brings to bear on his more generalized considerations of man's existential dilemma, somewhere truly between the Hebraic and the Christian, hence the separate category used here for talking about the novels of Baldwin and Ellison.

Baldwin, whose father was a preacher and who himself preached as a young man, has written directly about his religious experience in several places, notably in the essays of *Notes of a Native Son,* some of which is quoted above; in *Go Tell It on the Mountain* (New York: Alfred A. Knopf, 1953), his early autobiographical novel which covers in fictive terms some of the same material found in *Notes of a Native Son;* in *The Fire Next Time* (New York: Dial Press, 1963), a long and passionate essay which is itself a powerful sermon. In this long essay that quality of the prophetic voice, which Baldwin the essayist significantly shares in the world of contemporary American letters with Norman Mailer the essayist, is conspicuous. The prophetic voice is another attribute of the Hebraic temperament, and, while not absent in modern Christian writers by any means, it is most meaningfully present in the works of Negroes and Jews, where the rhetoric suits the substance.

The new black writers of the late sixties write more essays and autobiographical studies—often in a prophetic voice—than they write fictions because fiction is no longer sufficient to their dilemma. Richard Gilman examines the new black writing in a review of Eldridge Cleaver's book, *Soul on Ice* (New York: McGraw-Hill, 1968). Gilman says: "These Negro writers I am speaking of take their blackness not as a starting point . . . but as absolute theme and necessity. They make philosophies and fantasias out of their color. . . . For such men and women, to write is an almost literal means of survival and attack, a means—more radically than we have known it—to *be,* and their writing owes more, consciously at least, to the embattled historical moment in which American Negroes find themselves than to what is ordinarily thought of as literary expression or the ongoing elaboration of ideas." And, he says: "The kind of *Negro writing* I have been talking about, the act of the creation of the self in the face of that self's historic denial by our society, seems to me to be at this point beyond my right to intrude on" ("White Standards and Negro Writing," *The New Republic,* 158 [March 9, 1968], pp. 25–30). Thus, one of the critics who today represents the firmest, most fixed aesthetic standards ("white standards") opts out when it comes to judging the prophetic voice and the existential declaration of the new Negro writers.

28. Ralph Ellison, *Invisible Man* (New York: Random House, 1952).

29. R. V. Cassill, *Clem Anderson* (New York: Simon and Schuster, 1961).

30. Stevenson, *Daedalus*, p. 246.

31. Baldwin, *Another Country*, p. 363.

32. Ellison, *Invisble Man*, p. 10.

33. *Ibid.*, p. 501.

34. *Ibid.*, p. 498.

35. Irving Howe, "Black Boys and Native Sons," *Dissent*, X (Autumn, 1963), 353–368.

36. Ralph Ellison, *Shadow and Act* (New York: Random House, 1964), p. 109.

37. *Ibid.*, p. 177.

38. Ellison, *Invisible Man*, p. 501.

39. Martin Buber, "Kafka and Judaism," in *Kafka: A Collection of Critical Essays*, ed. Ronald Gray (Englewood Cliffs, New Jersey: Prentice Hall, Inc., 1962), p. 157.

40. *Ibid.*

41. Jean Genet, *Our Lady of the Flowers*, trans. Bernard Frechtman (New York: Grove Press, Inc., 1963).

42. David L. Stevenson, "The Novels of William Styron: Autonomy in the Case of the Environment" (Manuscript).

43. Styron, *Set This House on Fire*, frontispiece.

44. Buber, "Kafka," p. 161.

45. *Ibid.* The quotations from Kafka inside Buber's passage are among Kafka's parables, paradoxes, and aphorisms, which appear in a variety of collections and in the diaries, referred to elsewhere in this book. See Bibliography.

46. Another example of the hero's destruction of his body (through alcohol) for the sake of the spirit is provided in Malcolm Lowry's *Under the Volcano* (Philadelphia and New York: J. B. Lippincott Company, 1965). About this novel Stephen Spender writes: "The conclusion must be that [the novel] is religious: the contradictions of a hero who does not act and who fails to be a hero, the insistence implicit that the Consul is the writer, and living and dying for all of us, the concern for values which are outside the time in a world entirely contemporary, are resolved in the theme of the Divine Comedy, the progress of the soul" (Introduction, in *Under the Volcano*, p. xxvi).

In John Updike's *Rabbit, Run* (New York: Alfred A. Knopf, 1960), there is a picture of Harry "Rabbit" Angstrom, an ordinary man who rebels against the meaningless drift of his time and place, modern middle-class America, and asks for more, seeks the "something that wants me to find it" (p. 127). But rather than truly seeking, or yet finding, he runs from: he runs from the life of routine; and his "self-destructiveness" is characterized as much in this running-away as in his wish to give extraordinarily of himself in order to find the real self, the truth, the meaning of life, in order to be saved. This giving of the self in some wished-for completion of love is a positive alternative to the negative destructiveness of the body through alcohol or suicide, but it is also a way to lose the worldly self in order to transcend it. The Christian idea of self-transcendence is connected to the ideas of self-destructiveness that I have discussed in the text. (The Kafkan hero seeks a transcendent self not the self-transcendence of the spiritual activist in the Paulinist-Christian mode.) In his attempt to transcend his ordinary self, "Rabbit" Angstrom gives his finest love to a prostitute. (This sort of giving as virtuous is satirized in the heroine Candy Christian of Terry Southern's *Candy*. Another sort of Christian giving is satirized in Terry Southern's *The Magic Christian* [New York: Random House, 1960], and these two Pop novels together make an interesting set when seen as satirical studies in the masochism and sadism possible in Christian giving: Candy is the perfect masochist, and Guy Grand of *The Magic Christian* the perfect sadist.)

In his excellent chapter on John Updike's novels and in his especially perceptive section on *Rabbit, Run*, David Galloway in *The Absurd Hero in American Fiction* (Austin and London: University of Texas Press, 1966) speaks of the clear emphasis Updike has put on Harry's story as the story of a spiritual quest by taking a fragment from Pascal's *Penseés* as an epigraph for the novel. Galloway says: "It is perhaps only through the action of something akin to the Christian concept of grace that a voice calls to Harry that does not call to other men; his pursuit of that voice demands a hardness of the heart and a definite obliviousness to external circumstances. All of Pascal's religious writings rest on the foundation of a personal religious experience of a peculiarly intense nature" (p. 34). That Harry is on a spiritual quest clearly outside the church is underscored by his encounter with Eccles, the Episcopal minister. And Galloway says: Harry "has no taste for what Updike later calls 'the dark, tangled, visceral aspect of Christianity, the *going through* quality of it, the passage into suffering and death that redeems and inverts these things . . .'" (*ibid.*, p. 35). But I think that Harry retains the feel of Christianity though he may reject churchly forms for it: that which he rejects in the church he takes into himself and carries forward in his personal spiritual pilgrimage. He is a saintly sufferer, as Galloway has documented in his chapter on Updike.

Finally, the use of sex as salvationist is very apparent in *Rabbit, Run* and in other work by Updike; the sex-salvation connection comes up strikingly again in his most recent novel, *Couples* (New York: Alfred A. Knopf, 1968). Often in his work *eros* displaces *caritas* and *agape,* becoming a "divine" instrument in their stead, as it does in Baldwin's *Another Country.* About this Galloway comments: "Rabbit's peculiar saintliness demands, in fact, that he not be celibate, for it is largely through sex that he is able to express his desire to comfort and heal; it is through sex that he is able to see Ruth's [the prostitute's] 'heart' " (*ibid.,* p. 32). Ironically, salvationist physical love seems no more truly useful than the discarded concepts of love that the church has offered, if we take the evidence of the Updike novels. The failure of *eros,* its inability to save, is clear in *Rabbit, Run,* and it would seem to be the point Updike is making specifically in *Couples.* In *Couples* sex is still seen as a possible way to salvation; sex remains attractive but has become an ambiguous mixture of the diabolic and divine.

47. Cass, too, is an artist, a painter. The fact that Cass is a painter, as Clem is a poet, colors their quests. The artist-as-hero, however, is another subject. In *Set This House on Fire* and *Clem Anderson,* it is the spiritual activism of the heroes that is more important, and the fact of their being artists is somewhat incidental and does not govern the narrative.

48. Styron, *Set This House on Fire,* p. 501.

49. *Ibid.,* pp. 269–270.

50. Isaac Rosenfeld, "Approaches to Kafka," in *An Age of Enormity,* ed. Theodore Solotaroff (Cleveland and New York: The World Publishing Company, 1962), p. 174.

SELECTED BIBLIOGRAPHY

Aaron, Daniel. *Writers on the Left.* New York: Harcourt, Brace and World, 1961.

Aldrich, John W. *After the Lost Generation: A Critical Study of Two Wars.* New York: McGraw-Hill Book Company, 1951.

Alvarez, A. "Norman X," *Spectator* (May 7, 1965), 603.

Auerbach, Erich. *Mimesis: The Representation of Reality in Western Literature,* trans. Willard R. Trask. Princeton: Princeton University Press, 1953.

"Authors Discuss Sick-Book Trend," *The New York Times* (March 10, 1965), p. 34.

Baeck, Leo. *Judaism and Christianity.* Philadelphia: The Jewish Publication Society, 1958.

Baldwin, James. *Another Country.* New York: Dial Press, 1962.

———. *The Fire Next Time.* New York: Dial Press, 1963.

———. *Go Tell It on the Mountain.* New York: Alfred A. Knopf, 1953.

———. *Notes of a Native Son.* Boston: The Beacon Press, 1955.

Barrett, William. *Irrational Man: A Study in Existential Philosophy.* Garden City, New York: Doubleday and Company, 1958.

Barth, John. *The End of the Road.* New York: Doubleday and Company, 1960.

———. *Giles Goat-Boy.* New York: Doubleday and Company, 1966.

———. *The Sot-Weed Factor.* New York: Doubleday and Company, 1960.

Baumbach, Jonathan. *The Landscape of Nightmare: Studies in the Contemporary American Novel.* New York: New York University Press, 1965.

Beauvoir, Simone de. *The Ethics of Ambiguity*. New York: Philosophical Library, 1948.

——. *The Marquis de Sade*. Trans. Annette Michelson. New York: Grove Press, 1953.

Bellow, Saul. *The Adventures of Augie March*. New York: Viking Press, 1953.

——. "The Art of Fiction XXXVII," *The Paris Review*, IX (Winter, 1966), 48–73.

——. "A Comment on 'Form and Despair,'" *Location*, I (Summer, 1964), 10–12.

——. *Dangling Man*. New York: Meridian Fiction, 1960.

——. *Dangling Man*. New York: The Vanguard Press, 1944.

——. "Deep Readers of the World, Beware!" *The New York Times Book Review* (February 15, 1959), 1 and 34.

——. "Distractions of a Fiction Writer," *The Living Novel*. Ed. Granville Hicks. New York: Collier Books, 1962.

——. "From the Life of Augie March," *Partisan Review*, XVI (November, 1949), 1077–1089.

—— (ed.). *Great Jewish Short Stories*. New York: Dell Publishing Company, 1963.

——. *Henderson the Rain King*. New York: Viking Press, 1959.

——. *Herzog*. New York. Viking Press, 1964.

——. *The Last Analysis*. New York: Viking Press, 1965.

——. "Notes of a Dangling Man," *Partisan Review*, X (September–October, 1943), 402–409, 429–438.

——. *Seize the Day*. New York: Viking Press, 1956.

——. "Some Notes on Recent American Fiction, " *Encounter*, XXI (November, 1963), 22–29.

——. *The Victim*. New York: The Vanguard Press, 1947.

——. "Where Do We Go From Here: The Future of Fiction," *Michigan Quarterly Review*, I (January, 1962), 27–33.

——. "The Writer as Moralist," *The Atlantic*, CCXI (March, 1963), 58–62.

Berdyaev, Nicolas. *Slavery and Freedom*. New York: Charles Scribner's Sons, 1944.

Briggs, William A. (ed.). *Anthology of Zen*. New York: Grove Press, 1961.

Brod, Max. *Franz Kafka: A Biography*. Trans. G. Humphreys Roberts. New York: Schocken Books, 1947.

Brown, Norman O. *Life Against Death: The Psychoanalytical Meaning of History*. London: Routledge and K. Paul, 1959.

Buber, Martin. *Good and Evil*. New York: Charles Scribner's Sons, 1952.

——. *Hasidism*. New York: Philosophical Library, 1948.

——. *I and Thou*. New York: Charles Scribner's Sons, 1958.

——. *Israel and the World*. New York: Schocken Books, 1948.

——. *Tales of the Hasidim: Early Masters*. New York: Schocken Books, 1961.

——. *Tales of the Hasidim: Late Masters*. New York: Schocken Books, 1961.

——. *Ten Rungs: Hasidic Sayings*. New York: Schocken Books, 1962.

Burroughs, William. *Naked Lunch*. New York: Grove Press, 1959.

Camus, Albert. *The Myth of Sisyphus*. New York: Vintage Books, 1960.

——. *The Stranger*. Trans. Stuart Gilbert. New York: Alfred A. Knopf, 1946.

Cassill, R. V. *Clem Anderson*. New York: Simon and Schuster, 1961.

Chase, Richard. *The American Novel and Its Tradition*. New York: Doubleday Anchor Books, 1957.

Chester, Alfred. "Salinger: How to Love Without Love," *Commentary*, XXXV (June, 1963), 467–474.

Cook, Albert. *The Dark Voyage and The Golden Mean: A Philosophy of Comedy*. Cambridge: Harvard University Press, 1949.

——. *The Meaning of Fiction*. Detroit: Wayne State University Press, 1960.

Cowley, Malcolm. *The Literary Situation*. New York: Viking Press, 1954.

Diamond, Malcolm. *Martin Buber, Jewish Existentialist*. New York: Oxford University Press, 1960.

Dupee, F. W. "The Power of Positive Sex," *Partisan Review*, XXXI (Summer, 1964), 425–430.

Elliott, George P. "A Surfeit of Talk," *Commentary*, XXXIX (June, 1965), 97–100.

Ellison, Ralph. *Invisible Man*. New York: Random House, 1952.

———. *Shadow and Act.* New York: Random House, 1964.

Fallico, Arturo B. *Art and Existentialism.* Englewood Cliffs, New Jersey: Prentice-Hall, 1962.

Fiedler, Leslie. *Love and Death in the American Novel.* Cleveland and New York: World Publishing Company, 1962.

———. *No! In Thunder: Essays on Myth and Literature.* Boston: Beacon Press, 1960.

———. *Waiting for the End: The Crisis in American Culture and a Portrait of Twentieth Century American Literature.* New York: Stein and Day, 1964.

Friedman, Bruce (ed.). *Black Humor.* New York: Bantam Books, 1965.

———. *Stern.* New York: Simon and Schuster, 1962.

Frye, Northrop. *Anatomy of Criticism: Four Essays.* Princeton: Princeton University Press, 1957.

Galloway, David D. *The Absurd Hero in American Fiction.* Austin and London: University of Texas Press, 1966.

Genet, Jean. *Our Lady of the Flowers.* Trans. Bernard Frechtman. New York: Grove Press, 1963.

Gilman, Richard. "White Standards and Negro Writing," *The New Republic,* 158 (March 9, 1968), 25–30.

Gold, Herbert. *The Age of Happy Problems.* New York: Dial Press, 1962.

———. *The Birth of a Hero.* New York: Viking Press, 1951.

———. "The Discovered Self," *Nation,* CLXXXIII (November 17, 1956), 435–436.

———. *Fathers: A Novel in the Form of a Memoir.* New York: Random House, 1966.

——— (ed.). *Fiction of the Fifties.* Garden City, New York: Dolphin Books, Doubleday and Company, 1961.

———. *Love and Like.* New York: Dial Press, 1960.

———. *The Man Who Was Not With It.* Boston: Little, Brown and Company, 1956.

———. *The Optimist.* Boston: Little, Brown and Company, 1959.

———. *The Prospect Before Us.* Cleveland and New York: The World Publishing Company, 1954.

———. *Salt.* New York: Dial Press, 1963.

———. *Therefore Be Bold.* New York: Dial Press, 1960.

"The Good Guy," *Time* (September 25, 1964), 105.

Goodman, Paul. *Kafka's Prayer*. New York: The Vanguard Press, 1947.

———. *Making Do*. New York: Macmillan Company, 1963.

———. *The Structure of Literature*. Chicago: Univerity of Chicago Press, 1954.

Gray, Ronald (ed.). *Kafka: A Collection of Critical Essays* (Englewood Cliffs, New Jersey: Prentice-Hall, 1962.

Grene, Marjorie. *Dreadful Freedom*. Chicago: University of Chicago Press, 1948.

Grunwald, Henry A. (ed.). *Salinger: A Critical and Personal Portrait*. New York: Harper and Brothers, 1962.   ,

Gutwillig, Robert. "Talk with Saul Bellow," *The New York Times Book Review* (September 20, 1964), 40–41.

Gwynn, Frederick L. and Joseph L. Blotner. *The Fiction of J. D. Salinger*. Pittsburgh: Pittsburgh University Press, 1958.

Hassan, Ihab. *Radical Innocence: Studies in the Contemporary American Novel*. Princeton, New Jersey: Princeton University Press, 1962.

———. "Saul Bellow: Five Faces of a Hero," *Critique*, III (Summer, 1960), 28–36.

Hawkes, John. *The Cannibal*. New York: New Directions, 1949.

———. *Second Skin*. New York: New Direction, 1964.

Heller, Erich. *The Disinherited Mind*. New York: Meridian Books, 1959.

Heller, Joseph. *Catch-22*. New York: Simon and Schuster, 1961.

Hicks, Granville, (ed.). *The Living Novel*. New York: Collier Books, 1962.

Hoffman, Frederick, J. *The Mortal No*. Princeton: Princeton University Press, 1964.

———. *Samuel Beckett: The Language of the Self*. New York: E. P. Dutton and Company, 1964.

Howe, Irving. "Black Boys and Native Sons," *Dissent*, X (Autumn, 1963), 353–368.

Howe, Irving and Eliezer Greenberg (eds.). *A Treasury of Yiddish Stories*. Cleveland and New York: Meridian Books, 1961.

Kafka, Franz. *Amerika*. Trans. Edwin Muir. New York: New Directions, 1946.

———. *The Castle*. Trans. Willa and Edwin Muir. New York: Alfred A. Knopf, 1961.

———. *Dearest Father, Stories and Other Writings*. Trans. Ernst Kaiser and Eithne Wilkins. New York: Schocken Books, 1954.

———. *Diaries*. Ed. Max Brod. 2 vols. New York: Schocken Books, 1948, 1949.

———. *A Franz Kafka Miscellany: Pre-Fascist Exile*. New York: Twice a Year Press, rev. 2d. ed., 1946.

———. *The Great Wall of China: Stories and Reflections*. Trans. Willa and Edwin Muir. New York: Schocken Books, 1946.

———. *Letters to Milena*. Ed. Willi Haas. New York: Schocken Books, 1953.

———. *Parables and Paradoxes*. New York: Schocken Books, 1961.

———. *Selected Short Stories of Franz Kafka*. Trans. Willa and Edwin Muir. New York: The Modern Library, n.d.

———. *The Trial*. Trans. Willa and Edwin Muir. New York: The Modern Library, n.d

———. *Wedding Preparations in the Country and Other Posthumous Prose Writings*. Trans. Ernst Kaiser and Eithne Wilkins. London: Secker and Warburg, 1954.

Kaufmann, Walter. *Existentialism: From Dostoevsky to Sartre*. New York: Meridian Books, 1956.

——— (ed.). *The Portable Nietzsche*. New York: Viking Press, 1954.

Kazin, Alfred. "Bellow's Purgatory," *The New York Review of Books*, X (March 28, 1968), 32–36.

———. *On Native Grounds: An Interpretation of Modern American Prose Literature*. New York: Reynal and Hitchcock, 1942.

Kerouac, Jack. *On the Road*. New York: Viking Press, 1958.

Kierkegaard, Søren. *Fear and Trembling and the Sickness Unto Death*. Trans. Walter Lowrie. New York: Doubleday Anchor Books, n.d.

———. *A Kierkegaard Anthology*. Ed. Robert Bretall. New York: Modern Library, n.d.

Klein, Marcus. *After Alienation: American Novels in Mid-Century*. Cleveland and New York: The World Publishing Company, 1964.

Kostelanetz, Richard. "The Young Writers," *Writer's Yearbook 68*, XL (1968), 80–82, 110–113.

Krieger, Murray. *The Tragic Vision: Variations on a Theme*

in Literary Interpretation. New York: Holt, Rinehart and Winston, 1960.

Krutch, Joseph Wood. "In Back of Man, A World of Nature," *A Quarto of Modern Literature.* Ed. Leonard Brown. New York: Charles Scribner's Sons, 1964.

Leavis, F. R. *The Great Tradition.* New York: Doubleday and Company, 1954.

Lewis, R. W. B. *The Picaresque Saint: Representative Figures in Contemporary Fiction.* Philadelphia and New York: J. B. Lippincott Company, 1961.

Lowry, Malcolm. *Under the Volcano.* Philadelphia and New York: J. B. Lippincott Company, 1965.

Lubbock, Percy. *The Craft of Fiction.* New York: Charles Scribner's Sons, 1921.

Mailer, Norman. *Advertisements for Myself.* New York: G. P. Putnam's Sons, 1959.

———. *An American Dream.* New York: Dial Press, 1965.

———. *Armies of the Night: History as a Novel, The Novel as History.* New York: New American Library, 1968.

———. "The Art of Fiction XXXII," *The Paris Review,* VIII (Winter–Spring, 1964), 28–58.

———. *Barbary Shore.* New York: Rinehart and Company, 1951.

———. *Cannibals and Christians.* New York: The Dial Press, 1966.

———. *The Deer Park.* New York: G. P. Putnam's Sons, 1955.

———. *The Deer Park* (Play). New York: The Dial Press, 1967.

———. "Modes and Mutations: Quick Comments on The Modern American Novel," *Commentary,* XLI (March, 1966), 37–40.

———. *The Naked and the Dead.* New York: Rinehart and Company, 1948.

———. *The Presidential Papers.* New York: G. P. Putnam's Sons, 1963.

———. "The Steps of the Pentagon," *Harper's Magazine,* CCXXXVI (March, 1968), 47–142.

———. *Why Are We in Viet Nam?* New York: G. P. Putnam's Sons, 1967.

Malamud, Bernard. *The Assistant.* New York: Farrar, Straus and Cudahy, 1957.

———. *The Fixer.* New York: Farrar, Straus and Giroux, 1966.

——. *Idiots First*. New York: Farrar, Straus and Company, 1963.
——. *The Magic Barrel*. New York: Farrar, Straus and Cudahy, 1960.
——. *The Natural*. New York: Farrar, Straus and Cudahy, 1952.
——. *A New Life*. New York: Farrar, Straus and Cudahy, 1961.
Malin, Irving and Irwin Stark (eds.). *Breakthrough: A Treasury of Contemporary American-Jewish Literature*. Philadelphia: The Jewish Publication Society of America, 1963.
Malin, Irving. *Jews and Americans*. Carbondale: South Illinois University Press, 1965.
Marcel, Gabriel. *The Mystery of Being*. Chicago: Henry Regnery Company, 1950.
May, Rollo (ed.). *Existential Psychology*. New York: Random House, 1961.
McCarthy, Mary. "J. D. Salinger's Circuit," *Harper's Magazine*, CCV (October, 1962), 46–48.
Meehan, Thomas. "Claus," *The New Yorker* (January 9, 1965), 26–27.
Pearce, Roy Harvey. *The Continuity of American Poetry*. Princeton: Princeton University Press, 1961.
Percy, Walker. *The Moviegoer*. New York: Alfred A. Knopf, 1961.
——. *The Last Gentleman*. New York: Farrar, Straus and Giroux, 1966.
Philipson, Morris (ed.). *Aesthetics Today*. Cleveland and New York: Meridian Books, 1961.
Phillips, William (ed.). *Art and Psychoanalysis*. New York: Criterion Books, 1957.
Podhoretz, Norman. *Doings and Undoings: The Fifties and After in American Writing*. New York: Farrar, Straus and Company, 1964.
——. *Making It*. New York: Random House, 1968.
Poirier, Richard. "Bellows to Herzog," *Partisan Review*, XXXII (Spring, 1965), 264–271.
——. "Morbid-Mindedness," *Commentary*, XXXIX (June, 1965), 91–94.
Politzer, Heinz. *Franz Kafka: Parable and Paradox*. Ithaca, New York: Cornell University Press, 1962.

Potok, Chaim. *The Chosen*. New York: Simon and Schuster, 1967.

Powers, J. F. *Morte D'Urban*. New York: Doubleday & Company, 1962.

Pynchon, Thomas. *V*. Philadelphia: J. B. Lippincott and Company, 1963.

Rahv, Philip. *Image and Idea*. New York: New Directions Paperbook, 1957.

Reich, Wilhelm. *Character-Analysis*. New York: The Noonday Press, 1949.

Robbe-Grillet, Alain. *The Voyeur*. Trans. Richard Howard. New York: Grove Press, 1958.

Rosenberg, Harold. *The Tradition of the New*. New York: Grove Press, 1961.

Rosenfeld, Isaac. *An Age of Enormity: Life and Writing in the Forties and Fifties*. Ed. Theodore Solotaroff. Cleveland and New York: The World Publishing Company, 1962.

———. *Passage From Home*. New York: Dial Press, 1946.

Roth, Philip. "Civilization and Its Discontents," in Theodore Solotaroff, ed. *New American Review #3*. New York: New American Library, April 1968.

———. *Goodbye, Columbus*. New York: Houghton Mifflin Company, 1959.

———. "The Jewish Blues," in Theodore Solotaroff, ed. *New American Review #1*. New York: New American Library, September, 1967.

———. *Letting Go*. New York: Random House, 1962.

———. *Portnoy's Complaint*. New York: Random House, 1969.

———. "Whacking Off," *Partisan Review*, XXXIV (Summer, 1967), 385–399.

———. *When She Was Good*. New York: Random House, 1967.

Salinger, J. D. *The Catcher in the Rye*. Boston: Little, Brown and Company, 1951.

———. *Franny and Zooey*. Boston: Little, Brown and Company, 1961.

———. "Hapworth 16, 1924," *The New Yorker* (June 19, 1965), 32–113.

———. *Nine Stories*. Boston: Little, Brown and Company, 1953.

———. *Raise High the Roof Beam, Carpenters and Seymour—An*

Introduction. Boston: Little, Brown and Company, 1959.

Sarraute, Nathalie. *The Age of Suspicion: Essays on the Novel.* Trans. Maria Jolas. New York: George Braziller, 1963.

——. *The Planetarium.* Trans. Maria Jolas. New York: George Braziller, 1960.

Sartre, Jean-Paul. *Being and Nothingness.* Trans. Hazel E. Barnes. New York: Philosophical Library, 1956.

——. *Literary Essays.* Trans. Annette Michelson. New York: Philosophical Library, 1957.

——. *Nausea.* Trans. Lloyd Alexander. London: New Directions, 1949.

——. *What Is Literature?* Trans. Bernard Frechtman. New York: Philosophical Library, 1949.

Shapiro, Karl. *In Defense of Ignorance.* New York: Random House, 1960.

Singer, I. Bashevis. *Gimpel the Fool and Other Stories.* New York: Noonday Press, 1957.

Sokel, Walter H. *The Writer in Extremis: Expressionism in Twentieth Century German Literature.* Stanford, California: Stanford University Press, 1959.

Southern, Terry and Mason Hoffenberg. *Candy.* New York: G. P. Putnam's Sons, 1964.

Southern, Terry. *The Magic Christian.* New York: Random House, 1960.

Stevenson, David L. "The Activists," *Daedalus,* XCII (Spring, 1963), 238–249.

——. "The Novels of William Styron: Autonomy in the Cage of the Environment." (Manuscript.)

Styron, William. *The Confessions of Nat Turner.* New York: Random House, 1967.

——. *Lie Down in Darkness.* New York: The Bobbs-Merrill Company, 1951.

——. *Set This House on Fire.* New York: Random House, 1960.

Sykes, Gerald (ed.). *Alienation: The Cultural Climate of Our Time.* New York: George Braziller, 1964.

Sypher, Wylie. *Rococo to Cubism in Art and Literature.* New York: Vintage Books, 1960.

Tanner, Tony. "Saul Bellow: The Flight from Monologue," *Encounter,* XXIV (February, 1965), 58–70.

Tauber, Herbert. *Franz Kafka.* New Haven: Yale University Press, 1948.

Tennant, F. R. *The Sources of the Doctrines of the Fall and Original Sin.* New York: Schocken Books, 1968.

Trilling, Diana. "Norman Mailer," *Encounter,* XIX (November, 1962), 45–56.

Trilling, Lionel. *The Opposing Self: Nine Essays in Criticism.* New York: Viking Press, 1955.

Van Ghent, Dorothy. *The English Novel: Form and Function.* New York: Rinehart and Company, 1953.

Vivas, Eliseo. *Creation and Discovery, Essays in Criticism and Aesthetics.* New York: The Noonday Press, 1955.

"The Vocal Group," *The American Imagination* (Middletown, Connecticut: Special "Our Times" edition, 1960).

Wahl, Jean. *A Short History of Existentialism.* Trans. Forrest Williams and Stanley Maron. New York: Philosophical Library, 1949.

Weil, Simone. *Waiting for God.* New York: G. P. Putnam's Sons, 1951.

Wilson, Edmund. *A Literary Chronicle: 1920–1950.* Garden City: Doubleday and Company, 1956.

Wright, Richard. *Native Son.* New York: Harper and Brothers Publishers, 1940.

Updike, John. *Couples.* New York: Alfred A. Knopf, 1968.

———. *Rabbit, Run.* New York: Alfred A. Knopf, 1960.

INDEX

Fictional characters are alphabetized according to their first names or titles, as Augie March or Dr. Tamkin.